Latin American
Spanish

lonely planet

phrasebooks
and
Roberto Esposto

Latin American Spanish phrasebook
5th edition – September 2008

Published by
Lonely Planet Publications Pty Ltd ABN 36 005 607 983
90 Maribyrnong St, Footscray, Victoria 3011, Australia

Lonely Planet Offices
Australia Locked Bag 1, Footscray, Victoria 3011
USA 150 Linden St, Oakland CA 94607
UK 2nd Floor, 186 City Rd, London EC1V 2NT

Cover illustration
Purez by Philippe Bechervaise

ISBN 978 1 74059 712 8

text © Lonely Planet Publications Pty Ltd 2008
cover illustration © Lonely Planet Publications Pty Ltd 2008

10 9 8 7 6 5 4 3 2

Printed through The Bookmaker International Ltd.
Printed in China.

acknowledgments

Lonely Planet's Language Products and editor Francesca Coles would like to thank the following compadres for bringing this phrasebook to life:

Roberto Esposto (PhD), lecturer in Spanish and Latin American Studies at the University of Queensland, who supplied the translations and transliterations. Roberto wishes to thank his partner Maria Chiaroni for contributing her knowledge of Latin American Spanish gained in Peru and Central America.

Publishing manager Peter D'Onghia and his predecessor Jim Jenkin whose ingenuity gave birth to a new breed of phrasebook. Publishing manager Ben Handicott for the birth of this edition.

Commissioning editors Karin Vidstrup Monk, Karina Coates and Rachel Williams, as well as managing editor Annelies Mertens for her diligent supervision.

Project managers Fabrice Rocher and Charles Rawlings-Way for keeping the Latin American Express on the rails.

Assisting editors Piers Kelly, Quentin Frayne, Emma Koch, Branislava Vladisavljevic and Laura Crawford for their contributions.

Freelance proofers and Spanish language experts Peter and Marta Gibney for careful proofing of the Latin American Spanish.

Layout designers Yvonne Bischofberger and Katherine Marsh for efficient layout. Philippe Bechervaise for the cover and Patrick Marris for the inside illustrations. Series designer Yukiyoshi Kamimura for book and cover design.

Thanks also to cartographer Valentina Kremenchutskaya, managing cartographer Paul Piaia and cartographic designer Wayne Murphy for the language map. Gracias to in-house Argentinian Gus Balbontin for his advice, and to layout designer Nick Stebbing and macro-genius David Burnett for production support.

make the most of this phrasebook ...

Anyone can speak another language! It's all about confidence. Don't worry if you can't remember your school language lessons or if you've never learnt a language before. Even if you learn the very basics (on the inside covers of this book), your travel experience will be the better for it. You have nothing to lose and everything to gain when the locals hear you making an effort.

finding things in this book

For easy navigation, this book is in sections. The Tools chapters are the ones you'll thumb through time and again. The Practical section covers basic travel situations like catching transport and finding a bed. The Social section gives you conversational phrases, pick-up lines, the ability to express opinions – so you can get to know people. Food has a section all of its own: gourmets and vegetarians are covered and local dishes feature. Safe Travel equips you with health and police phrases, just in case. Sustainable Travel, finally, completes this book. Remember the colours of each section and you'll find everything easily; or use the comprehensive Index. Otherwise, check the two-way traveller's Dictionary for the word you need.

being understood

Throughout this book you'll see coloured phrases on each page. They're phonetic guides to help you pronounce the language. Start with them to get a feel for how the language sounds. The pronunciation chapter in Tools will explain more, but you can be confident that if you read the coloured phrase, you'll be understood. As you become familiar with the spoken language, move on to using the actual text in the language which will help you perfect your pronunciation.

communication tips

Body language, ways of doing things, sense of humour – all have a role to play in every culture. 'Local talk' boxes show you common ways of saying things, or everyday language to drop into conversation. 'Listen for ...' boxes supply the phrases you may hear. They start with the phonetic guide (because you'll hear it before you know what's being said) and then lead in to the language and the English translation.

CONTENTS

5

latin american spanish

United States of America

NORTH ATLANTIC OCEAN

MEXICO

Gulf of Mexico · Havana

DOMINICAN REPUBLIC

Mexico City · · Santo Domingo

CUBA

Haiti · **Puerto Rico (US)**
San Juan

Caribbean Sea

· Caracas

VENEZUELA

Guyana
Suriname
French Guiana (Fr)

see enlargement

· Bogotá

Galápagos Islands (ECUADOR)

Quito · **COLOMBIA**

ECUADOR

PERÚ

· Lima

Brazil

SOUTH PACIFIC OCEAN

BOLIVIA

Sucre

PARAGUAY

· Asunción

Easter Island (CHILE)

CHILE

BELIZE

Jamaica

Santiago ·

Buenos Aires · **URUGUAY**
· Montevideo

MEXICO · Belmopan

ARGENTINA

GUATEMALA **HONDURAS**
Tegucigalpa

Caribbean Sea

Guatemala City

· Managua

San Salvador **NICARAGUA**

SOUTH ATLANTIC OCEAN

EL SALVADOR

San José · Panama City
COSTA RICA **PANAMA**

PACIFIC OCEAN

COLOMBIA

Falkland Islands (UK)

◼ official language

◼ widely understood

For more details, see the **introduction**.

You may have thought that Spanish was the same the world over – but think again. Since the Spanish language was first introduced to the Americas following Columbus' discovery of the continent in 1492, it has developed a vast array of colourful characteristics that distinguish it from its European ancestor. Today, the umbrella term 'Latin American Spanish' embraces all manner of unique varieties of Spanish spoken in 19 Latin American nations as well as in parts of the Caribbean and in the southern states of the US.

There are plenty of good reasons to get into Latin American Spanish. Not only is it relatively easy for English speakers to come to grips with, but it's also one of the world's most widely spoken languages. Travellers are easily seduced by its melodic expressiveness and lilting rhythm – there's no doubting the richness of a language that has lent itself to the literary imagination of world-famous authors such as Mario Vargas Llosa, Gabriel García Márquez and Isabel Allende.

at a glance ...

language name:
Latin American Spanish

names in language:
castellano kas·te·*lya*·no
español es·pa·*nyol*

language family: Romance

approximate number of speakers: 300 million

close relatives:
Portuguese, Italian

donations to English:
barbecue, canoe, chili, chocolate, hammock, tomato, potato, tobacco and many more ...

Some say that the differences between Latin American Spanish and the Spanish spoken in Spain can be compared to the contrast between US English and UK English. While speakers of either variety of Spanish will understand each other, both varieties have been subject to very different influences. Many of the first migrants either came from, or passed through, the ports of Andalucia in southern Spain on their way to the New World and brought with them the local speech patterns.

introduction

The fact that Latin Americans do not lisp the letters *c* and *z* is considered evidence of this Andalucian influence. Equally, indigenous languages have left their mark on Latin American Spanish – a fact which is particularly evident in vocabulary to do with flora, fauna and cultural habits.

Latin American Spanish varies slightly from country to country and from region to region. This phrasebook gives some of the main features of regional variations in both accents and vocabulary. Despite this diversity, Latin American Spanish has retained a remarkable unity over time and across a vast geographical area. One exception is Mexico where a number of strong differences in vocabulary and common expressions distinguish it from the rest of Latin America (see Lonely Planet's Mexican Spanish phrasebook).

This book gives you all the practical words and phrases you need to get by as well as all the fun, spontaneous phrases that lead to a better understanding of Latin America and its people. Need more encouragement? Remember, the contact you make using Latin American Spanish will make your travels unique. Local knowledge, new relationships and a sense of satisfaction are on the tip of your tongue, so don't just stand there, say something!

grammatical abbreviations

m	masculine	**sg**	singular	**pol**	polite
f	feminine	**pl**	plural	**inf**	informal

country abbreviations

These are the countries where Latin American Spanish is the main language. The abbreviations are those given throughout the book to indicate regional variations:

Arg	Argentina	**Cub**	Cuba	**Par**	Paraguay
Bol	Bolivia	**Ecu**	Ecuador	**Per**	Peru
CAm	Central America	**Sal**	El Salvador	**Pue**	Puerto Rico
		Gua	Guatemala	**SAm**	South America
Chi	Chile	**Hon**	Honduras	**Uru**	Uruguay
Col	Colombia	**Nic**	Nicaragua	**Ven**	Venezuela
Cos	Costa Rica	**Pan**	Panama		

Latin American Spanish pronunciation is not difficult as many of the sounds are also found in English. The few sounds that are different aren't hard to produce and you'll probably find that revving up your *eres* (r's) and hissing out your *jotas* (j's) is fun.

Latin American Spanish pronunciation differs from the Castilian Spanish spoken in Spain. The most obvious difference is the lack of the lisping 'th' sound which is found in Castilian Spanish. Pronunciation in Latin America also varies from country to country and from region to region, just as English pronunciation varies from one place to another. In this book we use a generalised system for pronunciation which will allow you to be understood in all parts of Latin America.

vowel sounds

vocales

symbol	english equivalent	spanish example
a	f**a**ther	*agua*
e	r**e**d	*número*
ee	b**ee**	*día*
o	h**o**t	*ojo*
oo	m**oo**n	*gusto*

Vowels are pronounced crisply. They don't extend to form vowel sound combinations (diphthongs). Below are four vowel sounds, however, that roughly correspond to diphthongs in English:

symbol	english equivalent	spanish example
ai	**ai**sle	*bailar*
ay	s**ay**	*seis*
ow	h**ou**se	*autobús*
oy	b**oy**	*hoy*

consonant sounds

symbol	english equivalent	spanish example
b	**b**ig	**b**arco
ch	**ch**ili	**ch**ica
d	**d**in	**d**inero
f	**f**un	**f**iesta
g	**g**o	**g**ato
k	**k**ick	*cabeza*/**qu**eso
kh	as in the Scottish 'lo**ch**'	*jardín*/*gente*
l	**l**oud	*lago*
ly	mi**lli**on	*llamada*
m	**m**an	*mañana*
n	**n**o	*nuevo*
ny	can**y**on	*señora*
p	**p**ig	*padre*
r	**r**un, but stronger 'rolled' (especially as the first letter in a word and in all words with *rr*)	*mariposa*/*ritmo*/*burro*
s	**s**o	*semana*/*zarzuela*/*cinco*
t	**t**in	*tienda*
v	very soft 'v', somewhere between 'v' and 'b'	*severo*
w	**w**in	*guardia*
y	**y**es	*viaje*

regional variations

All transliterations in this book follow the system explained in the tables on pages 9-10. As we've said, pronunciation does vary across Latin America so you may expect to hear some of these variations as part of local accents:

The ly sound is simplified to 'y' (as in 'yes') in much of Latin America. Where this is the case, it drops out altogether before the vowel sounds e and ee. In Argentina, Uruguay and Highland Ecuador ly is pronounced like the 's' in 'measure'.

In much of Latin America s is reduced to just a slight 'h' sound when at the end of a syllable or a word, so *tos* 'cough' may sound like to followed by a barely audible 'h'.

Throughout Latin America there's confusion between the sounds r and l and you may hear one substituted for the other in a random way.

word stress

Latin American Spanish has stress. This means you emphasise one syllable of a word over another. Rule of thumb: when a word ends in *n*, *s* or a vowel, the stress falls on the second-last syllable. Otherwise, the last syllable is stressed. If you see an accent mark over a syllable, it cancels out these rules and you just stress that syllable instead. The stressed syllables are always italicised in our pronunciation guides so you needn't worry about these rules.

plunge in!

Don't worry too much about pronunciation. Just pick up your cue from the people around you. The phonetic guides we've given for every phrase account for the correct sounds and stress.

reading & writing

The relationship between Spanish sounds and their spelling is quite straightforward and consistent. The following rules will help you read any written Spanish you may come across:

c	before *e* or *i* pronounced 's'	**c**erveza, **c**inco
	before *a*, *o* and *u* pronounced as a 'k'	**c**arro, **c**orto, **c**ubo
h	never pronounced (silent)	**h**aber
q	pronounced as a 'k' and always followed by a *u* which is not pronounced	**q**uince
z	pronounced as an 's'	**z**orro
g	before *e* or *i* pronounced as the 'ch' in lo**ch** – elsewhere as in 'go'	**g**ente, **g**igante, **g**ato, **g**ordo, **g**uante
gue, gui	the *u* is not pronounced (silent) in these combinations (unless there are two dots over the *u*)	**g**uerra, **g**uinda, **g**üiski

alphabet

a	a	*j*	kho·ta	*r*	er
b	be *lar*·ga	*k*	ka	*rr**	e·re
c	se	*l*	e·le	*s*	e·se
ch*	che	*ll**	e·lye	*t*	te
d	de	*m*	e·me	*u*	oo
e	e	*n*	e·ne	*v*	be kor·tal
f	e·fe	*ñ*	e·nye	*w*	do·ble be
g	khe	*o*	o	*x*	e·kees
h	a·che	*p*	pe	*y*	ee grye·ga
i	ee	*q*	koo	*z*	se·ta

*The letters *ch*, *ll* and *rr* are no longer officially considered separate letters but they're still sounds in their own right.

This chapter will help you make your own sentences. It's arranged alphabetically for ease of navigation. If you can't find the exact phrase you need in this book, remember that with just a little grammar, a few gestures and a couple of well-chosen words, you'll generally get the message across.

a/an & some

I'd like a leather belt and an alpaca jumper.

Quisiera un cinto de cuero   kee·*sye*·ra oon *seen*·to de *kwe*·ro
y una chompa de alpaca.   ee *oo*·na *chom*·pa de al·*pa*·ka
  (lit: I-would-like a belt of
    leather and a jumper of alpaca)

Spanish has two words for the article 'a/an': *un* and *una*. The gender of the noun determines which one you use. *Un* and *una* also have plural forms: *unos* and *unas*, meaning 'some'.

masculine	*un* sg	*un huevo* oon *we*·vo	an egg
	unos pl	*unos huevos* *oo*·nos *we*·vos	some eggs
feminine	*una* sg	*una llama* *oo*·na *lya*·ma	a llama
	unas pl	*unas llamas* *oo*·na *lya*·mas	some llamas

adjectives see describing things

articles see a/an & some and the

be

Spanish has two words for the English verb 'be': *ser* and *estar*.

use *SER* to express	examples	
permanent characteristics of persons/things	*Ángel es muy amable.* an·khel es mooy a·ma·ble	Ángel is very nice.
occupations or nationality	*Pablo es de Puerto Rico.* pa·blo es de pwer·to ree·ko	Pablo is from Puerto Rico.
the time & location of events	*Son las tres.* son las tres	It's 3 o'clock.
possession	*¿De quién es esta mochila?* de kyen es es·ta mo·chee·la	Whose backpack is this?

use *ESTAR* to express	examples	
temporary characteristics of persons/things	*La comida está fría.* la ko·mee·da es·ta free·a	The meal is cold.
the time & location of persons/things	*Estamos en Buenos Aires.* es·ta·mos en bwe·nos ai·res	We are in Buenos Aires.
the mood of a person	*Estoy contento/a.* m/f es·toy kon·ten·to/a	I'm happy.

Forms of the verb *SER*					
I	am	a journalist	*yo*	*soy*	*reportero/a* m/f
you sg inf	are	from Cuba	*tú*	*eres**	*de Cuba*
you sg pol	are	an artist	*usted*	*es*	*artista*
he/she	is	an artist	*él/ella* m/f	*es*	*artista*
we	are	single	*nosostros/ as* m/f	*somos*	*solteros/as* m/f
you pl pol&inf	are	students	*ustedes*	*son*	*estudiantes*
they	are	students	*ellos/as* m/f	*son*	*estudiantes*

sos* in Arg, Uru & CAm (Also see **you page 25).

Forms of the verb *ESTAR*					
I	am	well	*yo*	*estoy*	*bien*
you sg inf	are	angry	*tú*	*estás*	*enojado/a* m/f
you sg pol	are	drunk	*usted*	*está*	*borracho/a* m/f
he/she	is	drunk	*él/ella*	*está*	*borracho/a* m/f
we	are	happy	*nosostros/ as* m/f	*estamos*	*contentos/ as* m/f
you pl pol&inf	are	reading	*ustedes*	*están*	*leyendo*
they	are	reading	*ellos/as* m/f	*están*	*leyendo*

describing things

I'm looking for a picturesque route.

Estoy buscando un camino pintoresco.	es·*toy* boos·*kan*·do oon ka·*mee*·no peen·to·*res*·ko
(lit: I-am looking-for a route picturesque)	

When using an adjective to describe a noun, you need to use a different ending depending on whether the noun is masculine or feminine, and singular or plural. Most adjectives have four forms which are easy to remember:

	singular	plural
masculine	*fantástico*	*fantásticos*
feminine	*fantástica*	*fantásticas*

un hotel fantástico	oon o·*tel* fan·*tas*·tee·ko	a fantastic hotel
una comida fantástica	oo·na ko·*mee*·da fan·*tas*·tee·ka	a fantastic meal
unos libros fantásticos	oo·nos *lee*·bros fan·*tas*·tee·kos	some fantastic books
unas tortas fantásticas	oo·nas *tor*·tas fan·*tas*·tee·kas	some fantastic cakes

Adjectives generally come after the noun in Spanish. However, 'adjectives' of quantity (such as 'much', 'a lot', 'little/few', 'too much'), and adjectives expressing possession ('my' and 'your') always precede the noun.

muchos turistas	*moo*·chos too·*rees*·tas	many tourists
primera clase	pree·*me*·ra *kla*·se	first class
mi carro	mee *ka*·ro	my car

diminutives

A distinctive and fun feature of Latin American Spanish is the use of diminutives. These are formed by adding endings such as *-ito/a*, *-cito/a* and *cillo/a* to words.

They're often used to indicate the smallness of something, eg, *gato* 'cat' becomes *gatito* 'kitten', but they're also a way of expressing how a speaker feels about something.

Diminutives may indicate that a speaker finds something charming, eg, to say *perrito* instead of *perro* 'dog' is akin to saying 'doggy' instead of 'dog' in English. Not surprisingly, many Spanish terms of endearment end in *-ito/a* or *-illo/a*, eg, *palomita* 'darling' is a diminutive of *paloma* 'dove'. Diminutives are used a lot in talking to children too.

Diminutive endings can give a friendly tone to a conversation. For instance, *un momentito* 'just a moment' sounds more light-hearted than *un momento*.

gender

In Spanish , all nouns – words which denote a thing, person or idea – are either masculine or feminine. Dictionaries will tell you what gender a noun is, but here are some handy tips to help you determine gender:

- the gender is masculine when talking about a man and feminine when talking about a female
- words ending in *-o* are usually masculine
- words ending in *-a* are usually feminine
- words ending in *-d*, *-z* or *-ión* are usually feminine

m (masculine) or f (feminine)?

In this book, masculine forms appear before the feminine forms. If you see a word ending in *-o/a*, it means the masculine form ends in *-o*, and the feminine form ends in *-a* (that is, you replace the *-o* ending with the *-a* ending to make it feminine). The same goes for the plural endings *-os/as*. If you see an *(a)* between brackets on the end of a word, it means you have to add that in order to make that word feminine. In other cases we spell out the whole word.

See also **a/an & some**, **describing things** and **the**.

have

I have two brothers.
> *Tengo dos hermanos.* ten·go dos er·man·os
> (lit: I-have two brothers)

Possession can be indicated in various ways in Spanish. The easiest way is by using the verb *tener*, 'have'.

I	have	a ticket	*yo*	*tengo*	*un boleto*
you sg inf	have	the key	*tú*	*tienes**	*la llave*
you sg pol	have	the key	*usted*	*tiene*	*la llave*
he/she	has	aspirin	*él/ella*	*tiene*	*aspirinas*
we	have	matches	*nosotros/ as* m/f	*tenemos*	*fósforos*
you pl pol&inf	have	cakes	*ustedes*	*tienen*	*tortas*
they	have	problems	*ellos/as* m/f	*tienen*	*problemas*

* *tenés* in Arg, Uru & CAm. (Also see **you** page 25).
See also **my & your** and **somebody's**.

is & are see be

more than one

I'd like a soft drink.
> *Quisiera un refresco.*   kee·*sye*·ra oon re·*fres*·ko
> (lit: I-would-like one soft-drink)

I'd like two soft drinks.
> *Quisiera dos refrescos.*   kee·*sye*·ra dos re·*fres*·kos
> (lit: I-would-like two soft-drinks)

In general, if the word ends in a vowel, you add *-s* for a plural. If the nouns ends in a consonant (or *y*), you add *-es*:

bed	*cama*	*ka*·ma	beds	*camas*	*ka*·mas
woman	*mujer*	moo·*kher*	women	*mujeres*	moo·*khe*·res

my & your

There are a number of words for 'my' and 'your' in Spanish. Choose the correct form according to the gender and quantity of the noun.

	singular		plural	
	masculine	feminine	masculine	feminine
	gift	visa	friends	houses
my	*mi regalo*	*mi visa*	*mis amigos*	*mis casas*
your sg inf	*tu regalo*	*tu visa*	*tus amigos*	*tus casas*
your sg pol	*su regalo*	*su visa*	*sus amigos*	*sus casas*
his/her/its	*su regalo*	*su visa*	*sus amigos*	*sus casas*
our	*nuestro regalo*	*nuestra visa*	*nuestros amigos*	*nuestras casas*
your pl pol&inf	*su regalo*	*su visa*	*sus amigos*	*sus casas*
their	*su regalo*	*su visa*	*sus amigos*	*sus casas*

See also **gender** and **more than one**.

negatives

Just add the the word *no* before the main verb of the sentence:

I don't live with my family.
No vivo con mi familia.   no *vee*·vo kon mee fa·*mee*·lya
(lit: no live-I with my family)

planning ahead

As in English, you can talk about your plans or future events
by using the verb *ir* (go) followed by the word *a* (to) and the
infinitive of another verb, for example:

Tomorow, I'm going to travel to Guatemala.
Mañana, yo voy a viajar   ma·*nya*·na yo voy a vya·*khar*
a Guatemala.   a gwa·te·*ma*·la
(lit: tomorrow I go-I to travel
to Guatemala)

I	am going	to call	yo	voy	a llamar
you sg inf	are going	to sleep	tú	vas	a dormir
you sg pol	are going	to dance	usted	va	a bailar
he/she	is going	to drink	él/ella	va	a beber
we	are going	to sing	nosotros/as m/f	vamos	a cantar
you pl pol&inf	are going	to eat	ustedes	van	a comer
they	are going	to write	ellos/as m/f	van	a escribir

plural see **more than one**

pointing something out

To point something out, the easiest phrases to use are *es* (it is), *esto es* (this is) or *eso es* (that is).

Es una guía de Lima.	es *oo·*na *gee·*a de *lee·*ma	It's a guide to Lima.
Esto es mi pasaporte.	*es·*to es mee pa·sa·*por·*te	This is my passport.
Eso es una empanada.	*e·*so es *oo·*na em·pa·*na·*da	That is an empanada.

See also **this & that**.

possession see **have**, **my & your** and **somebody's**

questions

When asking a question, simply make a statement, but raise your intonation towards the end of the sentence, as you would in English. The inverted question mark in written Spanish prompts you to do this.

Do you have a car?
   ¿Tienes un carro?   *tye·*nes oon *ka·*ro
   (lit: you-have a car)

question words

	question words	
Who?	¿Quién(es)? sg/pl	kyen/kye·nes
Who is it?	¿Quién es?	kyen es
Who are they?	¿Quiénes son ellos?	kye·nes son e·lyos
What?	¿Qué?	ke
What are you saying?	¿Qué estás diciendo?	ke es·tas dee·syen·do
Which?	¿Cuál(es)? sg/pl	kwal/kwal·es
Which is the best restaurant?	¿Cuál es el mejor restaurante?	kwal es el me·khor res·tow·ran·te
Which local dishes do you recommend?	¿Cuáles platos típicos puedes recomendar?	kwa·les pla·tos tee·pee·kos pwe·des re·ko·men·dar
When?	¿Cuándo?	kwan·do
When does the bus arrive?	¿Cuándo llega el autobús?	kwan·do lye·ga el ow·to·boos
Where?	¿Dónde?	don·de
Where can I buy tickets?	¿Dónde puedo comprar boletos?	don·de pwe·do kom·prar bo·le·tos
How?	¿Cómo?	ko·mo
How do you say that in Spanish?	¿Cómo se dice eso en castellano?	ko·mo se dee·se e·so en kas·te·lya·no
How much?	¿Cuánto?	kwan·to
How much is it?	¿Cuánto cuesta?	kwan·to kwes·ta
How many?	¿Cuántos/as? m/f pl	kwan·tos/kwan·tas
For how many days?	¿Por cuántos días?	por kwan·tos dee·as
Why?	¿Por qué?	por ke
Why is the museum closed?	¿Por qué está cerrado el museo?	por ke es·ta se·ra·do el moo·se·o

some see a/an & some

somebody's

In Spanish, ownership is expressed through the word *de* (of).

This is my friend's tent.
   Esta es la carpa de mi amiga.   es·ta es la *kar*·pa de mee a·*mee*·ga
   (lit: this is the tent of my
     friend)

See also **have** and **my & your**.

this & that

There are three 'distance words' in Spanish, depending on whether something or someone is close (this), away from you (that) or even further away in time or distance (that over there).

masculine	singular	plural
close	*éste* (this)	*éstos* (these)
away	*ése* (that)	*ésos* (those)
further away	*aquél* (that over there)	*aquéllos* (those over there)
feminine	singular	plural
close	*ésta* (this)	*éstas* (these)
away	*ésa* (that)	*ésas* (those)
further away	*aquélla* (that over there)	*aquéllas* (those over there)

See also **pointing something out**.

the

The Spanish articles *el* and *la* both mean 'the'. Whether you use *el* or *la* depends on the gender of the thing, person or idea talked about, which in Spanish will always be either masculine or feminine. The gender is not really concerned with the sex of something, for example, a llama is a feminine noun, even if it's male! There's no rule as to why, say, the sun is masculine but a cloud is feminine.

When talking about plural things, persons or ideas, you use *los* instead of *el* and *las* instead of *la*.

	singular	plural
masculine	*el*	*los*
feminine	*la*	*las*

el carro m	el *ka*·ro	the car
la tienda f	la *tyen*·da	the shop
los carros m pl	los *ka*·ros	the cars
las tiendas f pl	las *tyen*·das	the shops

See also **gender** and **a/an & some**.

word order

Sentences in Spanish have a basic word order of subject-verb-object, just as English does.

I study business.
    Yo estudio comercio.   yo es·*too*·dyo ko·*mer*·syo
    (lit: I study-I English)

However, the subject pronoun is often omitted: *'Estudio comercio'* is enough. Subject pronouns are used if a speaker wishes to emphasise who is the 'doer' of an action.

yes/no questions

It's not impolite to answer questions with a simple *sí* (yes) or *no* (no) in Spanish. There's no way to say 'Yes it is/does', or 'No, it isn't/doesn't'.

See also **questions**.

you

Latin American Spanish has two forms for the singular 'you'. When talking to someone familiar to you or younger than you, use the informal form *tú*, too, rather than the polite form *usted*, oos·te. Use the polite form when you're meeting someone for the first time, talking to someone much older than you or when you're in a formal situation (eg, talking to the police, customs officers etc). All phrases in this book use the form of 'you' that is appropriate to the situation. In Latin American Spanish there's no informal/formal distinction for plural 'you' – you just use *ustedes* oos·te·des.

In many Latin-American countries (particularly in Argentina, Chile, Paraguay and Uruguay and in some Central American countries), you'll hear *vos* instead of *tú*. The form of the verb that goes with *vos* may differ slightly from the form of the verb that goes with *tú* (even when the *vos* is understood from the context). The *vos* verb form that you're likely to hear most is *sos* from the verb *ser* (to be). So, for example, instead of *¿Eres de Australia?* (Are you from Australia?) you may hear *¿Sos de Australia?* In this book we've just used *tú* (and the verb form that goes with it) to keep things simple. You'll be perfectly well understood if you use *tú* – just be aware that locals may use *vos* (and *vos* verb forms) instead.

false friends

Beware of false friends – words which look, and even sound, like an English word but have a different meaning altogether. Using them in the wrong context could confuse, or even amuse, Spanish speakers.

injuria	een·*khoo*·ree·a	insult
herida	e·*ree*·da	injury
parientes	pa·*ryen*·tes	relatives
padres	*pa*·dres	parents
éxito	*ek*·see·to	success
salida	sa·*lee*·da	exit

Estoy embarazada.
  es·*toy* em·ba·ra·*sa*·da   I'm pregnant.

Estoy avergonzado/a. m/f
  es·*toy* a·ver·gon·*sa*·do/a   I'm embarrassed.

Do you speak (English)?
¿Habla/Hablas (inglés)? pol/inf   *a*·bla/*a*·blas (een·*gles*)

Does anyone speak (English)?
¿Hay alguien que hable   ai al·*gyen* ke *a*·ble
(inglés)?   (een·*gles*)

Do you understand?
¿Me entiende/entiendes? pol/inf   me en·*tyen*·de/en·*tyen*·des

I understand.
Entiendo.   en·*tyen*·do

I don't understand.
No entiendo.   no en·*tyen*·do

I speak (Spanish).
Hablo (castellano).   *a*·blo (kas·te·*lya*·no)

I speak a little (Spanish).
Hablo un poco   *a*·blo oon *po*·ko
(de castellano).   (de kas·te·*lya*·no)

I speak (English).
Hablo (inglés).   *a*·blo (een·*gles*)

speaking of Spanish

In the Spanish-speaking world Spanish is known as both *español* and *castellano*. Latin Americans favour the term *castellano*. The underlying reason for this is probably that *español* is heard more as a nationality than as the name of a language.

How do you pronounce this word?

¿Como se pronuncia esta palabra?

ko·mo se pro·*noon*·sya es·ta pa·*la*·bra

How do you write 'ciudad'?

¿Como se escribe 'ciudad'?

ko·mo se es·*kree*·be syoo·*da*

What does 'entrada' mean?

¿Qué significa 'entrada'?

ke seeg·nee·*fee*·ka en·*tra*·da

Could you please ...?	¿Puede ..., por favor?	pwe·de ... por fa·vor
repeat that	repetirlo	re·pe·*teer*·lo
speak more slowly	hablar más despacio	a·*blar* mas des·*pa*·syo
write it down	escribirlo	es·kree·*beer*·lo

tongue twisters

Tongue twisters are known as *trabalenguas* in Spanish. Try exercising your tongue with these two:

From Chile:

Comí chirimoyas, me enchirimoyé. Ahora, para desenchirimoyarme, ¿cómo me desenchirimoyaré?

ko·*mee* chee·ree·*mo*·yas me en·chee·ree·*mo*·ye a·o·ra *pa*·ra des·en·chee·ree·mo·*yar*·me *ko*·mo me des·en·chee·ree·mo·ya·*re*

(I ate custard apples, I got myself custard-appled. Now, in order to get un-custard-appled, how shall I un-custard-apple myself?)

From Venezuela:

Poquito a poquito Paquito empaca poquitas copitas en pocos paquetes.

po·*kee*·to a po·*kee*·to pa·*kee*·to em·*pa*·ka po·*kee*·tas ko·*pee*·tas en *po*·kos pa·*ke*·tes

(Little by little Paquito is packing a few small wineglasses in a few boxes.)

cardinal numbers

		los números cardinales
0	*cero*	*se*·ro
1	*uno*	*oo*·no
2	*dos*	dos
3	*tres*	tres
4	*cuatro*	*kwa*·tro
5	*cinco*	*seen*·ko
6	*seis*	says
7	*siete*	*sye*·te
8	*ocho*	*o*·cho
9	*nueve*	*nwe*·ve
10	*diez*	dyes
11	*once*	*on*·se
12	*doce*	*do*·se
13	*trece*	*tre*·se
14	*catorce*	ka·*tor*·se
15	*quince*	*keen*·se
16	*dieciséis*	dye·see·*says*
17	*diecisiete*	dye·see·*sye*·te
18	*dieciocho*	dye·see·*o*·cho
19	*diecinueve*	dye·see·*nwe*·ve
20	*veinte*	*vayn*·te
21	*veintiuno*	vayn·tee·*oo*·no
22	*veintidos*	vayn·tee·*dos*
30	*treinta*	*trayn*·ta
40	*cuarenta*	kwa·*ren*·ta
50	*cincuenta*	seen·*kwen*·ta
60	*sesenta*	se·*sen*·ta
70	*setenta*	se·*ten*·ta
80	*ochenta*	o·*chen*·ta
90	*noventa*	no·*ven*·ta
100	*cien*	*syen*
200	*doscientos*	do·*syen*·tos

1,000	*mil*	meel
2,000	*dos mil*	dos meel
1,000,000	*un millón*	oon mee·*lyon*

ordinal numbers

		los numeros ordinales
1st	*primero/a* m/f	pree·*me*·ro/a
2nd	*segundo/a* m/f	se·*goon*·do/a
3rd	*tercero/a* m/f	ter·*se*·ro/a
4th	*cuarto/a* m/f	*kwar*·to/a
5th	*quinto/a* m/f	*keen*·to/a

fractions

		las fracciónes
a quarter	*un cuarto*	oon *kwar*·to
a third	*un tercio*	oon *ter*·syo
a half	*medio/a* m/f	*me*·dee·o/a
three-quarters	*tres cuartos*	tres *kwar*·tos
all	*todo/a* m/f sg	*to*·do/a
	todos/as m/f pl	*to*·dos/as
none	*nada*	*na*·da

useful amounts

		cantidades utiles
How much?	*Cuánto/a?* m/f	*kwan*·to/a
How many?	*Cuántos/as?* m/f pl	*kwan*·tos/as
Please give me ...	*Por favor, deme ...*	por fa·*vor de*·me ...
(just) a little	*(solo) un poco*	(*so*·lo) oon *po*·ko
some	*algunos/as* m/f pl	al·*goo*·nos/as
much	*mucho/a* m/f	*moo*·cho/a
many	*muchos/as* m/f pl	*moo*·chos/as
less	*menos*	*me*·nos
more	*más*	mas

telling the time

dando la hora

When telling the time in Spanish, 'It's …' is expressed by *Son las* … followed by a number. However, one o'clock is *Es la una* and 'It's midnight' and 'It's midday' are *Es el mediodía* and *Es la medianoche* respectively. Both the 12-hour and the 24-hour clock are commonly used.

What time is it?	*¿Qué hora es?*	ke *o*·ra es
It's one o'clock.	*Es la una.*	es la *oo*·na
It's (ten) o'clock.	*Son las (diez).*	son las (dyes)
Quarter past (two).	*(Las dos) y cuarto.*	(las dos) ee *kwar*·to
Twenty past (two).	*(Las dos) y veinte.*	(las dos) ee *vayn*·te
Half past (two).	*(Las dos) y media.*	(las dos) ee *me*·dya
Twenty to (three).	*(Las tres)*	(las tres)
	menos veinte.	*me*·nos *vayn*·te
Quarter to (three).	*(Las tres)*	(las tres)
	menos cuarto.	*me*·nos *kwar*·to
It's early.	*Es temprano.*	es tem·*pra*·no
It's late.	*Es tarde.*	es *tar*·de
am (in the morning)	*de la mañana*	de la ma·*nya*·na
pm (in the afternoon)	*de la tarde*	de la *tar*·de
in the morning	*por la mañana*	por la ma·*nya*·na
in the afternoon	*por la tarde*	por la *tar*·de
in the evening	*por la tarde*	por la *tar*·de
at night	*por la noche*	por la *no*·che
At what time …?	*¿A qué hora …?*	a ke *o*·ra …
At one.	*A la una.*	a la *oo*·na
At (six).	*A las (seis).*	a las (says)
At 7.57 pm.	*A las ocho menos tres de la tarde.*	a las *o*·cho *me*·nos tres de la *tar*·de

days of the week

Monday	*lunes*	*loo*·nes
Tuesday	*martes*	*mar*·tes
Wednesday	*miércoles*	*myer*·ko·les
Thursday	*jueves*	*khwe*·ves
Friday	*viernes*	*vyer*·nes
Saturday	*sábado*	*sa*·ba·do
Sunday	*domingo*	do·*meen*·go

the calendar

el calendario

months

January	*enero*	e·*ne*·ro
February	*febrero*	fe·*bre*·ro
March	*marzo*	*mar*·so
April	*abril*	a·*breel*
May	*mayo*	*ma*·yo
June	*junio*	*khoo*·nyo
July	*julio*	*khoo*·lyo
August	*agosto*	a·*gos*·to
September	*septiembre*	sep·*tyem*·bre
October	*octubre*	ok·*too*·bre
November	*noviembre*	no·*vyem*·bre
December	*diciembre*	dee·*syem*·bre

dates

What date?	*¿Qué fecha?*	ke *fe*·cha
What's today's date?	*¿Qué día es hoy?*	ke *dee*·a es oy
It's (18 October).	*Es (el dieciocho de octubre).*	es (el dye·see·o·cho de ok·*too*·bre)

seasons

summer	*verano*	ve·*ra*·no
autumn	*otoño*	o·*to*·nyo
winter	*invierno*	een·*vyer*·no
spring	*primavera*	pree·ma·*ve*·ra

present

now	*ahora*	a·o·ra
today	*hoy*	oy
tonight	*esta noche*	es·ta *no*·che

this ...
afternoon	*esta tarde*	es·ta *tar*·de
month	*este mes*	es·te mes
morning	*esta mañana*	es·ta ma·*nya*·na
week	*esta semana*	es·ta se·*ma*·na
year	*este año*	es·te *a*·nyo

past

| (three days) ago | *hace (tres días)* | a·se (tres *dee*·as) |
| day before yesterday | *anteayer* | an·te·a·*yer* |

last ...
month	*el mes pasado*	el mes pa·*sa*·do
night	*anoche*	a·*no*·che
week	*la semana pasada*	la se·*ma*·na pa·*sa*·da
year	*el año pasado*	el *a*·nyo pa·*sa*·do

| since (May) | *desde (mayo)* | *des*·de (*ma*·yo) |
| yesterday | *ayer* | a·*yer* |

yesterday ...	*ayer por la ...*	a·*yer* por la ...
afternoon	*tarde*	*tar*·de
evening	*noche*	*no*·che
morning	*mañana*	ma·*nya*·na

time & dates

33

future

el futuro

day after tomorrow	*pasado mañana*	pa·*sa*·do ma·*nya*·na
in (six days)	*dentro de (seis días)*	*den*·tro de (says *dee*·as)
next ...	*... que viene*	... ke *vye*·ne
month	*el mes*	el mes
week	*la semana*	la se·*ma*·na
year	*el año*	el *a*·nyo
tomorrow	*mañana*	ma·*nya*·na
tomorrow ...	*mañana por la ...*	ma·*nya*·na por la ...
afternoon	*tarde*	*tar*·de
evening	*noche*	*no*·che
morning	*mañana*	ma·*nya*·na
until (June)	*hasta (junio)*	*as*·ta (*khoo*·nyo)

during the day

durante el día

afternoon	*tarde* f	*tar*·de
dawn	*alba* f	*al*·ba
day	*día* m	*dee*·a
evening	*noche* f	*no*·che
midday	*mediodía* m	me·dyo·*dee*·a
midnight	*medianoche* f	me·dya·*no*·che
morning	*mañana* f	ma·*nya*·na
night	*noche* f	*no*·che
sunrise	*amanecer* m	a·ma·ne·*ser*
sunset	*atardecer* m	a·tar·de·*ser*

How much is it?
  ¿Cuánto cuesta?   kwan·to kwes·ta

It's free.
  Es gratis.   es gra·tees

It's … (pesos).
  Cuesta … (pesos).   kwes·ta … (pe·sos)

Can you write down the price?
  ¿Puede escribir el precio?   pwe·de es·kree·beer el pre·syo

Do you change money here?
  ¿Se cambia dinero aquí?   se kam·bya dee·ne·ro a·kee

Do you accept …?	*¿Aceptan …?*	a·sep·tan …
credit cards	*tarjetas de crédito*	tar·khe·tas de kre·dee·to
debit cards	*tarjetas de débito*	tar·khe·tas de de·bee·to
travellers cheques	*cheques de viajero*	che·kes de vya·khe·ro

I'd like to …	*Me gustaría …*	me goos·ta·ree·a …
cash a cheque	*cobrar un cheque*	ko·brar oon che·ke
change money	*cambiar dinero*	kam·byar dee·ne·ro
change a travellers cheque	*cambiar un cheque de viajero*	kam·byar oon che·ke de vya·khe·ro
withdraw money	*sacar dinero*	sa·kar dee·ne·ro

What's the …?	*¿Cuál es la …?*	kwal es la …
commission	*comisión*	ko·mee·syon
exchange rate	*tasa de cambio*	ta·sa de kam·byo

I'd like …, please.	*Quisiera …, por favor.*	kee·sye·ra … por fa·vor
a receipt	*un recibo*	oon re·see·bo
my change	*mi cambio*	mee kam·byo
my money back	*que devuelva el dinero*	ke de·vwel·va el dee·ne·ro

There's a mistake in the bill.
Hay un error en la cuenta. ai oon e·*ror* en la *kwen*·ta

I don't want to pay the full price.
No quiero pagar el precio no *kye*·ro pa·*gar* el *pre*·syo
íntegro. *een*·te·gro

Do I need to pay upfront?
¿Hay que pagar por adelantado? ai ke pa·*gar* por a·de·lan·*ta*·do

Where's the nearest automatic teller machine?
¿Dónde está el cajero *don*·de es·*ta* el ka·*khe*·ro
automático más cercano? ow·to·*ma*·tee·ko mas ser·*ka*·no

latin american currencies

Argentina	*peso**	*pe*·so
Bolivia	*boliviano*	bo·lee·*vya*·no
Chile	*peso**	*pe*·so
Colombia	*peso**	*pe*·so
Costa Rica	*colón* (in honour of Columbus)	ko·*lon*
Cuba	*peso**	*pe*·so
Ecuador	*sucre* (named after a general who helped liberate Ecuador from colonial rule)	*soo*·kre
Guatemala	*quetzal* (the name of a native bird)	*ket*·sal
Honduras	*lempira* (the name of a chief of the Lenca tribe who lead the resistance against the Spanish)	lem·*pee*·ra
Nicaragua	*córdoba* (in honour of a Spanish explorer)	*kor*·do·ba
Panama	*dolár/balboa* (the latter named after a Spanish explorer)	do·*lar*/bal·*bo*·a
Paraguay	*guaraní* (an Amerindian people)	gwa·ra·*nee*
Peru	*nuevo sol* (lit: new sun)	*nwe*·vo sol
Uruguay	*peso**	*pe*·so
Venezuela	*bolivár* (named after Simón Bolivár who freed several countries from Spanish rule)	bo·lee·*var*

*The word peso literally means 'weight'.

getting around

desplazándose

What time does the ... leave?	*¿A qué hora sale ...?*	a ke *o*·ra *sa*·le ...
boat	*el barco*	el *bar*·ko
bus (city)	*el autobús*	el ow·to·*boos*
(Col) *la chiva*		la *chee*·va
(Arg) *el colectivo*		el ko·lek·*tee*·vo
(Cub) *la guagua*		la *gwa*·gwa
(Bol, Chi) *el micro*		el *mee*·kro
bus (intercity)	*el ómnibus*	el *om*·nee·boos
(Arg) *el micro*		el *mee*·kro
ferry	*la ferry*	la *fe*·ree
metro	*el subterráneo*	el soob·te·*ra*·ne·o
(Arg) *el subte*		el *soob*·te
plane	*el avión*	el a·*vyon*
train	*el tren*	el tren
tram	*el tranvía*	el tran·*vee*·a

listen for ...

el (*vwe*·lo) es·*ta* kan·se·*la*·do
El (vuelo) está cancelado.   **The (flight) is cancelled.**

el (*om*·nee·boos) es·*ta* re·tra·*sa*·do
El (ómnibus) está retrasado.   **The (bus) is delayed.**

es·*ta* kom·*ple*·to
Está completo.   **It's full.**

What time's the ... bus?	*¿A qué hora es el ... autobús?*	a ke *o*·ra es el ... ow·to·*boos*
first	*primer*	pree·*mer*
last	*último*	*ool*·tee·mo
next	*próximo*	*prok*·see·mo

When's the next flight to (Machala)?

¿Cuándo sale el próximo kwan·do sa·le el prok·see·mo
vuelo para (Machala)? vwe·lo pa·ra (ma·cha·la)

Can you tell me when we get to (San Miguel)?

¿Me puede decir cuándo me pwe·de de·seer kwan·do
lleguemos a (San Miguel)? lye·ge·mos a (san mee·gel)

I want to get off here.

Quiero bajarme aquí. kye·ro ba·khar·me a·kee

Is this seat free?

¿Está libre este asiento? es·ta lee·bre es·te a·syen·to

That's my seat.

Ése es mi asiento. e·se es mee a·syen·to

For phrases about getting through customs and immigration,
see **border crossing**, page 49.

buying tickets

Where can I buy a ticket?
¿Dónde puedo comprar   *don*·de *pwe*·do kom·*prar*
un boleto?   oon bo·*le*·to

Do I need to book?
¿Tengo que reservar?   *ten*·go ke re·ser·*var*

Can I get a stand-by ticket?
¿Puede ponerme en la lista   *pwe*·de po·*ner*·me en la *lees*·ta
de espera?   de es·*pe*·ra

How much is it?
¿Cuánto cuesta?   *kwan*·to *kwes*·ta

How long does the trip take?
¿Cuánto se tarda?   *kwan*·to se *tar*·da

Is it a direct route?
¿Es un viaje directo?   es oon *vya*·khe dee·*rek*·to

What time do I have to check in?
¿A qué hora tengo que facturar   a ke *o*·ra *ten*·go ke fak·too·*rar*
mi equipaje?   mee e·kee·*pa*·khe

I'd like to … my ticket, please.	*Quisiéra … mi boleto, por favor.*	kee·*sye*·ra … mee bo·*le*·to por fa·*vor*
cancel	*cancelar*	kan·se·*lar*
change	*cambiar*	kam·*byar*
confirm	*confirmar*	kon·feer·*mar*

A … ticket to (Lima), please.	*Un boleto … a (Lima), por favor.*	oon bo·*le*·to … a (*lee*·ma) por fa·*vor*
1st-class	*de primera clase*	de pree·*me*·ra *kla*·se
2nd-class	*de segunda clase*	de se·*goon*·da *kla*·se
child's	*infantil*	een·fan·*teel*
one-way	*de ida*	de *ee*·da
return	*de ida y vuelta*	de *ee*·da ee *vwel*·ta
student's	*de estudiante*	de es·too·*dyan*·te

I'd like a/an …	Quisiéra un	kee·sye·ra oon
seat.	asiento …	a·syen·to …
aisle	de pasillo	de pa·see·lyo
(non-)smoking	de (no) fumadores	de (no) foo·ma·do·res
window	junto a la ventana	khoon·to a la ven·ta·na

Is there (a) …?	¿Hay … ?	ai …
air-conditioning	aire acondicionado	ai·re a·kon·dee·syo·na·do
blanket	una frazada	oo·na fra·sa·da
toilet	baños	ba·nyos
video	vídeo	vee·de·o

luggage

el equipaje

My luggage hasn't arrived.

| Mi equipage no ha llegado. | mee e·kee·pa·khe no a lye·ga·do |

My luggage has been …	Mi equipaje ha sido …	mee e·kee·pa·khe a see·do …
damaged	dañado	da·nya·do
lost	perdido	per·dee·do
stolen	robado	ro·ba·do

I'd like …	Quisiera …	kee·sye·ra …
a luggage locker	un casillero de consigna	oon ka·see·lye·ro de kon·seeg·na
some coins	unas monedas	oo·nas mo·ne·das
some tokens	unas fichas	oo·nas fee·chas

PRACTICAL

bus, tram & metro

Which bus goes to (the centre of town)?
¿Qué autobús va al   ke ow·to·*boos* va al
(centro de la cuidad)?   (*sen*·tro de la syoo·*da*)

Which bus goes to (Cochabamba)?
¿Qué ómnibus va a   ke *om*·nee·boos va a
(Cochabamba)?   (ko·cha·*bam*·ba)

This/That one.
Éste/Ése.   *es*·te/*es*·e

Tram number (three).
El tranvía número   el tran·*vee*·a *noo*·me·ro
(tres).   (tres)

How many stops to (the museum)?
¿Cuantas paradas hay hasta   *kwan*·tas pa·*ra*·das ai *as*·ta
(el museo)?   (el moo·*se*·o)

Do you stop at (the market)?
¿Tiene parada en   *tye*·ne pa·*ra*·da en
(el mercado)?   (el mer·*ka*·do)

bussing it

The most common way to get around Latin America is by bus.
Throughout Latin America the general name for a bus station
is *una estación de autobúses* although in Argentina, it's known
as *una terminal de ómnibuses*. In Venezuela and Colombia
you'll find the term *una terminal terrestre* (lit: land terminal) or
una terminal de pasajeros (lit: passenger terminal). Travelling
by bus can be slow and crowded but it's often a great way to
meet local people – just pull out your phrasebook and get
chatting.

train

What station is this?
¿Cuál es esta estación?　　kwal es *es*·ta es·ta·*syon*

What's the next station?
¿Cuál es la próxima estación?　　kwal es la *prok*·see·ma es·ta·*syon*

Does this train stop at (Veracruz)?
¿Para el tren en (Veracruz)?　　*pa*·ra el tren en (ve·ra·*kroos*)

Do I need to change trains?
¿Tengo que cambiar de tren?　　*ten*·go ke kam·*byar* de tren

Which carriage is …?	*¿Cuál es el coche …?*	kwal es el *ko*·che …
1st class	*de primera clase*	de pree·*me*·ra *kla*·se
for (Buenos Aires)	*para (Buenos Aires)*	para (*bwe*·nos *ai*·res)
for dining	*comedor*	ko·me·*dor*

boat

Where do we get on the boat?
¿Donde subimos al barco?　　*don*·de soo·*bee*·mos al *bar*·ko

Are there life jackets?
¿Hay chalecos salvavidas?　　ai cha·*le*·kos sal·va·*vee*·das

What's the sea like today?
¿Cómo está el mar hoy?　　*ko*·mo es·*ta* el mar oy

I feel seasick.
Estoy mareado/a. m/f　　es·*toy* ma·re·*a*·do/a

barge/ferry (CAm)	*panga* f	*pan*·ga
canoe	*canoa* f	ka·*no*·a
dugout canoe	*cayuco* m	ka·*yoo*·ko
port	*puerto* m	*pwer*·to
raft	*balsa* f	*bal*·sa
wharf	*embarcadero* m	em·bar·ka·*de*·ro
(Per, CAm)	*malecón* m	ma·le·*kon*

taxi

I'd like a taxi …	*Quisiera un taxi …*	kee·*sye*·ra oon *tak*·see …
at (9am)	*a las (nueve de la mañana)*	a las (*nwe*·ve de la ma·*nya*·na)
now	*ahora*	a·*o*·ra
tomorrow	*mañana*	ma·*nya*·na

Is this taxi free?
¿Está libre este taxi?   es·*ta lee*·bre *es*·te *tak*·see

How much is it (to the airport)?
¿Cuánto cuesta ir (al aeropuerto)?   *kwan*·to *kwes*·ta eer (al a·e·ro·*pwer*·to)

Please put the meter on.
Por favor, ponga el taxímetro.   por fa·*vor pon*·ga el tak·*see*·me·tro

Please take me to (this address).
Por favor, lléveme a (esta dirección).   por fa·*vor lye*·ve·me a (*es*·ta dee·rek·*syon*)

typical addresses

avenue	*avenida* f	a·ve·*nee*·da
	(Per) *paseo* m	pa·*se*·o
	(Arg) *rambla* f	*ram*·bla
lane	*callejón* m	ka·lye·*khon*
street	*calle* f	*ka*·lye

Please …	*Por favor, …*	por fa·*vor* …
slow down	*vaya más despacio*	*va*·ya mas des·*pa*·syo
wait here	*espere aquí*	es·*pe*·re a·*kee*
Stop …	*Pare …*	*pa*·re …
at the corner	*en la esquina*	en la es·*kee*·na
here	*aquí*	a·*kee*

car & motorbike

car & motorbike hire

I'd like to	*Quisiera*	kee·sye·ra
hire a/an ...	*alquilar ...*	al·kee·lar ...
4WD	*un todo terreno*	oon to·do te·re·no
automatic	*un carro*	oon ka·ro
(car)	*automático*	ow·to·ma·tee·ko
car	*un carro*	oon ka·ro
(SAm)	*un auto*	oon ow·to
manual (car)	*un carro manual*	oon ka·ro man·wal
motorbike	*una moto*	oo·na mo·to

with ...	*con ...*	kon ...
air-	*aire*	ai·re
conditioning	*acondicionado*	a·kon·dee·syo·na·do
a driver	*un chofer*	oon cho·fer

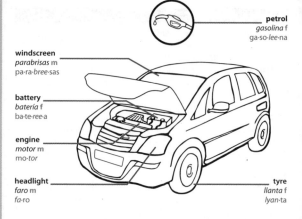

petrol
gasolina f
ga·so·lee·na

windscreen
parabrisas m
pa·ra·bree·sas

battery
batería f
ba·te·ree·a

engine
motor m
mo·tor

headlight
faro m
fa·ro

tyre
llanta f
lyan·ta

How much for	¿Cuánto cuesta	kwan·to kwes·ta
... hire?	alquilar por ...?	al·kee·lar por ...
daily	día	dee·a
hourly	hora	o·ra
weekly	semana	se·ma·na

on the road

What's the ...	¿Cuál es el límite	kwal es el lee·mee·te
speed limit?	de velocidad ...?	de ve·lo·see·da ...
city	en la ciudad	en la syoo·da
country	en el campo	en el kam·po

Is this the road to (Tegucigalpa)?
¿Se va a (Tegucigalpa) por
esta carretera?
se va a (te·goo·see·gal·pa) por
es·ta ka·re·te·ra

(How long) Can I park here?
¿(Por cuánto tiempo)
Puedo aparcar aquí?
(por kwan·to tyem·po)
pwe·do a·par·kar a·kee

Where's a petrol station?
¿Dónde hay una
gasolinera?
don·de ai oo·na
ga·so·lee·ne·ra

gas guzzlers

The word *gasolinera* for 'petrol station' is the standard term that will be understood throughout Latin America but you may come across some other country-specific terms:

Argentina:	estación f de servicio	es·ta·syon de ser·vee·syo
Bolivia:	surtidor m	soor·tee·dor
Chile:	bencinera f	ben·see·ne·ra
Colombia and Central America:	bomba f	bom·ba
Peru:	grifo m	gree·fo

transport

45

Please fill it up.
   Lleno, por favor.   *lye·*no por fa·*vor*

I'd like (20) litres.
   Quiero (veinte) litros.   *kye·*ro (*vayn·*te) *lee·*tros

Where do I pay?
   ¿Dónde se paga?   *don·*de se *pa·*ga

diesel	*diesel*	*dee·*sel
leaded (regular)	*gasolina con plomo*	ga·so·*lee·*na kon *plo·*mo
petrol (gas)	*gasolina*	ga·so·*lee·*na
	(Arg) *nafta*	*naf·*ta
	(Chi) *bencina*	ben·*see·*na
unleaded	*gasolina sin plomo*	ga·so·*lee·*na seen *plo·*mo

Please check the ...	*Por favor, revise ...*	por fa·*vor* re·*vee·*se ...
oil	*el nivel del aceite*	el nee·*vel* del a·*say·*te
tyre pressure	*la presión de las llantas*	la pre·*syon* de las *lyan·*tas
water	*el nivel del agua*	el nee·*vel* del *a·*gwa

road signs

Acceso	ak·*se·*so	**Entrance**
Aparcamiento	a·par·ka·*myen·*to	**Parking**
Ceda el Paso	se·da el *pa·*so	**Give way**
Dirección Única	dee·rek·*syon* oo·nee·ka	**One-way**
Peaje	pe·*a·*khe	**Toll**
Peligro	pe·*lee·*gro	**Danger**
Prohibido Aparcar	pro·ee·*bee·*do a·par·*kar*	**No Parking**
Prohibido el Paso	pro·ee·*bee·*do el *pa·*so	**No Entry**
Pare	*pa·*re	**Stop**
Stop	e·*stop*	**Stop**
Salida de Autopista	sa·*lee·*da de ow·to·*pees·*ta	**Exit Freeway**

PRACTICAL

46

problems

I need a mechanic.
Necesito un mecánico.
ne·se·*see*·to oon
me·*ka*·nee·ko

The car has broken down (in Granada).
El carro se ha averiado (en Granada).
el *ka*·ro se a a·ve·*rya*·do (en gra·*na*·da)

I had an accident.
Tuve un accidente.
too·ve oon ak·see·*den*·te

The motorbike won't start.
No arranca la moto.
no a·*ran*·ka la *mo*·to

The battery is flat.
La batería está descargada.
la ba·te·*ree*·a es·*ta* des·kar·*ga*·da

I have a flat tyre.
Tengo un pinchazo.
ten·go oon peen·*cha*·so

I've lost my car keys.
He perdido las llaves de mi carro.
e per·*dee*·do las *lya*·ves de mee *ka*·ro

I've locked the keys inside.
Dejé las llaves encerradas dentro.
de·*khe* las *lya*·ves en·se·*ra*·das *den*·tro

I've run out of petrol.
Me quedé sin gasolina.
me ke·*de* seen ga·so·*lee*·na

Can you fix it (today)?
¿Puede arreglarlo (hoy)?
pwe·de a·re·*glar*·lo (oy)

How long will it take?
¿Cuánto tardará?
kwan·to tar·da·*ra*

listen for ...

de ke *mar*·ka es
¿De qué marca es?
What make/model is it?

ten·go ke pe·*deer* e·se re·*pwes*·to
Tengo que pedir ese repuesto.
I have to order that part.

bicycle

la bicicleta

Where can I …?	¿Dónde se puede …?	don·de se pwe·de …
hire a bicycle	alquilar una bicicleta	al·kee·lar oo·na bee·see·kle·ta
buy a second-hand bike	comprar una bicicleta de segunda mano	kom·prar oo·na bee·see·kle·ta de se·goon·da ma·no

How much is it per …?	¿Cuánto cuesta por …?	kwan·to kwes·ta por …
afternoon	una tarde	oo·na tar·de
day	un día	oon dee·a
hour	hora	o·ra
morning	una mañana	oo·na ma·nya·na

I have a puncture.
Se me pinchó una rueda.   se me peen·cho oo·na rwe·da

---

trucking it

In rural areas of Latin America, where bus services are infrequent, drivers of pick-up trucks and other vehicles transport others in need of a ride for a fare similar to a bus fare. We don't recommend hitchhiking per se, but if you find yourself in a situation where this informal taxi service is your only option, these phrases might come in handy:

Could you give me a ride in your (pick-up)?
¿Me podría llevar en su (pick-up)?   me po·dree·a lye·var en soo (peek·oop)

How much do I owe you?
¿Cuánto le debo?   kwan·to le de·bo

Are you waiting for more people?
¿Está esperando a más gente?   es·ta es·pe·ran·do a mas khen·te

I'm here …	Estoy aquí …	es·toy a·kee …
in transit	en tránsito	en tran·see·to
on business	de negocios	de ne·go·syos
on holiday	de vacaciones	de va·ka·syo·nes

I'm here for …	Estoy aquí por …	es·toy a·kee por …
(four) days	(cuatro) días	(kwa·tro) dee·as
(two) weeks	(dos) semanas	(dos) se·ma·nas
(three) months	(tres) meses	(tres) me·ses

I have a	Tengo un	ten·go oon
… permit.	permiso de …	per·mee·so de …
residency	residencia	re·see·den·sya
study	estudios	es·too·dyos
work	trabajo	tra·ba·kho

border crossing

I have a visa.
Tengo un visado.   ten·go oon vee·sa·do

I have nothing to declare.
No tengo nada que declarar.   no ten·go na·da ke de·kla·rar

I have something to declare.
Tengo algo que declarar.   ten·go al·go ke de·kla·rar

I didn't know I had to declare it.
No sabía que tenía que   no sa·bee·a ke te·nee·a ke
declararlo.   de·kla·rar·lo

Do you have this form in English?
¿Tiene ese formulario   tye·ne e·se for·moo·la·ryo
en inglés?   en een·gles

Where's (the bank)?
¿Dónde está (el banco)?   don·de es·ta (el ban·ko)

I'm looking for (the public toilets).
Busco (los baños).   boos·ko (los ba·nyos)

Which way's (the post office)?
¿Por dónde se va (a correos)?   por don·de se va (a ko·re·os)

How can I get there?
¿Cómo puedo ir?   ko·mo pwe·do eer

How far is it?
¿A cuánta distancia está?   a kwan·ta dees·tan·sya es·ta

Can you show me (on the map)?
¿Me lo podría indicar   me lo po·dree·a een·dee·kar
(en el mapa)?   (en el ma·pa)

What's the address?
¿Cuál es la dirección?   kwal es la dee·rek·syon

It's ...	Está ...	es·ta ...
behind ...	detrás de ...	de·tras de ...
far away	lejos	le·khos
here	aquí	a·kee
in front of ...	adelante de ...	a·de·lan·te de ...
left	a la izquierda	a la ees·kyer·da
near	cerca	ser·ka
next to ...	al lado de ...	al la·do de ...
on the corner	en la esquina	en la es·kee·na
opposite ...	frente a ...	fren·te a ...
right	a la derecha	a la de·re·cha
straight ahead	todo derecho	to·do de·re·cho
there	ahí	a·ee
	(Arg) acá	a·ka

Turn ...	Doble ...	do·ble ...
left/right	*a la izquierda/ derecha*	a la ees·*kyer*·da/ de·*re*·cha
at the corner	*en la esquina*	en la es·*kee*·na
at the traffic lights	*en el semáforo*	en el se·*ma*·fo·ro

It's ...	Está a ...	es·*ta* a ...
(100) metres	*(cien) metros*	(syen) *me*·tros
(two) kilometres	*(dos) kilómetros*	(dos) kee·*lo*·me·tros
(five) minutes	*(cinco) minutos*	(*seen*·ko) mee·*noo*·tos

by bus	*en autobús*	en ow·to·*boos*
on foot	*a pie*	a pye
by taxi	*en taxi*	en *tak*·see
by train	*en tren*	en tren

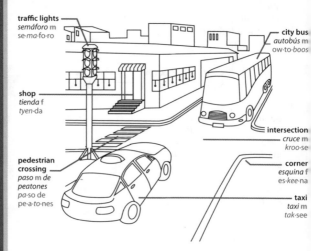

traffic lights
semáforo m
se·*ma*·fo·ro

shop
tienda f
tyen·da

pedestrian crossing
paso m *de peatones*
pa·so de pe·a·*to*·nes

city bus
autobús m
ow·to·*boos*

intersection
cruce m
kroo·se

corner
esquina f
es·*kee*·na

taxi
taxi m
tak·see

finding accommodation

buscar alojamiento

Where's a ...?	¿Dónde hay ...?	don·de ai ...
bed and breakfast	una pensión con desayuno	oo·na pen·syon kon de·sa·yoo·no
cabin	una cabaña	oo·na ka·ba·nya
camping ground	un terreno de cámping	oon te·re·no de kam·peen
guesthouse	una pensión	oo·na pen·syon
	una casa de huéspedes	oo·na ka·sa de wes·pe·des
(Arg, Chi)	una hostería	oo·na os·te·ree·a
hotel	un hotel	oon o·tel
youth hostel	un albergue juvenil	oon al·ber·ge khoo·ve·neel

Can you recommend somewhere ...?	¿Puede recomendar algún sitio ...?	pwe·de re·ko·men·dar al·goon see·tyo ...
cheap	barato	ba·ra·to
good	bueno	bwe·no
luxurious	de lujo	de loo·kho
nearby	cercano	ser·ka·no
romantic	romántico	ro·man·tee·ko

What's the address?
¿Cuál es la dirección?   kwal es la dee·rek·syon

For more on asking and giving directions, see **directions**, page 51.

accommodation

dive	*pocilga* f	po·*seel*·ga
rat-infested	*plagado/a* m/f	pla·*ga*·do/a
	de ratas	de *ra*·tas
top spot	(Arg) *lugar* m *bárbaro*	loo·*gar* bar·ba·ro
	(Per) *lugar* m *paja*	loo·*gar* pa·kha

booking ahead & checking in

hacer una reserva & registrándose

Do you have a	*¿Tiene una*	tye·ne oo·na
… room?	*habitación …?*	a·bee·ta·*syon* …
double	*doble*	*do*·ble
single	*individual*	een·dee·vee·*dwal*
twin	*con dos camas*	kon dos *ka*·mas
How much is it	*¿Cuánto cuesta*	*kwan*·to *kwes*·ta
per …?	*por …?*	por …
night	*noche*	*no*·che
person	*persona*	per·*so*·na
week	*semana*	se·*ma*·na

I'd like to book a room, please.
Quisiera reservar una   kee·*sye*·ra re·ser·*var* oo·na
habitación.   a·bee·ta·*syon*

I have a reservation.
Tengo una reserva.   *ten*·go oo·na re·*ser*·va

My name's …
Me llamo …   me *lya*·mo …

For (three) nights/weeks.
Para (tres) noches/semanas.   *pa*·ra (tres) *no*·ches/se·*ma*·nas

From (July 2) to (July 6).
Desde (el dos de julio)
hasta (el seis de julio).

des·de (el dos de *khoo*·lyo)
as·ta (el says de *khoo*·lyo)

Can I see it?
¿Puedo verla?

pwe·do *ver*·la

It's fine. I'll take it.
OK. La alquilo.

o·*kay* la al·*kee*·lo

Do I need to pay upfront?
¿Necesito pagar por
adelantado?

ne·se·*see*·to pa·*gar* por
a·de·lan·*ta*·do

Can I pay by …?   *¿Puedo pagar*
                          con …?

     credit card   *tarjeta de*
                          crédito
     travellers   *cheques de*
     cheque   *viajero*

pwe·do pa·*gar*
kon …

     tar·*khe*·ta de
     kre·dee·to
     che·kes de
     vya·*khe*·ro

For other methods of payment, see **money**, page 35.

requests & queries

peticiones & preguntas

When/Where's breakfast served?
¿Cuándo/Dónde se sirve
el desayuno?

kwan·do/*don*·de se *seer*·ve
el de·sa·*yoo*·no

Please wake me at (seven).
Por favor, despiérteme
a (las siete).

por fa·*vor* des·*pyer*·te·me
a (las *sye*·te)

Can I get another …?
¿Puede darme otro/a …? m/f

pwe·de *dar*·me o·tro/a …

Can I use the …?	¿Puedo usar …?	pwe·do oo·sar …
kitchen	la cocina	la ko·see·na
laundry	la lavandería	la la·van·de·ree·a
telephone	el teléfono	el te·le·fo·no

Do you have a/an …?	¿Hay …?	ai …
elevator	ascensor	a·sen·sor
laundry service	servicio de lavandería	ser·vee·syo de la·van·de·ree·a
message board	tablón de anuncios	ta·blon de a·noon·syos
(CAm)	pizarra de anuncios	pee·sa·ra de a·noon·syos
(Chi)	diario mural	dya·ryo moo·ral
safe	una caja fuerte	oo·na ka·kha fwer·te
swimming pool	piscina	pee·see·na
(SAm)	pileta	pee·le·ta

Do you … here?	¿Aquí …?	a·kee …
arrange tours	organizan paseos guiados	or·ga·nee·san pa·se·os gee·a·dos
change money	cambian dinero	kam·byan dee·ne·ro

---

listen for …

la *lya*·ve es·*ta* en re·sep·*syon*
La llave está en recepción. — **The key is at reception.**

lo *syen*·to es·*ta* kom·*ple*·to
Lo siento, está completo. — **I'm sorry, we're full.**

por *kwan*·tas *no*·ches
¿Por cuántas noches? — **For how many nights?**

soo pa·sa·*por*·te por fa·*vor*
Su pasaporte, por favor. — **Your passport, please.**

PRACTICAL

Can I leave a message for someone?
¿Puedo dejar un   *pwe·*do de·*khar* oon
mensaje para alguien?   men·*sa·*khe *pa·*ra al·gyen

Is there a message for me?
¿Hay algún mensaje   ai al·*goon* men·*sa·*khe
para mí?   *pa·*ra mee

I'm locked out of my room.
Cerré la puerta y se me   se·*re* la *pwer·*ta ee se me
olvidaron las llaves   ol·vee·*da·*ron las *lya·*ves
dentro.   *den·*tro

The (bathroom) door is locked.
La puerta (del baño) está   la *pwer·*ta (del *ba·*nyo) es·*ta*
cerrada con llave.   se·*ra·*da kon *lya·*ve

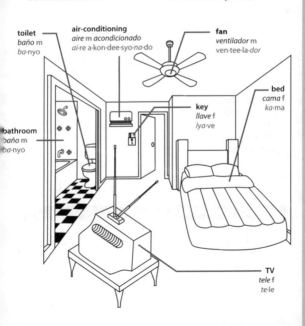

toilet
baño m
*ba·*nyo

air-conditioning
aire m *acondicionado*
*ai·*re a·kon·dee·syo·*na·*do

fan
ventilador m
ven·tee·la·*dor*

bathroom
baño m
*ba·*nyo

key
llave f
*lya·*ve

bed
cama f
*ka·*ma

TV
tele f
*te·*le

complaints

The room is too ...	La habitación es demasiado ...	la a·bee·ta·syon es de·ma·sya·do ...
cold	fría	free·a
dark	oscura	os·koo·ra
dirty	sucia	soo·sya
expensive	cara	ka·ra
light/bright	luminosa	loo·mee·no·sa
noisy	ruidosa	rwee·do·sa
small	pequeña	pe·ke·nya
The ... doesn't work.	No funciona ...	no foon·syo·na ...
air-conditioning	el aire acondicionado	el ai·re a·kon·dee·syo·na·do
fan	el ventilador	el ven·tee·la·dor
heater	la estufa	la es·too·fa
toilet	el baño	el ba·nyo
window	la ventana	la ven·ta·na

The room smells.
La habitación huele mal.   la a·bee·ta·syon we·le mal

The toilet smells.
El baño huele mal.   el ba·nyo we·le mal

There's no hot water.
No hay agua caliente.   no ai a·gwa ka·lyen·te

This ... isn't clean.
Éste/a ... no está limpio/a. m/f   es·te/a ... no es·ta leem·pyo/a

a knock at the door ...

Who is it?	¿Quién es?	kyen es
Just a moment.	Un momento.	oon mo·men·to
Come in.	Adelante.	a·de·lan·te
Come back later, please.	¿Puede volver más tarde, por favor?	pwe·de vol·ver mas tar·de por fa·vor

checking out

What time is checkout?
*¿A qué hora hay que dejar
libre la habitación?*
a ke *o*·ra ai ke de·*khar
lee*·bre la a·bee·ta·*syon*

Can I have a late checkout?
*¿Puedo dejar libre la
habitación más tarde?*
pwe·do de·*khar lee*·bre la
a·bee·ta·*syon* mas *tar*·de

How much extra to stay until (6 o'clock)?
*¿Cuánto más cuesta
quedarse hasta (las seis)?*
kwan·to mas *kwes*·ta
ke·*dar*·se *as*·ta (las says)

Can I leave my luggage here?
*¿Puedo dejar el
equipaje aquí?*
pwe·do de·*khar* el
e·kee·*pa*·khe a·*kee*

I'm leaving now.
Me voy ahora.
me voy a·*o*·ra

There's a mistake in the bill.
Hay un error en la cuenta.
ai oon e·*ror* en la *kwen*·ta

Can you call a taxi for me (for 11 o'clock)?
*¿Me puede pedir un
taxi (para las once)?*
me *pwe*·de pe·*deer* oon
tak·see (*pa*·ra las *on*·se)

**Could I have
my ..., please?**
  deposit
  passport
  valuables
*¿Me puede dar
..., por favor?*
  mi depósito
  mi pasaporte
  *mis objetos
  de valor*
me *pwe*·de dar
... por fa·*vor*
  mee de·*po*·see·to
  mee pa·sa·*por*·te
  mees ob·*khe*·tos
  de va·*lor*

**I'll be back ...
  in (three) days
  on (Tuesday)**
*Volveré ...
  en (tres) días
  el (martes)*
vol·ve·*re* ...
  en (tres) *dee*·as
  el (*mar*·tes)

accommodation

I had a great stay, thank you.
  Tuve una estancia muy agradable, gracias.
  too·ve oo·na es·tan·sya mooy a·gra·da·ble gra·syas

You've been terrific.
  Fueron muy amables.
  fwe·ron mooy a·ma·bles

I'll recommend it to my friends.
  Se lo recomendaré a mis amigos.
  se lo re·ko·men·da·re a mees a·mee·gos

camping

acampar

Where's the nearest …?	*¿Dónde está …?*	don·de es·ta …
campsite	*el terreno de cámping más cercano*	el te·re·no de kam·peen mas ser·ka·no
shop	*la tienda más cercana*	la tyen·da mas ser·ka·na
Where are the nearest …?	*Donde están …?*	don·de es·tan …
showers	*las duchas más cercanas*	las doo·chas mas ser·ka·nas
toilets	*los baños más cercanos*	los ba·nyos mas ser·ka·nos
Do you have …?	*¿Tiene …?*	tye·ne …
electricity	*electricidad*	e·lek·tree·see·da
shower facilities	*duchas*	doo·chas
a site	*un lugar*	oon loo·gar
tents for hire	*carpas para alquilar*	kar·pas pa·ra al·kee·lar

How much is it per …?	¿Cuánto vale por …?	kwan·to va·le por …
caravan	caravana	ka·ra·va·na
person	persona	per·so·na
tent	carpa	kar·pa
vehicle	vehículo	ve·ee·koo·lo

Can I …?	¿Se puede …?	se pwe·de …
camp here	acampar aquí	a·kam·par a·kee
park next to my tent	estacionar al lado de mi carpa	es·ta·syo·nar al la·do de mee kar·pa

Who do I ask to stay here?
¿Con quién tengo que hablar   kon kyen ten·go ke a·blar
para quedarme aquí?   pa·ra ke·dar·me a·kee

Is it coin-operated?
¿Funciona con monedas?   foon·syo·na kon mo·ne·das

Is the water drinkable?
¿Se puede beber el agua?   se pwe·de be·ber el a·gwa

Could I borrow (a mallet)?
¿Me podría prestar   me po·dree·a pres·tar
(un mazo)?   (oon ma·so)

For more words related to camping, see the **dictionary**.

renting

alquilar

I'm here about (the room) for rent.
Vengo por (la habitación)   ven·go por (la a·bee·ta·syon)
que anuncian para alquilar.   ke a·noon·syan pa·ra al·kee·lar

Do you have a/an … for rent?	¿Tiene … para alquilar?	tye·ne … pa·ra al·kee·lar
apartment	un departamento	oon de·par·ta·men·to
cabin	una cabaña	oo·na ka·ba·nya
house	una casa	oo·na ka·sa
room	una habitación	oo·na a·bee·ta·syon
villa	un chalet	oon cha·le

furnished	*amueblado/a* m/f	a·mwe·*bla*·do/a
partly	*parcialmente*	par·syal·*men*·te
furnished	*amueblado/a* m/f	a·mwe·*bla*·do/a
unfurnished	*sin amueblar*	seen a·mwe·*blar*

staying with locals

hospedárse con la gente de la zona

Can I stay at your place?

| *¿Me podría quedar en* | me po·*dree*·a ke·*dar* en |
| *su/tu casa?* pol/inf | soo/too *ka*·sa |

Is there anything I can do to help?

| *¿Puedo ayudar en algo?* | *pwe*·do a·yoo·*dar* en *al*·go |

I have my own ...	*Tengo mi*	*ten*·go mee
	propio/a ... m/f	*pro*·pyo/a ...
mattress	*colchón* m	kol·*chon*
sleeping bag	*bolsa* f *de dormir*	*bol*·sa de dor·*meer*

Can I ...?	*¿Puedo ...?*	*pwe*·do ...
bring anything	*traer algo para*	tra·*er al*·go *pa*·ra
for the meal	*la comida*	la ko·*mee*·da
do the dishes	*lavar los platos*	la·*var* los *pla*·tos
set/clear the	*poner/quitar la*	po·*ner*/kee·*tar* la
table	*mesa*	*me*·sa
take out the	*sacar la basura*	sa·*kar* la ba·*soo*·ra
rubbish		

Thanks for your hospitality.

| *Gracias por su/tu* | *gra*·syas por soo/too |
| *hospitalidad.* pol/inf | os·pee·ta·lee·*da* |

If you're dining with your hosts, see **eating out**, page 146 for more phrases.

looking for ...

buscando ...

Where's (a supermarket)?
¿Dónde hay   don·de ai
(un supermercado)?   (oon soo·per·mer·ka·do)

Where can I buy (bread)?
¿Dónde puedo comprar (pan)?   don·de pwe·do kom·prar (pan)

For asking and giving directions, see **directions**, page 51 and for types of shops, see the **dictionary**.

shop till you drop

In Latin America the generic term for 'general store' is *una tienda*. Look out for some of these regional variations:

Argentina:
  un almacén   oon al·ma·sen
Central America, Colombia, Bolivia, Ecuador and Peru:
  una tienda de abarrrotes oo·na tyen·da de a·ba·ro·tes
Central America:
  una bodega   oo·na bo·de·ga
Costa Rica and Chile:
  una pulpería   oo·na pool·pe·ree·a
Venezuela:
  un abasto   oon a·bas·to

making a purchase

I'd like to buy …
Quisiera comprar …
kee·sye·ra kom·prar …

I'm just looking.
Sólo estoy mirando.
so·lo es·toy mee·ran·do

How much is this?
¿Cuánto cuesta esto?
kwan·to kwes·ta es·to

Can you write down the price?
¿Puede escribir el precio?
pwe·de es·kree·beer el pre·syo

Do you have any others?
¿Tiene otros?
tye·ne o·tros

Can I look at it?
¿Puedo verlo?
pwe·do ver·lo

market hopping

Markets or *mercados* are a colourful feature of Latin American life and you'll find a vast array of comestibles and consumables there. Smaller, open-air street markets are known as *ferias*. If it's vibrant folk art you're after, the place to visit is a *mercado de artesanía* or craft market.

Could I have it wrapped?
¿Me lo podría envolver?
me lo po·dree·a en·vol·ver

Does it have a guarantee?
¿Tiene garantía?
tye·ne ga·ran·tee·a

Can I have it sent overseas?
¿Pueden enviarlo por
correo a otro país?
pwe·den en·vyar·lo por
ko·re·o a o·tro pa·ees

Can you order it for me?
¿Me lo puede pedir?
me lo pwe·de pe·deer

Can I pick it up later?
¿Puedo recogerlo más tarde?
pwe·do re·ko·kher·lo mas tar·de

al·go mas	¿Algo más?	**Anything else?**
kwan·tos/as	¿Cuántos/as	**How many**
kye·re	quiere? m/f pl	**would you like?**
no no te·ne·mos	No, no tenemos	**No, we don't**
neen·goo·no	ninguno.	**have any.**

Do you have change?
¿Tiene cambio?   tye·ne kam·byo

It's faulty.
Es defectuoso.   es de·fek·two·so

I don't like it.
No me gusta.   no me goos·ta

Do you accept ...?   ¿Aceptan ...?   a·sep·tan ...

   American dollars   dólares americanos   do·la·res a·me·ree·ka·nos

   credit cards   tarjetas de crédito   tar·khe·tas de kre·dee·to

   debit cards   tarjetas de débito   tar·khe·tas de de·bee·to

   travellers cheques   cheques de viajero   che·kes de vya·khe·ro

Could I have a ..., please?   ¿Podría darme ..., por favor?   po·dree·a dar·me ... por fa·vor

   bag   una bolsa   oo·na bol·sa

   receipt   un recibo   oon re·see·bo

I'd like ..., please.   Quisiera ..., por favor.   kee·sye·ra ... por fa·vor

   my change   mi cambio   mee kam·byo

   my money back   que me devuelva el dinero   ke me de·vwel·va el dee·ne·ro

   to return this   devolver esto   de·vol·ver es·to

bargaining

el regateo

That's too expensive.
Es muy caro.   es mooy *ka*·ro

The price is very high.
Cuesta demasiado.   *kwes*·ta de·ma·*sya*·do

Can you lower the price (a little)?
¿Podría bajar   po·*dree*·a ba·*khar*
(un poco) el precio?   (oon *po*·ko) el *pre*·syo

Do you have something cheaper?
¿Tiene algo más barato?   *tye*·ne *al*·go mas ba·*ra*·to

I'll give you …
Le/La daré … m/f   le/la da·*re* …

What's your final price?
¿Cuál es su precio final?   kwal es soo *pre*·syo fee·*nal*

local talk

bargain	*ganga* f	*gan*·ga
bargain hunter	*cazador* m *de ofertas*	ka·sa·*dor* de o·*fer*·tas
rip-off	*estafa* f	es·*ta*·fa
specials	*saldos* m pl	*sal*·dos
sale	*venta* f	*ven*·ta

clothes

la ropa

Can I try it on?
¿Me lo puedo probar?   me lo *pwe*·do pro·*bar*

My size is (medium).
Uso la talla (mediana).   *oo*·so la *ta*·lya (me·*dya*·na)

It doesn't fit.
No me queda bien.   no me *ke*·da byen

For different types of clothing, see the **dictionary**.

repairs

Can I have my ... repaired here?	¿Puede reparar mi ... aquí?	pwe·de re·pa·rar mee ... a·kee
backpack	mochila	mo·chee·la
camera	cámara	ka·ma·ra

When will my ... be ready?	¿Cuándo estarán listos mis ...?	kwan·do es·ta·ran lees·tos mees ...
(sun)glasses	anteojos (de sol)	an·te·o·khos (de sol)
shoes	zapatos	sa·pa·tos

hairdressing

I'd like (a) ...	Quisiera ...	kee·sye·ra ...
blow wave	un secado a mano	oon se·ka·do a ma·no
colour	un tinte de pelo	oon teen·te de pe·lo
haircut	un corte de pelo	oon kor·te de pe·lo
highlights	reflejos	re·fle·khos
my beard trimmed	que me recorte la barba	ke me re·kor·te la bar·ba
shave	que me afeite	ke me a·fay·te
trim	que me recorte el pelo	ke me re·kor·te el pe·lo

Don't cut it too short.
No me lo corte   no me lo kor·te
demasiado corto.   de·ma·sya·do kor·to

Shave it all off!
¡Aféitelo todo!   a·fay·te·lo to·do

Please use a new blade.
Por favor, use una   por fa·vor oo·se oo·na
cuchilla nueva.   koo·chee·lya nwe·va

I should never have let you near me!
¡No debía haberle/haberla   no de·bee·a a·ber·le/a·ber·la
dejado tocarme! m/f   de·kha·do to·kar·me

books & reading

Is there a/an (English-language) ...?   *¿Hay alguna ... (en inglés)?*   ai al·*goo*·na ... (en een·*gles*)

bookshop	*librería*	lee·bre·*ree*·a
entertainment guide	*guía de espectáculos*	*gee*·a de es·pek·*ta*·koo·los
section	*sección*	sek·*syon*

Do you have a book by (Gabriel García Márquez)?
¿Tiene un libro de (Gabriel García Márquez)?   tye·ne oon *lee*·bro de (ga·*bryel* gar·*see*·a mar·*kes*)

I like (Isabel Allende).
Me gusta (Isabel Allende).   me *goos*·ta (ee·sa·*bel* a·*lyen*·de)

Do you have Lonely Planet guidebooks?
¿Tiene guías de Lonely Planet?   tye·ne *gee*·as de *lon*·lee *pla*·net

music

I'd like (a) ...   *Quisiera ...*   kee·*sye*·ra ...

blank tape	*una cinta virgen*	*oo*·na *seen*·ta *veer*·khen
CD	*un cómpact*	oon *kom*·pak
headphones	*unos auriculares*	*oo*·nos ow·ree·koo·*la*·res

I heard a singer called (Omara Portuondo).
Escuché un cantante que se llama (Omara Portuondo).   es·koo·*che* oon kan·*tan*·te ke se *lya*·ma (o·*ma*·ra por·*twon*·do)

I heard a band called (Maná).
Escuché un grupo que se llama (Maná).   es·koo·*che* oon *groo*·po ke se *lya*·ma (ma·*na*)

What's his/her best recording?
¿Cuál es su mejor disco?   kwal es soo me·*khor* *dees*·ko

Can I listen to this?
¿Puedo escuchar este?   *pwe*·do es·koo·*char* *es*·te

photography

I need … film for this camera.	*Necesito un carrete de película … para esta cámara.*	ne·se·*see*·to oon ka·*re*·te de pe·*lee*·koo·la … *pa*·ra *es*·ta *ka*·ma·ra
APS	*APS*	a pe *e*·se
B&W	*en blanco y negro*	en *blan*·ko ee *ne*·gro
colour	*en color*	en ko·*lor*
slide	*para diapositivas*	*para* dya·po·*see*·*tee*·vas
(400) speed	*de sensibilidad (cuatro cientos)*	de sen·*see*·bee·lee·*da* (*kwa*·tro *syen*·tos)
Can you … ?	*¿Puede …?*	*pwe*·de …
load my film	*cargar el carrete*	kar·*gar* el ka·*re*·te
develop this film	*revelar este carrete*	re·ve·*lar es*·te ka·*re*·te

How much is it to develop this film?
¿Cuánto cuesta revelar este carrete? — *kwan*·to *kwes*·ta re·ve·*lar es*·te ka·*re*·te

When will it be ready?
¿Cuándo estará listo? — *kwan*·do es·ta·*ra lees*·to

I need passport photos taken.
Necesito fotos de pasaporte. — ne·se·*see*·to *fo*·tos de pa·sa·*por*·te

I'm not happy with these photos.
No estoy contento/a con estas fotos. m/f — no es·*toy* kon·*ten*·to/a kon *es*·tas *fo*·tos

For more photographic equipment, see the **dictionary**.

souvenirs

alpaca jumper	*chompa* f *de alpaca*	*chom·*pa de al·*pa·*ka
basketwork	*cestería* f	ses·te·*ree·*a
cigars	*cigarros* m pl	see·*ga·*ros
coffee	*café* m	ka·*fe*
earrings	*pendientes* m pl	pen·*dyen·*tes
(Arg, CAm)	*aritos* m pl	a·*ree·*tos
(Uru)	*caravanas* f pl	ka·ra·*va·*nas
(Nic)	*chapas* f pl	*cha·*pas
hammock	*hamaca* f	a·*ma·*ka
jewellery	*joyería* f	kho·ye·*ree·*a
leather belt	*cinto* m *de cuero*	*seen·*to de *kwe·*ro
leather boots	*botas* f pl *de cuero*	*bo·*tas de *kwe·*ro
leather handbag	*cartera* f *de cuero*	kar·*te·*ra de *kwe·*ro
necklace	*collar* m	ko·*lyar*
Panamanian appliqué textile	*mola* f	*mo·*la
panpipes	*zampoña* f	sam·*po·*nya
Peruvian hat	*chullo* m	*choo·*lyo
pottery	*alfarería* f	al·fa·re·*ree·*a
ring	*anillo* m	a·*nee·*lyo
rug	*alfombra* f	al·*fom·*bra
silverware	*plata* f	*pla·*ta
weaving	*tejido* m	te·*khee·*do
woodcarving	*talla* f *de madera*	*ta·*lya de ma·*de·*ra

post office

correos

I want to send a …	*Quisiera enviar …*	kee·*sye*·ra en·*vyar* …
fax	*un fax*	oon faks
letter	*una carta*	*oo*·na *kar*·ta
parcel	*un paquete*	oon pa·*ke*·te
(Arg)	*una encomienda*	*oo*·na en·ko·*myen*·da
postcard	*una postal*	*oo*·na pos·*tal*
I want to buy …	*Quisiera comprar …*	kee·*sye*·ra kom·*prar* …
an aerogram	*un aerograma*	oon a·e·ro·*gra*·ma
an envelope	*un sobre*	oon *so*·bre
stamps	*unos sellos*	*oo*·nos *se*·lyos

airmail	*correo* m *aéreo*	ko·*re*·o a·*e*·re·o
customs declaration	*declaración* f *de aduana*	de·kla·ra·*syon* de a·*dwa*·na
domestic	*nacional*	na·syo·*nal*
express mail	*correo* m *urgente*	ko·*re*·o oor·*khen*·te
fragile	*frágil*	*fra*·kheel
international	*internacional*	een·ter·na·syo·*nal*
mailbox	*buzón* m	boo·*son*
postcode	*código* m *postal*	*ko*·dee·go pos·*tal*
(Arg)	*característica* f	ka·rak·te·*rees*·tee·ka
registered mail	*correo* m *certificado*	ko·*re*·o ser·tee·fee·*ka*·do
regular mail	*correo* m *normal*	ko·*re*·o nor·*mal*
surface mail	*por vía terrestre*	por *vee*·a te·*res*·tre

Please send it by airmail (to England).
Por favor, mándelo por vía aérea (a Inglaterra).
por fa·*vor* man·de·lo por *vee*·a a·e·re·a (a een·gla·*te*·ra)

Please send it by surface mail (to Buenos Aires).
Por favor, mándelo por vía terrestre (a Buenos Aires).
por fa·*vor* man·de·lo por *vee*·a te·*res*·tre (a *bwe*·nos *ai*·res)

It contains …
Contiene …
kon·*tye*·ne …

Where's the poste restante section?
¿Dónde está la lista de correos?
don·de es·*ta* la *lees*·ta de ko·*re*·os

Is there any mail for me?
¿Hay alguna carta para mí?
ai al·*goo*·na *kar*·ta *pa*·ra mee

---

listen for …

a·*don*·de lo *man*·da
¿Adónde lo manda? **Where are you sending it?**

por ko·*re*·o oor·*khen*·te o nor·*mal*
¿Por correo urgente o normal? **By express post or regular post?**

---

phone

el teléfono

What's your phone number?
¿Cuál es su número de teléfono?
kwal es soo *noo*·me·ro de te·*le*·fo·no

Where's the nearest public phone?
¿Dónde está la cabina telefónica más cercana?
don·de es·*ta* la ka·*bee*·na te·le·*fo*·nee·ka mas ser·*ka*·na

I want to make a (reverse-charge/collect) call to Singapore.
Quiero hacer una llamada (a cobro revertido) a Singapur.
kye·ro a·*ser* oo·na lya·*ma*·da (a *ko*·bro re·ver·*tee*·do) a seen·ga·*poor*

I want ...	Quiero ...	kye·ro ...
to buy a phone card	comprar una tarjeta telefónica	kom·prar oo·na tar·khe·ta te·le·fo·nee·ka
to speak for (three) minutes	hablar por (tres) minutos	a·blar por (tres) mee·noo·tos

How much does ... cost?	¿Cuánto cuesta ...?	kwan·to kwes·ta ...
a (three)-minute call	una llamada de (tres) minutos	oo·na lya·ma·da de (tres) mee·noo·tos
each extra minute	cada minuto extra	ka·da mee·noo·to ek·stra

The number is ...
El número es ...　　el noo·me·ro es ...

What's the area code for (Lima)?
¿Cuál es el prefijo de (Lima)?　　kwal es el pre·fee·kho de (lee·ma)

What's the country code for (Chile)?
¿Cuál es el prefijo de (Chile)?　　kwal es el pre·fee·kho de (chee·le)

It's engaged.
Está ocupada.　　es·ta o·koo·pa·da

The connection's bad.
Es mala conexión.　　es ma·la ko·nek·syon

I've been cut off.
Me han cortado (la comunicación).　　me an kor·ta·do (la ko·moo·nee·ka·syon)

Hello. (making a call)
¡Hola!　　o·la

Hello. (answering a call)
¿Diga?　　dee·ga

It's … (when identifying yourself)
Habla …   a·bla …

Can I speak to (Pedro)?
¿Está (Pedro)?   es·ta pe·dro

Can I leave a message?
¿Puedo dejar un   pwe·do de·khar oon
mensaje?   men·sa·khe

Please tell him/her I called.
Dile/Dila que llamé,   dee·le/dee·la ke lya·me
por favor. m/f   por fa·vor

I'll call back later.
Ya llamaré más tarde.   ya lya·ma·re mas tar·de

My number is …
Mi número es …   mee noo·me·ro es …

I don't have a contact number.
No tengo número de   no ten·go noo·me·ro de
contacto.   kon·tak·to

---

listen for …

de par·te de kyen
  ¿De parte de quién?   **Who's calling?**

kon kyen kye·re a·blar
  ¿Con quién quiere   **Who do you want to**
  hablar?   **speak to?**

lo syen·to pe·ro a·o·ra no es·ta
  Lo siento, pero ahora   **I'm sorry he's/she's**
  no está.   **not here.**

lo syen·to tye·ne el noo·me·ro e·kee·vo·ka·do
  Lo siento, tiene el   **Sorry, wrong number.**
  numero equivocado.

oon mo·men·to
  Un momento.   **One moment.**

see a·kee es·ta
  Sí, aquí está.   **Yes, he's/she's here.**

mobile/cell phone

el teléfono móvil

I'd like a/an …	*Quisiera …*	kee·*sye*·ra …
adaptor plug	*un adaptador*	oon a·dap·ta·*dor*
charger for	*un cargador*	oon kar·ga·*dor*
my phone	*para mi*	*pa*·ra mee
	teléfono	te·*le*·fo·no
mobile/cell	*un móvil para*	oon *mo*·veel *pa*·ra
phone for hire	*alquilar*	al·kee·*lar*
prepaid mobile/	*un móvil*	oon *mo*·veel
cell phone	*pagado por*	pa·*ga*·do por
	adelantado	a·de·lan·*ta*·do
SIM card for	*una tarjeta*	*oo*·na tar·*khe*·ta
your network	*SIM para su red*	seem *pa*·ra soo re

What are the rates?
 ¿Cuáles son las tarifas?   *kwa*·les son las ta·*ree*·fas

(30c) per (30) seconds.
 (Treinta centavos) por   (*trayn*·ta sen·*ta*·vos) por
 (treinta) segundos.   (*trayn*·ta) se·*goon*·dos

the internet

el internet

Where's the local Internet cafe?
 ¿Dónde hay un cibercafé   *don*·de ai oon see·ber·ka·*fe*
 cercano?   ser·*ka*·no

I'd like to …	*Quisiera …*	kee·*sye*·ra …
get Internet	*usar el*	oo·*sar* el
access	*Internet*	een·ter·*net*
check my email	*revisar mi*	re·vee·*sar* mee
	correo	ko·*re*·o
	electrónico	e·lek·*tro*·nee·ko
use a printer	*usar una*	oo·*sar* *oo*·na
	impresora	eem·pre·*so*·ra
use a scanner	*usar un escáner*	oo·*sar* oon es·*ka*·ner

How much per …?	¿Cuánto cuesta por …?	kwan·to kwes·ta por …
CD	cómpact	kom·pak
(10) minutes	(diez) minutos	(dyes) mee·noo·tos
hour	hora	o·ra
page	página	pa·khee·na

Do you have …?	¿Tiene …?	tye·ne …
PCs	PC	pe se
Macs	MacIntosh	ma·keen·tosh
a Zip drive	unidad de Zip	oo·nee·da de seep

How do I log on?
¿Cómo me conecto al sistema?
ko·mo me ko·nek·to al sees·te·ma

I need help with the computer.
Necesito ayuda con la computadora.
ne·se·see·to a·yoo·da kon la kom·poo·ta·do·ra

It's crashed.
Se ha quedado colgado.
se a ke·da·do kol·ga·do

I've finished.
He terminado.
e ter·mee·na·do

---

return to sender

In Latin America dwellings may not be numbered and addresses are sometimes short descriptive passages. Be prepared to decipher an exotic address like the following:

Marirosa Ferrer Botero	Marirosa Ferrer Botero
la casa azul en la	the blue house on the
esquina de Avenida de	corner of Avenida de
la Paz y Calle 12	la Paz and 12th Street
cerca de la farmacia	near the pharmacy
una manzana al norte de	one block north of
la catedral	the cathedral
Tegucigalpa Honduras	Tegucigalpa Honduras

If you're having trouble finding your way to such an address, try using the **dictionary** to translate the various elements, or ask for help using the phrases in **directions**, page 51.

Where can I …?	*¿Dónde puedo …?*	*don·de pwe·do …*
I'd like to …	*Me gustaría …*	*me goos·ta·ree·a …*
arrange a transfer	*organizar una transferencia*	*or·ga·nee·sar oo·na trans·fe·ren·sya*
cash a cheque	*cobrar un cheque*	*ko·brar oon che·ke*
change a travellers cheque	*cambiar un cheque de viajero*	*kam·byar oon che·ke de vya·khe·ro*
change money	*cambiar dinero*	*kam·byar dee·ne·ro*
get a cash advance	*obtener un adelanto*	*ob·te·ner oon a·de·lan·to*
use internet banking	*usar la banca por internet*	*oo·sar la ban·ka por een·ter·net*
withdraw money	*sacar dinero*	*sa·kar dee·ne·ro*
Where's the nearest …?	*¿Dónde está …?*	*don·de es·ta …*
automatic teller machine	*el cajero automático más cercano*	*el ka·khe·ro ow·to·ma·tee·ko mas ser·ka·no*
foreign exchange office	*la oficina de cambio más cercana*	*la o·fee·see·na de kam·byo mas ser·ka·na*

What time does the bank open?
¿A qué hora abre el banco? a ke o·ra a·bre el ban·ko

The automatic teller machine took my card.
El cajero automático se ha tragado mi tarjeta. el ka·khe·ro ow·to·ma·tee·ko se a tra·ga·do mee tar·khe·ta

I've forgotten my PIN.
Me he olvidado del NPI. me e ol·vee·da·do del e·ne pe ee

Can I use my credit card to withdraw money?
¿Puedo usar mi tarjeta de crédito para sacar dinero? pwe·do oo·sar mee tar·khe·ta de kre·dee·to pa·ra sa·kar dee·ne·ro

What's the exchange rate?
¿Cuál es la tasa de cambio?   kwal es la *ta*·sa de *kam*·byo

What's the commission?
¿Cuál es la comisión?   kwal es la ko·mee·*syon*

What's the charge for that?
¿Cuánto hay que pagar por eso?   *kwan*·to ai ke pa·*gar* por *e*·so

Can I have smaller notes?
¿Me lo puede dar en   me lo *pwe*·de dar en
billetes más pequeños?   bee·*lye*·tes mas pe·*ke*·nyos

Has my money arrived yet?
¿Ya ha llegado mi dinero?   ya a lye·*ga*·do mee dee·*ne*·ro

How long will it take to arrive?
¿Cuánto tiempo tardará   *kwan*·to *tyem*·po tar·da·*ra*
en llegar?   en lye·*gar*

For other useful phrases, see **money**, page 35.

For other useful phrases, see **money**, page 35.

---

listen for ...

ai oon pro·*ble*·ma kon soo *kwen*·ta		
Hay un problema	**There's a problem**	
con su cuenta.	**with your account.**	
no po·*de*·mos a·*ser e*·so		
No podemos hacer eso.	**We can't do that.**	
pwe·de es·kree·*beer*·lo		
¿Puede escribirlo?	**Could you write it down?**	
por fa·*vor* feer·me a·*kee*		
Por favor firme aquí.	**Please sign here.**	

soo ...	Su ...	Your ...
en ...	*En ...*	**In ...**
(kwa·tro) dee·as	*(cuatro) días*	**(four)**
la·bo·*ra*·bles	*laborables*	**working days**
(kwa·tro) dee·as	**(SAm)** *(cuatro) días*	
a·*bee*·les	*hábiles*	
soo ...	*Su ...*	**Your ...**
ee·den·tee·fee·ka·*syon*	*identificación*	**ID**
pa·sa·*por*·te	*pasaporte*	**passport**

I'd like a/an …	Quisiera …	kee·sye·ra …
audio set	un equipo audio	oon e·kee·po ow·dyo
catalogue	un catálogo	oon ka·ta·lo·go
guide (person)	un/una guía m/f	oon/oo·na gee·a
guidebook in English	una guía turística en inglés	oo·na gee·a too·rees·tee·ka en een·gles
(local) map	un mapa (de la zona)	oon ma·pa (de la so·na)

Do you have information on … sights?	¿Tiene información sobre los lugares … de interés?	tye·ne een·for·ma·syon so·bre los loo·ga·res … de een·te·res
cultural	culturales	kool·too·ra·les
local	locales	lo·ka·les
religious	religiosos	re·lee·khyo·sos
unique	únicos	oo·nee·kos

I'd like to see …
Me gustaría ver … me goos·ta·ree·a ver …

What's that?
¿Qué es eso? ke es e·so

Who made it?
¿Quién lo hizo? kyen lo ee·so

How old is it?
¿De cuándo es? de kwan·do es

Could you take a photograph of me?
¿Me puede sacar una foto? me pwe·de sa·kar oo·na fo·to

Can I take photographs (of you)?
¿(Le/Te) Puedo sacar fotos? pol/inf (le/te) pwe·do sa·kar fo·tos

I'll send you the photograph.
Le/Te mandaré la foto. pol/inf le/te man·da·re la fo·to

getting in

What time does it open/close?
¿A qué hora abre/cierra?　　　a ke o·ra a·bre/sye·ra

What's the admission charge?
¿Cuánto cuesta la entrada?　　kwan·to kwes·ta la en·tra·da

It costs (100 pesos).
Cuesta (cien pesos).　　　　　kwes·ta (syen pe·sos)

Is there a discount for ...?	*¿Hay descuentos para ...?*	ai des·kwen·tos pa·ra ...
children	*niños*	nee·nyos
families	*familias*	fa·mee·lyas
groups	*grupos*	groo·pos
pensioners	*pensionados*	pen·syo·na·dos
	(Arg) *jubilados*	khoo·bee·la·dos
students	*estudiantes*	es·too·dyan·tes

what's in a name?

Many Latin American place names are linked to historical events. *Argentina* comes from the Latin *argentum* 'silver' allegedly because the first Europeans to arrive observed the indigenous people wearing silver jewellery. *Bolivia* is named after Simón Bolívar, the famous revolutionary general who helped liberate many Latin American countries from Spanish rule and became the country's first president. *Costa Rica* means 'rich coast' and was named by Christopher Columbus for the precious metals that the land was expected to yield. *Honduras* literally means 'depths' and was named by Columbus for the deep waters off the country's north coast. *Colombia* was named after Columbus himself, though not until the 19th century.

tours

Can you recommend a ...?	¿Puede recomendar algún ...?	pwe·de re·ko·men·dar al·goon ...
boat trip	paseo en barca	pa·se·o en bar·ka
tour	recorrido	re·ko·ree·do
When's the next ...?	¿Cuándo es la próxima ...?	kwan·do es la prok·see·ma ...
daytrip	excursión de un día	ek·skoor·syon de oon dee·a
excursion	excursión	ek·skoor·syon
Is ... included?	¿Incluye ...?	een·kloo·ye ...
accommodation	alojamiento	a·lo·kha·myen·to
equipment	equipo	e·kee·po
food	comida	ko·mee·da
transport	transporte	trans·por·te

Can we hire a guide?
¿Podemos alquilar un guía?
po·de·mos al·kee·lar oon gee·a

The guide will pay.
El guía va a pagar.
el gee·a va a pa·gar

The guide has paid.
El guía ha pagado.
el gee·a a pa·ga·do

Do I need to take (lunch) with me?
¿Necesito llevar (el almuerzo)?
ne·se·see·to lye·var (el al·mwer·so)

sightseeing

81

How long is the tour?
¿Cuánto dura el recorrido?
kwan·to doo·ra el re·ko·ree·do

What time should I be back?
¿A qué hora tengo que volver?
a ke o·ra ten·go ke vol·ver

Be back here at (four).
Vuelva a (las cuatro).
vwel·va a (las kwa·tro)

I'm with them.
Voy con ellos.
voy kon e·lyos

I've lost my group.
He perdido mi grupo.
e per·dee·do mee groo·po

signs

Abierto	*a·byer·to*	**Open**
Baños	*ba·nyos*	**Toilets**
Caliente	*ka·lyen·te*	**Hot**
Cerrado	*se·ra·do*	**Closed**
Entrada	*en·tra·da*	**Entry**
Frío	*free·o*	**Cold**
Información	*een·for·ma·syon*	**Information**
No Tocar	*no to·kar*	**Don't Touch**
Prohibido Tomar Fotos	*pro·ee·bee·do to·mar fo·tos*	**No Photography**
Prohibido Usar el Flash	*pro·ee·bee·do oo·sar el flash*	**No Flash Photography**
Reservado	*re·ser·va·do*	**Reserved**
Salida	*sa·lee·da*	**Exit**
Salida de Emergencia	*sa·lee·da de e·mer·khen·sya*	**Emergency Exit**
Servicios	*ser·vee·syos*	**Toilets**

I'm attending a …   *Asisto a …*   a·*sees*·to a …
   conference   *un congreso*   oon kon·*gre*·so
   course   *un curso*   oon *koor*·so
   meeting   *una reunión*   oo·na re·oo·*nyon*
   trade fair   *una feria de*   oo·na *fe*·rya de
     muestras   *mwes*·tras

I'm here with …   *Estoy aquí con …*   es·*toy* a·*kee* kon …
   my company   *mi compañía*   mee kom·pa·*nyee*·a
   my colleague(s)   *mi(s) colega(s)*   mee(s) ko·*le*·ga(s)
   (two) others   *otros (dos)*   o·tros (dos)

I'm alone.
   Estoy solo/a. m/f   es·*toy* so·lo/a

I'm staying at the (Hotel Libertad), room (82).
   Me estoy alojando en el   me es·*toy* a·lo·*khan*·do en el
   (Hotel Libertad), habitación   (o·tel lee·ber·*ta*) a·bee·ta·*syon*
   (ochenta y dos).   (o·*chen*·ta ee dos)

I'm here for (two) days/weeks.
   Estoy aquí por (dos)   es·toy a·*kee* por (dos)
   días/semanas.   *dee*·as/se·*ma*·nas

I have an appointment with (Mr Gonzáles).
   Tengo una cita con   *ten*·go *oo*·na *see*·ta kon
   (el Señor Gonzáles).   (el se·*nyor* gon·*sa*·les)

Here's my business card.
   Aquí tiene mi tarjeta   a·*kee* tye·ne mee tar·*khe*·ta
   de visita.   de vee·*see*·ta

Let me introduce you to my colleague.
   ¿Puedo presentarle   *pwe*·do pre·sen·*tar*·le
   a mi colega?   a mee ko·*le*·ga

That went very well.
   Eso salió muy bien.   e·so sa·*lyo* mooy byen

Shall we go for a drink/meal?
   ¿Vamos a tomar/comer algo?   *va*·mos a to·*mar*/ko·*mer* al·go

Where's the ...?	¿Dónde está ...?	don·de es·ta ...
business	el servicio	el ser·vee·syo
centre	secretarial	se·kre·ta·ryal
conference	el congreso	el kon·gre·so
meeting	la reunión	la re·oo·nyon

I need ...	Necesito ...	ne·se·see·to ...
a computer	una	oo·na
	computadora	kom·poo·ta·do·ra
a connection	una conexión	oo·na ko·nek·syon
to the Net	al Internet	al een·ter·net
an interpreter	un/una	oon/oo·na
	intérprete m/f	een·ter·pre·te
more business	más tarjetas de	mas tar·khe·tas de
cards	visita	vee·see·ta
some space to	espacio para	es·pa·syo pa·ra
set up	disponer	dees·po·ner
to send an	enviar un	en·vyar oon
email/fax	email/fax	ee·mayl/faks

I'm expecting a ...	Estoy esperando ...	es·toy es·pe·ran·do ...
call	una llamada	oo·na lya·ma·da
fax	un fax	oon faks

don't worry, don't hurry

The attitude towards time is more relaxed in Latin American countries than in the English-speaking world. Latin Americans do differentiate, however, between formal and social occasions and are usually more punctual for the former.

When arranging a business meeting, try adding the expres–sion *en punto* (equivalent to the English 'sharp') to the time expression, eg, *a las once en punto* means 'at 11 o'clock sharp'.

For social occasions, it's common to show up at least half an hour later than the designated time. If you don't want to be kept waiting, you could ask, when arranging to meet, if the appointed time is *a la hora inglesa* (lit: on English time) meaning promptly, or *a la hora latina* (lit: on Latin American time), ie, approximately half an hour later than specified.

I have a disability.
Soy discapacitado/a. m/f — soy dees·ka·pa·see·*ta*·do/a

I need assistance.
Necesito asistencia. — ne·se·*see*·to a·sees·*ten*·sya

I have a hearing aid.
Llevo audífono. — *lye*·vo ow·*dee*·fo·no

I'm deaf.
Soy sordo/a. m/f — soy *sor*·do/a

What services do you have for people with a disability?
¿Qué servicios tienen para — ke ser·*vee*·syos *tye*·nen *pa*·ra
discapacitados? — dees·ka·pa·see·*ta*·dos

Is there wheelchair access?
¿Hay acceso para silla — ai ak·*se*·so *pa*·ra *see*·lya
de ruedas? — de *rwe*·das

Is there a lift?
¿Hay ascensor? — ai a·sen·*sor*

How many steps are there?
¿Cuántos escalones hay? — *kwan*·tos es·ka·*lo*·nes ai

How wide is the entrance?
¿Cuánto es de ancha la — *kwan*·to es de *an*·cha la
entrada? — en·*tra*·da

Are guide dogs permitted?
¿Se permite la entrada — se per·*mee*·te la en·*tra*·da
a los perros guía? — a los *pe*·ros *gee*·a

Is there somewhere I can sit down?
¿Hay algún sitio dónde me — ai al·*goon* *see*·tyo *don*·de me
pueda sentar? — *pwe*·da sen·*tar*

Could you call me a disabled taxi please?

¿Me podría llamar a
un taxi para
discapacitados?

me po·*dree*·a lya·*mar* a
oon tak·*see* pa·ra
dees·ka·pa·see·*ta*·dos

Could you help me cross this street?

¿Me puede ayudar a
cruzar la calle?

me *pwe*·de a·yoo·*dar* a
kroo·*sar* la *ka*·lye

Braille library	*biblioteca* f *Braille*	bee·blyo·*te*·ka *brai*·e·le
disabled person	*persona* f *discapacitada*	per·*so*·na dees·ka·pa·see·*ta*·da
guide dog	*perro* m *guía*	*pe*·ro *gee*·a
ramp	*rampa* f	*ram*·pa
space (to move around)	*espacio* m *(para moverse)*	es·*pa*·syo (*pa*·ra mo·*ver*·se)
wheelchair	*silla* f *de ruedas*	*see*·lya de *rwe*·das

---

gender rules

When you see an m it means masculine, so the article you use should be either *un* or *el* . When you see an f it means feminine, so the article should be either *una* or *la*.

Where an *-o* ending and an *-a* ending mark masculine and feminine forms respectively we've used a slash. For example, the two forms of the word 'beautiful' *lindo* and *linda* are written *lindo/a*.

Where the only difference between masculine and feminine forms is the addition of an *-a* ending for the feminine form, we've used brackets. Hence the two forms of the word 'doctor', *doctor* and *doctora,* are abbreviated to *doctor(a)*.

Also see **gender** in the **a–z phrasebuilder**, page 17.

Is there a/an …?	*¿Hay …?*	ai …
baby change room	*una sala en la que pueda cambiarle el pañal al bebé*	oo·na sa·la en la ke pwe·da kam·byar·le el pa·nyal al be·be
child-minding service	*servicio de cuidado de niños*	ser·vee·syo de kwee·da·do de nee·nyos
children's menu	*menú infantil*	me·noo een·fan·teel
creche	*guardería*	gwar·de·ree·a
(English-speaking) babysitter	*niñera (de habla inglesa)*	nee·nye·ra (de a·bla een·gle·sa)
family discount	*descuento familiar*	des·kwen·to fa·mee·lyar
highchair	*trona*	tro·na
park	*un parque*	oon par·ke
playground nearby	*un parque infantil cercano*	oon par·ke een·fan·teel ser·ka·no
theme park	*un parque de atracciones*	oon par·ke de a·trak·syo·nes
toyshop	*una juguetería*	oo·na khoo·ge·te·ree·a
I need a …	*Necesito …*	ne·se·see·to …
baby seat	*un asiento de seguridad para bebés*	oon a·syen·to de se·goo·ree·da pa·ra be·bes
booster seat	*un asiento de seguridad para niños*	oon a·syen·to de se·goo·ree·da pa·ra nee·nyos
potty	*una bacinica*	oo·na ba·see·nee·ka
	(SAm) *una pelela*	oo·na pe·le·la
stroller	*un cochecito*	oon ko·che·see·to

Do you mind if I breast-feed here?

¿Le molesta que dé
de pecho aquí?

le mo·les·ta ke de
de pe·cho a·kee

Are children allowed?

¿Se admiten niños?

se ad·mee·ten nee·nyos

Is this suitable for (two)-year-old children?

¿Es apto para niños de
(dos) años?

es ap·to pa·ra nee·nyos de
(dos) a·nyos

---

kids' talk

When's your birthday?

¿Cuándo es tu
cumpleaños?

kwan·do es too
koom·ple·a·nyos

Do you go to school or kindergarten?

¿Vas al colegio o
a la guardería?

vas al ko·le·khyo o
a la gwar·de·ree·a

What grade are you in?

¿En qué grado estás?

en ke gra·do es·tas

Do you like school?

¿Te gusta el colegio?

te goos·ta el ko·le·khyo

Do you like sport?

¿Te gusta el deporte?

te goos·ta el de·por·te

What do you do after school?

¿Qué haces después del
colegio?

ke a·ses des·pwes del
ko·le·khyo

Do you learn English?

¿Aprendes inglés?

a·pren·des een·gles

I come from very far away.

Vengo de muy lejos.

ven·go de mooy le·khos

Show me how to play.

Dime cómo se juega.

dee·me ko·mo se khwe·ga

Well done!

¡Muy bien!

mooy byen

basics

lo básico

Yes.	*Sí.*	see
No.	*No.*	no
Please.	*Por favor.*	por fa·*vor*
Thank you (very much).	*(Muchas) Gracias.*	(*moo*·chas) *gra*·syas
You're welcome.	*De nada.*	de *na*·da
(CAm)	*Con mucho gusto.*	kon *moo*·cho *goo*·sto
Sorry. (condolence)	*Lo siento.*	lo *syen*·to
Sorry. (apology)	*Perdón.*	per·*don*

Excuse me. (regret)
Perdón.   per·*don*

Excuse me. (for attention or apology)
Discúlpe.   dees·*kool*·pe
Con permiso. **(CAm)**   kon per·*mee*·so

greetings

saludos

Latin Americans are cordial yet polite when dealing with others and will expect you to reciprocate. Never address a stranger without extending a greeting such as *buenos días* (good morning) or *buenas tardes* (good afternoon). These are shortened to *buenos* and *buenas* in Central America and the Andean countries.

Hello./Hi.	*¡Hola!*	o·la
(Chi)	*¿Qué hubo?*	ke *oo*·bo
Good day.	*Buen día.*	bwen *dee*·a
Good morning.	*Buenos días.*	*bwe*·nos *dee*·as
Good afternoon. (until 8pm)	*Buenas tardes.*	*bwe*·nas *tar*·des
Good evening/night.	*Buenas noches.*	*bwe*·nas *no*·ches

See you later.	Hasta luego.	*as*·ta *lwe*·go
Goodbye.	¡Adiós!	a·*dyos*
Bye.	Chao./Chaucito.	chow/chow·*see*·to

getting friendly

Spanish has two forms for the singular 'you'. With people you know well, with your peers and with children, use the informal form *tú*. When addressing strangers, older people, or people that you've just met, use the polite form *usted*. Once your new-found friends feel it's time to switch to *tú* they may say:

Let's use the tú form.
Hablemos de tú.   a·*ble*·mos de too

Also see **you** in the **a–z phrasebuilder**.

How are you?
¿Cómo está? pol	*ko*·mo es·*ta*
¿Cómo estás? inf	*ko*·mo es·*tas*
¿Cómo están? pl pol&inf	*ko*·mo es·*tan*

Fine, thank you.
| Bien, gracias. | byen *gra*·syas |

And you?
| ¿Y usted/tú? pol/inf | ee oos·*te*/too |

What's your name?
| ¿Cómo se llama usted? pol | *ko*·mo se *lya*·ma oos·*te* |
| ¿Cómo te llamas? inf | *ko*·mo te *lya*·mas |

My name is …
| Me llamo … | me *lya*·mo … |

I'd like to introduce you to …
| Quisiera presentarle/te a … pol/inf | kee·*sye*·ra pre·sen·*tar*·le/te a … |

I'm pleased to meet you.
| Mucho gusto. | *moo*·cho *goos*·to |

titles & addressing people

Women are mostly addressed as *Señora* regardless of age or marital status, though some older unmarried women may prefer to be called *Señorita*. Men are usually addressed as *Señor*. Professional titles are important and should be used before the surname when addressing someone directly.

Mr	*Señor*	se·*nyor*
Ms/Mrs	*Señora*	se·*nyo*·ra
Miss	*Señorita*	se·nyo·*ree*·ta

Architect
  Arquitecto/a m/f   ar·kee·*tek*·to/a

Doctor (holder of a PhD or medical doctor)
  Doctor/Doctora m/f   dok·*tor*/dok·*to*·ra

Graduate
  Licenciado/a m/f   lee·sen·*sya*·do/a

Engineer
  Ingeniero/a m/f   een·khe·*nye*·ro/a

Lawyer
  Abogado/a m/f   a·bo·*ga*·do/a

Professor (teacher or university lecturer or professor)
  Profesor/Profesora m/f   pro·fe·*sor*/pro·fe·*so*·ra

Master (teacher or skilled musician or craftsman)
  Maestro/a m/f   ma·*es*·tro/a

---

hey mate!

Friends may call each other *tío* tee·o (lit: uncle) or *tía* tee·a (lit: aunt). It's a bit like saying 'bloke' or 'sheila' in Australian slang. Guys may call each other *colega* ko·*le*·ga (lit: colleague) or may be addressed, or address one another, as *hombre* om·bre (lit: man). Women may be addressed, or address one another, as *mujer* moo·*kher* (lit: woman). In the Southern Cone countries of Argentina, Paraguay and Uruguay you may also hear the term *che* che used to address a man or boy.

making conversation

Do you live here?
¿Vive/Vives aquí? pol/inf
vee·ve/vee·ves a·*kee*

Where are you going?
¿Adónde va/vas? pol/inf
a·*don*·de va/vas

What are you doing?
¿Qué hace/haces? pol/inf
ke a·se/a·ses

Are you waiting (for a bus)?
*¿Está/Estás esperando
(un autobús)?* pol/inf
es·ta/es·tas es·pe·*ran*·do
(oon ow·to·*boos*)

Can I have a light, please?
*¿Tiene/Tienes fuego,
por favor?* pol/inf
tye·ne/tye·nes fwe·go
por fa·*vor*

What's this called?
¿Cómo se llama esto?
ko·mo se lya·ma es·to

What a beautiful baby!
¡Qué niño/a más lindo/a! m/f
ke nee·nyo/a mas leen·do/a

That's (beautiful), isn't it?
Qué (precioso), ¿no?
ke (pre·syo·so) no

Are you here on holiday?
*¿Está/Estás aquí de
vacaciones?* pol/inf
es·ta/es·tas a·kee de
va·ka·syo·nes

How long are you here for?
*¿Cuánto tiempo le va a
quedar?* pol
*¿Cuánto tiempo te vas a
quedar?* inf
kwan·to tyem·po le va a
ke·dar
kwan·to tyem·po te vas a
ke·dar

I'm here for (four) weeks/days.
*Estoy aquí por (cuatro)
semanas/días.*
es·toy a·kee por (kwa·tro)
se·ma·nas/dee·as

Do you like it here?
¿Le/Te gusta esto? pol/inf
le/te goos·ta es·to

I love it here.
Me encanta esto.
me en·kan·ta es·to

I'm here ...	*Estoy aquí ...*	es·toy a·kee ...
for a holiday	*de vacaciones*	de va·ka·syo·nes
on business	*en viaje de negocios*	en *vya*·khe de ne·*go*·syos
to study	*estudiando*	es·too·*dyan*·do
with my family	*con mi familia*	kon mee fa·*mee*·lya
with my partner	*con mi pareja* m&f	kon mee pa·*re*·kha

This is my ...	*Éste/a es mi ...* m/f	es·ta/e es mee ...
child	*hijo/a* m/f	ee·*kho*/a
colleague	*colega* m&f	ko·*le*·ga
friend	*amigo/a* m/f	a·*mee*·go/a
husband	*esposo*	es·*po*·so
partner (intimate)	*pareja* m&f	pa·*re*·kha
wife	*esposa*	es·*po*·sa

local talk

Hey!	*¡Eh, tú!*	e too
What's up?	*¿Qué onda?*	ke *on*·da
What's happening?	*¿Qué pasó?*	ke pa·*so*
It's/I'm OK.	*Está/Estoy bien.*	es·*ta*/es·*toy* byen
Listen (to this)!	*¡Escucha (esto)!*	es·*koo*·cha (*es*·to)
Look!	*¡Mira!*	*mee*·ra
How cool!	*¡Qué bárbaro!*	ke *bar*·ba·ro
(Arg)	*¡Se pasa!*	se *pa*·sa
(Ven)	*¡Chévere!*	*che*·ve·re
Just joking.	*Te estoy tomando el pelo.*	te es·*toy* to·*man*·do el *pe*·lo
(Arg)	*Te estoy cargando.*	te es·*toy* kar·*gan*·do
No problem.	*No hay drama.*	no ai *dra*·ma
Maybe.	*Quizás.*	kee·*sas*
No way!	*¡De ningún modo!*	de neen·*goon mo*·do
Sure.	*Macanudo.*	ma·ka·*noo*·do

nationalities

Where are you from?
    ¿De dónde es/eres? pol/inf   de *don*·de es/*e*·res

I'm from …   *Soy de …*   soy de …
    Australia   *Australia*   ow·*stra*·lya
    Germany   *Alemania*   a·le·*ma*·nya
    Scotland   *Escocia*   es·*ko*·sya
    the USA   *Los Estados*   los es·*ta*·dos
        Unidos   oo·*nee*·dos

For more countries, see the **dictionary**.

age

How old …?   *¿Cuántos años …?*   *kwan*·tos *a*·nyos …
    are you   *tiene/tienes* pol/inf   *tye*·ne/*tye*·nes
    is your   *tiene su/tu*   *tye*·ne soo/too
      daughter   *hija* pol/inf   *ee*·kha
    is your son   *tiene su/tu*   *tye*·ne soo/too
        hijo pol/inf   *ee*·kho

I'm … years old.
    Tengo … años.   *ten*·go … *a*·nyos
He's/She's … years old.
    Tiene … años.   *tye*·ne … *a*·nyos
Too old!
    ¡Demasiado viejo/a! m/f   de·ma·*sya*·do *vye*·kho/a
I'm younger than I look.
    Soy más joven de lo que   soy mas *kho*·ven de lo ke
    parezco.   pa·*res*·ko

For your age, see **numbers**, page 29.

occupations & studies

What's your occupation?
¿A qué le dedica? pol	a *ke* le de·*dee*·ka
¿A qué te dedicas? inf	a *ke* te de·*dee*·kas

I'm self-employed.
Soy trabajador/	soy tra·ba·kha·*dor*/
trabajadora	tra·ba·kha·*do*·ra
autónomo/a. m/f	ow·*to*·no·mo/a

I'm a/an ...   *Soy ...*   soy ...
architect	*arquitecto/a* m/f	ar·kee·*tek*·to/a
mechanic	*mecánico/a* m/f	me·*ka*·nee·ko/a
writer	*escritor/*	es·kree·*tor*/
	escritora m/f	es·kree·*to*·ra

I work in ...   *Trabajo en ...*   tra·*ba*·kho en ...
communications	*comunicaciones*	ko·moo·nee·ka·*syo*·nes
education	*enseñanza*	en·se·*nyan*·sa
hospitality	*hostelería*	os·te·le·*ree*·a

I'm ...   *Estoy ...*   es·*toy* ...
retired	*jubilado/a* m/f	khoo·bee·*la*·do/a
unemployed	*desempleado/a* m/f	des·em·ple·*a*·do/a

What are you studying?
¿Qué estudia/estudias? pol/inf	ke es·*too*·dya/es·*too*·dyas

I'm studying ...   *Estudio ...*   es·*too*·dyo ...
business	*economía*	e·ko·no·*mee*·a
languages	*idiomas*	ee·*dyo*·mas
science	*ciencias*	*syen*·syas

I'm studying at …	Estudio en …	es·too·dyo en …
college	un instituto	oon een·stee·too·to
school	un colegio	oon ko·le·khyo
trade school	un instituto	oon een·stee·too·to
	técnico	tek·nee·ko
university	una	oo·na
	universidad	oo·nee·ver·see·da

For more occupations and studies, see the **dictionary**.

family

la familia

Do you have (a brother)?
  ¿Tiene/Tienes   tye·ne/tye·nes
  (hermano)? pol/inf   (er·ma·no)

I have (a partner).
  Tengo (pareja). m&f   ten·go (pa·re·kha)

Do you live with (your family)?
  ¿Vive/Vives con (su/tu   vee·ve/vee·ves kon (soo/too
  familia)? pol/inf   fa·mee·lya)

I live with (my sister).
  Vivo con (mi hermana).   vee·vo kon (mee er·ma·na)

This is (my mother).
  Ésta es (mi madre).   es·ta es (mee ma·dre)

Are you married?
  ¿Está casado/a? m/f pol es·ta ka·sa·do/a
  ¿Estás casado/a? m/f inf es·tas ka·sa·do/a

I live with someone.
  Vivo con alguien.   vee·vo kon al·gyen

I'm single.
  Soy soltero/a. m/f   soy sol·te·ro/a

I'm …	Estoy …	es·toy …
married	casado/a m/f	ka·sa·do/a
separated	separado/a m/f	se·pa·ra·do/a

For more kinship terms, see the **dictionary**.

farewells

Tomorrow is my last day here.
Mañana es mi   ma·*nya*·na es mee
último día aquí.   ool·*tee*·mo *dee*·a a·kee

Here's my ...	*Ésta es mi ...*	*es*·ta es mee ...
What's your ...?	*¿Cuál es tu ...?*	kwal es too ...
(email) address	*dirección*	dee·rek·*syon*
	(de email)	(de *ee*·mayl)
fax number	*número de fax*	*noo*·me·ro de faks
mobile number	*número de*	*noo*·me·ro de
	móvil	*mo*·veel
work number	*número de*	*noo*·mero de
	teléfono en el	te·*le*·fo·no en el
	trabajo	tra·*ba*·kho

If you ever visit (Scotland) come and visit us.
Si algún día visitas   see al·*goon dee*·a vee·*see*·tas
(Escocia) ven a vernos.   (es·ko·sya) ven a *ver*·nos

If you ever visit (the USA) you can stay with me.
Si algún día visitas (los   see al·*goon dee*·a vee·*see*·tas (los
Estados Unidos) te puedes   es·*ta*·dos oo·*nee*·dos) te *pwe*·des
quedar conmigo.   ke·*dar* kon·*mee*·go

body language

Personal space boundaries vary from culture to culture and in Latin America they're set closer than in Anglo-Saxon countries. You'll probably find that people stand closer to you when talking than you're used to. Casual touching on the arm or shoulder during conversation is not outside the norm so don't be taken aback if it happens to you. You'll observe good friends greeting each other with an *abrazo* a·*bra*·so (hug) or *beso be*·so (kiss) and and it's quite usual to see people of the same sex walking down the street arm-in-arm.

I want to come and visit you.
Quiero venir a visitarte.   kye·ro ve·neer a vee·see·tar·te

I'll send you copies of the photos.
Te enviaré copias de   te en·vya·re ko·pyas de
las fotos.   las fo·tos

It's been great meeting you.
Me ha encantado conocerte.   me a en·kan·ta·do ko·no·ser·te

I'll miss you.
Te voy a echar de menos.   te voy a e·char de me·nos

Keep in touch!
¡Nos mantendremos en   nos man·ten·dre·mos en
contacto!   kon·tak·to

---

melting pot

Latin American Spanish reflects the rich ethnic mix of the region. A good example of this are the few words coined to refer to people with respect to their heritage. These terms aren't racially loaded labels and are used by people to refer to themselves and their background.

criollo/a m/f   kree·o·lo/a
   person born in Latin America of Spanish ancestry. On the Caribbean Coast, a person of mixed African and European ancestry.

ladino/a m/f   la·dee·no/a
   Spanish-speaking person of mixed Indian and European ancestry

mestizo/a m/f   mes·tee·so/a
   person of mixed ancestry (usually Spanish and Indian)

zambo/a m/f   sam·bo/a
   person of mixed African and Indian ancestry

Avoid using the term *indio/a* m/f 'Indian' which can be offensive to indigenous people. *Indígena* een·dee·khe·na is the preferred option.

common interests

What do you do in your spare time?
¿Qué te gusta hacer en tu tiempo libre?
ke te *goos*·ta a·*ser* en too *tyem*·po *lee*·bre

Do you like …?	*¿Te gusta/ gustan …?* sg/pl	te *goos*·ta/ *goos*·tan …
I (don't) like …	*(No) Me gusta/ gustan …* sg/pl	(no) me *goos*·ta/ *goos*·tan …
board games	*los juegos* m pl *de tablero*	los *khwe*·gos de ta·*ble*·ro
cooking	*cocinar*	ko·see·*nar*
films	*el cine* sg	el *see*·ne
travelling	*viajar*	vya·*khar*

For more hobbies and types of sports, see **sport**, page 125, and the **dictionary**.

---

like it or not

In Spanish, in order to say you like something, you say *me gusta* (lit: me it-pleases). If what you're referring to is plural, use *me gustan* (lit: me they-please). If you're referring to an activity, eg, cooking or travelling, use *me gusta* followed by the verb.

I like that song.
Me gusta esta canción.
me *goos*·ta *es*·ta kan·*syon*

I like soap operas.
Me gustan las telenovelas.
me *goos*·tan las te·le·no·*ve*·las

I like dancing.
Me gusta bailar.
me *goos*·ta bai·*lar*

music

Do you like to …?	*Te gusta …?*	te *goos*·ta …
dance	*bailar*	bai·*lar*
go to concerts	*ir a conciertos*	eer a kon·*syer*·tos
listen to music	*escuchar*	es·koo·*char*
	música	*moo*·see·ka
play an	*tocar un*	to·*kar* oon
instrument	*instrumento*	een·stroo·*men*·to
sing	*cantar*	kan·*tar*

What bands do you like?
  ¿Qué grupos te gustan?   ke *groo*·pos te *goos*·tan
What music do you like?
  ¿Qué música te gusta?   ke *moo*·see·ka te *goos*·ta

classical music	*música* f *clásica*	*moo*·see·ka *kla*·see·ka
electronic music	*música* f	*moo*·see·ka
	electrónica	e·lek·*tro*·nee·ka
merengue	*merengue* m	me·*ren*·ge
pop	*música* f *pop*	*moo*·see·ka pop
R&B	*rhythm and blues* m	*ree*·dem en bloos
rock	*música* f *rock*	*moo*·see·ka rok
salsa	*salsa* f	*sal*·sa
tango	*tango* m	*tan*·go
traditional	*música* f	*moo*·see·ka
music	*folclórica*	fol·*klo*·ree·ka
world music	*música* f *étnica*	*moo*·see·ka *et*·nee·ka

Planning to go to a concert? See **buying tickets**, page 39 and **going out**, page 109.

---

idiosyncratic interests

Here's a quirky Latin American equivalent of the English saying 'To each his own'.

Cada perico a su estaca, cada changa a su mecate.
ka·da pe·*ree*·ko a soo es·*ta*·ka *ka*·da *chan*·ga a soo me·*ka*·te
(lit: each parrot on its perch, each monkey on its rope)

cinema & theatre

I feel like going to a ...	*Tengo ganas de ir a ...*	ten·go ga·nas de eer a ...
ballet	*un ballet*	oon ba·le
comedy	*una comedia*	oo·na ko·me·dya
film	*una película*	oo·na pe·lee·koo·la
play	*una obra*	oo·na o·bra

What's showing at the cinema (tonight)?
¿Qué película dan en el cine (esta noche)?
ke pe·lee·koo·la dan en el see·ne (es·ta no·che)

Is it in English/Spanish?
¿Es en inglés/castellano?
es en een·gles/kas·te·lya·no

Does it have (English) subtitles?
¿Tiene subtítulos (en inglés)?
tye·ne soob·tee·too·los (en een·gles)

I want to sell this ticket.
Quiero vender esta entrada.
kye·ro ven·der es·ta en·tra·da

Are those seats taken?
¿Están libres estos asientos?
es·tan lee·bres es·tos a·syen·tos

Have you seen ...?
¿Has visto ...?
as vees·to ...

Who's in it?
¿Quién actúa?
kyen ak·too·a

It stars ...
Actúa ...
ak·too·a ...

Did you like (the film)?
Te gustó (la película)?
te goos·to (la pe·lee·koo·la)

I thought it was ...	*Pienso que fue ...*	pyen·so ke fwe ...
crap	*una porquería*	oo·na por·ke·ree·a
excellent	*excelente*	ek·se·len·te
long	*larga*	lar·ga

animated films	*películas* f pl *de dibujos animados*	pe·*lee*·koo·las de dee·*boo*·khos a·nee·*ma*·dos
comedies	*comedias* f pl	ko·*me*·dyas
documentaries	*documentales* m pl	do·koo·men·*ta*·les
drama	*drama* m	*dra*·ma
film noir	*cine* m *negro*	*see*·ne *ne*·gro
(Latin American) cinema	*cine* m *(latino-americano)*	*see*·ne (la·tee·no·a·me·ree·*ka*·no)
horror movies	*cine* m *de terror*	*see*·ne de te·*ror*
sci-fi	*cine* m *de ciencia ficción*	*see*·ne de *syen*·sya feek·*syon*
short films	*cortos* m pl	*kor*·tos
thrillers	*cine* m *de suspenso*	*see*·ne de soos·*pen*·so

reading

la lectura

What kind of books do you read?
¿Qué tipo de libros lees?   ke *tee*·po de *lee*·bros *le*·es

Which (Latin American) author do you recommend?
¿Qué autor (latino-americano) recomiendas?   ke ow·*tor* (la·tee·no·a·me·ree·*ka*·no) re·ko·*myen*·das

Have you read (Pablo Neruda)?
¿Has leído a (Pablo Neruda)?   as le·*ee*·do a (*pa*·blo ne·*roo*·da)

On this trip I'm reading (One Hundred Years of Solitude).
En este viaje estoy leyendo (Cien años de soledad).   en *es*·te *vya*·khe es·*toy* ley·*en*·do (syen *a*·nyos de so·le·*da*)

I'd recommend (Jorge Luís Borges).
Recomiendo a (Jorge Luís Borges).   re·ko·*myen*·do a (*khor*·khe loo·*ees* bor·khes)

Where can I exchange books?
¿Dónde puedo cambiar libros?   *don*·de *pwe*·do kam·*byar* *lee*·bros

For more on books, see **shopping**, page 68.

feelings & opinions

feelings

los sentimientos

Feelings are described with either nouns or adjectives: the nouns use 'have' in Spanish (eg, 'I have hunger') and the adjectives use 'be' (like in English).

I'm (not) …	*(No) Tengo …*	(no) *ten·go …*
Are you …?	*¿Tiene(s)…?* pol/inf	*tye·ne(s) …*
cold	*frío*	*free·o*
hot	*calor*	ka·*lor*
hungry	*hambre*	*am·*bre

I'm (not) …	*(No) Estoy …*	(no) es·*toy …*
Are you …?	*¿Está(s) …?* pol/inf	es·*ta(s) …*
annoyed	*enojado/a* m/f	e·no·*kha·*do/a
embarrassed	*avergonzado/a* m/f	a·ver·gon·*sa·*do/a
tired	*cansado/a* m/f	kan·*sa·*do/a

opinions

opiniones

Did you like it?
¿Le/Te gustó? pol/inf   le/te goos·*to*

What did you think of it?
¿Qué pensó/pensaste   ke pen·*so*/pen·*sas·*te
de eso? pol/inf   de *e·*so

I thought it was …	*Pienso que fue …*	*pyen·*so ke fwe …
It's …	*Es …*	es …
beautiful	*bonito/a* m/f	bo·*nee·*to/a
bizarre	*raro/a* m/f	*ra·*ro/a
crap	*un coñazo*	oon ko·*nya·*so
entertaining	*entretenido/a* m/f	en·tre·te·*nee·*do/a
excellent	*fantástico/a* m/f	fan·*tas·*tee·ko/a
full-on	*total*	to·*tal*

mixed emotions

Generally, *un poco*, *bastante* and *muy* are used to qualify feelings.

a little	*un poco*	oon *po*·ko
I'm a little sad.	*Estoy un poco triste.*	es·*toy* oon *po*·ko *trees*·te
quite	*bastante*	bas·*tan*·te
I'm quite disappointed.	*Estoy bastante decepcionado/a.* m/f	es·*toy* bas·*tan*·te de·sep·syo·*na*·do/a
very	*muy*	mooy
I feel very lucky.	*Me siento muy afortunado/a.* m/f	me *syen*·to mooy a·for·too·*na*·do/a

politics & social issues

la política & los temas sociales

The political scene is notoriously volatile in many Latin American countries and politics are the subject of much conversation and debate. People will probably be interested to hear your opinions but be tactful as passions can run high on certain issues.

Who do you vote for?

    ¿A quién vota/votas? pol/inf   a kyen *vo*·ta/*vo*·tas

I support	*Apoyo al*	a·*po*·yo al
the … party.	*partido …*	par·*tee*·do …
I'm a member	*Soy miembro del*	soy *myem*·bro del
of the … party.	*partido …*	par·*tee*·do …
communist	*comunista*	ko·moo·*nees*·ta
conservative	*conservador*	kon·ser·va·*dor*
green	*verde*	*ver*·de
labour	*laborista*	la·bo·*rees*·ta
liberal	*progre*	*pro*·gre
(progressive)		
social democratic	*socialdemócrata*	so·syal·de·*mo*·kra·ta
socialist	*socialista*	so·sya·*lees*·ta

Do you agree with it?
¿Está/Estás de acuerdo con eso? pol/inf — es·ta/es·tas de a·kwer·do kon e·so

I (don't) agree with …
(No) Estoy de acuerdo con … — (no) es·toy de a·kwer·do kon …

Are you against …?
¿Está/Estás en contra de …? pol/inf — es·ta/es·tas en kon·tra de …

Are you in favour of …?
¿Está/Estás a favor de …? pol/inf — es·ta/es·tas a fa·vor de …

How do people feel about …?
¿Cómo se siente la gente de …? — ko·mo se syen·te la khen·te de …

abortion	*aborto* m	a·bor·to
corruption	*corrupción* f	ko·roop·syon
crime	*crimen* m	kree·men
discrimination	*discriminación* f	dees·kree·mee·na·syon
drugs	*drogas* f pl	dro·gas
the economy	*economía* f	e·ko·no·mee·a
education	*educación* f	e·doo·ka·syon
the environment	*medio* m *ambiente*	me·dyo am·byen·te
equal opportunity	*igualdad* f de oportunidades	ee·gwal·da de o·por·too·nee·da·des
euthanasia	*eutanasia* f	e·oo·ta·na·sya
globalisation	*globalización* f	glo·ba·lee·sa·syon
human rights	*derechos* m pl humanos	de·re·chos oo·ma·nos
immigration	*inmigración* f	een·mee·gra·syon
party politics	*política* f de partido	po·lee·tee·ka de par·tee·do
privatisation	*privatización* f	pree·va·tee·sa·syon
racism	*racismo* m	ra·sees·mo
sexism	*sexismo* m	sek·sees·mo
social welfare	*estado* m *del bienestar*	es·ta·do del byen·es·tar
terrorism	*terrorismo* m	te·ro·rees·mo
unemployment	*desempleo* m	des·em·ple·o

the environment

Is there a/an (environmental) problem here?

¿Aquí hay un problema (con el medio ambiente)?   a·*kee* ai oon pro·*ble*·ma (kon el *me*·dyo am·*byen*·te)

conservation	*conservación* f	kon·ser·va·*syon*
deforestation	*deforestación* f	de·fo·res·ta·*syon*
drought	*sequía* f	se·*kee*·a
ecosystem	*ecosistema* m	e·ko·sees·*te*·ma
hunting	*caza* f	*ka*·sa
hydroelectricity	*hidroelectricidad* f	ee·dro·e·lek·tree·see·da
irrigation	*irrigación* f	ee·ree·ga·*syon*
ozone layer	*capa* f *de ozono*	*ka*·pa de o·*so*·no
pesticides	*pesticidas* f pl	pes·tee·*see*·das
pollution	*contaminación* f	kon·ta·mee·na·*syon*
recycling programme	*programa* m *de reciclaje*	pro·*gra*·ma de re·see·*kla*·khe
toxic waste	*residuos* m pl *tóxicos*	re·*see*·dwos tok·*see*·kos
water supply	*suministro* m *de agua*	soo·*mee*·nees·tro de *a*·gwa

Is this a protected …?	*¿Es este/a … protegido/a?* m/f	es *es*·te/a … pro·te·*khee*·do/a
forest	*un bosque* m	oon *bos*·ke
park	*un parque* m	oon *par*·ke
species	*una especie* f	*oo*·na es·*pe*·sye

local talk

Absolutely!	*¡Por supuesto!*	por soo·*pwes*·to
Come off it!	*¡No me jodas!*	no me *kho*·das
Exactly!	*¡Exactamente!*	ek·sak·ta·*men*·te
How interesting!	*¡Qué interesante!*	ke een·te·re·*san*·te
In your dreams!	*¡Anda ya!*	*an*·da ya
No way!	*¡Ni hablar!*	nee a·*blar*
Sure!	*¡Claro!*	*kla*·ro
That's not true!	*¡Eso no es verdad!*	*e*·so no es ver·*da*

where to go

What's there to do in the evenings?
¿Qué se puede hacer por las noches?
ke se *pwe*·de a·*ser* por las *no*·ches

What's on ...?	¿Qué hay ...?	ke ai ...
locally	en la zona	en la *so*·na
this weekend	este fin de semana	*es*·te feen de se·*ma*·na
today	hoy	oy
tonight	esta noche	*es*·ta *no*·che

Where are the ...?	¿Dónde hay ...?	*don*·de ai ...
clubs	clubs nocturnos	kloobs nok·*toor*·nos
gay venues	lugares gay	loo·*ga*·res gay
places to eat	lugares donde comer	loo·*ga*·res *don*·de ko·*mer*
pubs	bares	*ba*·res

Is there a local ... guide?	¿Hay una guía de ... de la zona?	ai oo·na *gee*·a de ... de la *so*·na
entertainment	espectáculos	es·pek·*ta*·koo·los
film	cine	*see*·ne
music	música	*moo*·see·ka

put on your dancing shoes

In dance-crazy Latin America the general term for a dance club is *discoteca*. Dance clubs are also known by these regional terms:

Argentina:	*boliche* m	bo·*lee*·che
Colombia:	*salseadero* m	sal·se·a·*de*·ro
	rumbeadero m	room·be·a·*de*·ro
Ecuador:	*salsoteca* f	sal·so·*te*·ka

| Come on! | ¡Venga, vamos! | ven·ga va·mos |
| This place is great! | ¡Es un lugar bárbaro! | es oon loo·gar bar·ba·ro |

I feel like going to …	Tengo ganas de ir …	ten·go ga·nas de eer …
a bar	a un bar	a oon bar
a cafe	a una cafetería	a oo·na ka·fe·te·ree·a
a concert	a un concierto	a oon kon·syer·to
a nightclub	a una discoteca	a oo·na dees·ko·te·ka
a party	a una fiesta	a oo·na fyes·ta
a restaurant	a un restaurante	a oon res·tow·ran·te
a salsa dance club	a una salsoteca	a oo·na sal·so·te·ka
a tango club	a un club de tango	a oon kloob de tan·go
the movies	al cine	al see·ne
the theatre	al teatro	al te·a·tro

What's the cover charge?
¿Cuánta cuesta entrar?   kwan·ta kwes·ta en·trar

It's free.
Es gratis.   es gra·tees

Am I likely to be harassed for being gay?
¿Me van a molestar por ser   me van a mo·les·tar por ser
homosexual?   o·mo·sek·swal

invitations

What are you doing …?	*¿Qué haces/ hacen …?* sg/pl	ke a·ses/ a·sen …
right now	*ahora*	a·o·ra
this evening	*esta noche*	es·ta no·che
this weekend	*este fin de semana*	es·te feen de se·ma·na

Would you like to go for a …?	*¿Te/Les gustaría ir a …?* sg/pl	te/les goos·ta·ree·a eer a …
coffee	*tomar un café*	to·mar oon ka·fe
drink	*tomar unos tragos*	to·mar oo·nos tra·gos
meal	*comer*	ko·mer
walk	*pasear*	pa·se·ar

I feel like going …	*Tengo ganas de …*	ten·go ga·nas·de …
dancing	*ir a bailar*	eer a bai·lar
out somewhere	*salir*	sa·leer
out to lunch	*ir a almorzar*	eer a al·mor·sar
out to dinner	*ir a cenar*	eer a se·nar

Do you know a good restaurant?
¿Conoces/Conocen un   ko·no·ses/ko·no·sen oon
buen restaurante? sg/pl   bwen res·tow·ran·te

Do you want to come to the (Inti-Illimani) concert with me?
¿Quieres/Quieren venir   kye·res/kye·ren ve·neer
conmigo al concierto   kon·mee·go al kon·syer·to
(de Inti-Illimani)? sg/pl   (de een·tee ee·lyee·ma·nee)

We're having a party.
Vamos a dar una fiesta. va·mos a dar oo·na fyes·ta

You should come.
¿Por qué no vienes/vienen? sg/pl por ke no vye·nes/vye·nen

responding to invitations

Sure!
¡Por supuesto! por soo·pwes·to

Yes, I'd love to.
Me encantaría. me en·kan·ta·ree·a

Yes, let's go.
Sí, vamos. see va·mos

No, I'm afraid I can't.
Lo siento pero no puedo. lo syen·to pe·ro no pwe·do

What about tomorrow?
¿Qué tal mañana? ke tal ma·nya·na

Sorry, I can't sing/dance.
Lo siento, no sé cantar/bailar. lo syen·to no se kan·tar/bai·lar

party animals

Latin Americans know how to let down their hair and *pasarlo guay* pa·sar·lo gway (have a good time). Here are some expressions which all mean 'going out drinking and partying' to help you get a slice of the action:

ir de copas	eer de ko·pas
ir de farra	eer de fa·ra
ir de rumba	eer de room·ba
ir de juerga	eer de khwer·ga
ir de fiesta	eer de fyes·ta
ir de pachanga	eer de pa·chan·ga

SOCIAL

arranging to meet

What time shall we meet?
¿A qué hora quedamos?　　　a ke *o*·ra ke·*da*·mos

Where will we meet?
¿Dónde quedamos?　　　*don*·de ke·*da*·mos

Let's meet at (eight o'clock).
Quedamos a (las ocho).　　　ke·*da*·mos a (las *o*·cho)

Let's meet at the entrance.
Quedamos en la entrada.　　　ke·*da*·mos en la en·*tra*·da

I'll pick you up.
Paso a recogerte/　　　*pa*·so a re·ko·*kher*·te/
recogerles. sg/pl　　　re·ko·*kher*·les

I'll be coming later.
Iré más tarde.　　　ee·*re* mas *tar*·de

Where will you be?
¿Dónde estarás/estarán? sg/pl　　　*don*·de es·ta·*ras*/es·ta·*ran*

If I'm not there by (nine), don't wait for me.
Si no estoy a (las nueve),　　　see no es·*toy* a (las *nwe*·ve)
no me esperes/esperen. sg/pl　　　no me es·*pe*·res/es·*pe*·ren

OK!
¡OK!　　　*o*·key

I'll see you then.
Nos vemos.　　　nos *ve*·mos

See you later/tomorrow.
Hasta luego/mañana.　　　*as*·ta *lwe*·go/ma·*nya*·na

I'm looking forward to it.
Tengo muchas ganas de ir.　　　*ten*·go *moo*·chas *ga*·nas de eer

Sorry I'm late.
Siento llegar tarde.　　　*syen*·to lye·*gar tar*·de

Never mind.
No importa.　　　no eem·*por*·ta

drugs

las drogas

I don't take drugs.
*No consumo ningún
tipo de drogas.*
no kon·*soo*·mo neen·*goon*
tee·po de *dro*·gas

I have … occasionally.
Tomo … de vez en cuando.
to·mo … de ves en *kwan*·do

Do you want to have a smoke?
¿Nos fumamos un porro?
nos foo·*ma*·mos oon *po*·ro

I'm high.
Estoy volado/a. m/f
es·*toy* vo·*la*·do/a

latin american rhythms

Latin America has a profusion of musical styles. Pre-Colombian, Latin, Caribbean and African styles mesh to create a rich variety of rhythms, dances, regional styles and songs.

Música Andina   *moo*·see·ka an·*dee*·na
Well known in the West, Andean music incorporates woodwind instruments of pre-Columbian origin such as the *quena* (reed flute), the *zampoña* (pan flute), the *caja* (tamourine-like drums) and the ukulele-like *charango*.

Música de Los Llanos   *moo*·see·ka de los *lya*·nos
A Venezuelan and Colombian song style accompanied by a *cuatro* (harp) and maracas.

Música Criolla   *moo*·see·ka kree·o·la
With its roots in Spain and Africa, the main instruments of Creole music are guitars and a *cajón* (wooden box drum).

Reggae   *re*·gay
The reggae influence is strongly felt along the Caribbean coast of Central America.

Salsa   *sal*·sa
This immensely popular dance style originated in New York but spread through the Caribbean in the 1960s.

Tango   *tan*·go
Argentina is the birthplace of this musical style and it remains hugely popular today. A visit to a *club de tango* in Buenos Aires is an unforgettable experience.

romance

asking someone out

invitando a alguien a salir

Would you like to do something (tonight)?
¿Quieres hacer algo (esta noche)?
kye·res a·*ser* al·go (*es*·ta *no*·che)

Yes, I'd love to.
Me encantaría.
me en·kan·ta·*ree*·a

No, I'm afraid I can't.
Lo siento, pero no puedo.
lo *syen*·to *pe*·ro no *pwe*·do

I'm busy.
Estoy ocupado/a. m/f
es·*toy* o·koo·*pa*·do/a

Not if you were the last person on Earth!
¡Ni aunque fueras la última persona en el mundo!
nee *own*·ke *fwe*·ras la *ool*·tee·ma per·*so*·na en el *moon*·do

pick-up lines

frases para ligar

Would you like a drink?
¿Puedo ofrecerte una copa?
pwe·do o·fre·*ser*·te oo·na *ko*·pa

What star sign are you?
¿Cuál es tu signo del horóscopo?
kwal es too *seeg*·no del o·*ros*·ko·po

Shall we get some fresh air?
¿Vamos a tomar el aire?
va·mos a to·*mar* el *ai*·re

Do you study or do you work?
¿Estudias o trabajas?
es·*too*·dyas o tra·*ba*·khas

Do you have a light?
¿Tienes fuego?
tye·nes *fwe*·go

You have (a) beautiful ...	Tienes ...	tye·nes ...
body	un cuerpo precioso	oon kwer·po pre·syo·so
eyes	unos ojos preciosos	oo·nos o·khos pre·syo·sos
hands	unas manos preciosas	oo·nas ma·nos pre·syo·sas
laugh	una risa preciosa	oo·na ree·sa pre·syo·sa
personality	una personalidad preciosa	oo·na per·so·na·lee·da pre·syo·sa

local talk

What a babe. (referring to a woman)
Qué hembra. — ke *em*·bra
Qué mamacita. **(Per)** — ke ma·ma·*see*·ta
Qué mina. **(Arg)** — ke *mee*·na

He's/She's a hot guy/girl.
Está buenísimo/a. **m/f** — es·*ta* bwe·*nee*·see·mo/a

He/She gets around.
Se va a la cama con cualquiera. — se va a la *ka*·ma kon kwal·*kye*·ra

He's/She's a virgin and proud of it.
Es virgen y está orgulloso/a de eso. **m/f** — es *veer*·khen ee es·*ta* or·goo·*lyo*·so/a de *e*·so

He's a jerk.
Él es un cabrón. **m** — el es oon ka·*bron*

She's ...	Ella es ...	el·ya es ...
a babe	un bombón	oon bom·bon
a bitch	una loca	oo·na lo·ka
	(SAm) una yegua	oo·na ye·gwa

He's/She's ...	Él/Ella es ...	el/el·ya es ...
hot	caliente **m&f**	ka·lyen·te
gorgeous	guapísimo/a **m/f**	gwa·pee·see·mo/a
an idiot	**(SAm)** conchudo/a **m/f**	kon·choo·do/a

rejections

No, thank you.
No, gracias.　　　　　　　　　no gra·syas

I have a boyfriend/girlfriend.
Tengo novio/a. m/f　　　　　　ten·go no·vyo/a

I'm here with my boyfriend/girlfriend.
Estoy aquí con mi novio/a. m/f　es·toy a·kee kon mee no·vyo/a

Excuse me, I have to go now.
Lo siento, pero me tengo　　　lo syen·to pe·ro me ten·go
que ir.　　　　　　　　　　ke eer

Your ego is out of control.
Tu ego está fuera de　　　　too e·go es·ta fwe·ra de
control.　　　　　　　　　kon·trol

I'm not interested.
No estoy interesado/a. m/f　　no es·toy een·te·re·sa·do/a

Hey, I'm not interested in talking to you.
Mira tío/a, es que no me　　mee·ra tee·o/a es ke no me
interesa hablar contigo. m/f　een·te·re·sa a·blar kon·tee·go

Leave me alone!
Déjame en paz.　　　　　　de·kha·me en pas

Piss off!
¡Andate a la mierda!　　　　an·da·te a la myer·da

getting closer

You're very nice.
Eres muy simpático/a. m/f　　e·res mooy seem·pa·tee·ko/a

You're great.
Eres estupendo/a. m/f　　　　e·res es·too·pen·do/a

You're very attractive.
Eres muy guapo/a. m/f　　　　e·res mooy gwa·po/a

I'm interested in you.
Me fascinas mucho. me fa·*see*·nas *moo*·cho

I like you very much.
Me gustas mucho. me *goos*·tas *moo*·cho

Do you like me too?
¿Me tienes algo de me tye·nes *al*·go de
cariño también? ka·*ree*·nyo tam·*byen*

Can I kiss you?
¿Te puedo besar? te *pwe*·do be·*sar*

Will you take me home?
¿Me acompañas a casa? me a·kom·*pa*·nyas a *ka*·sa

Do you want to come inside for a while?
¿Quieres entrar a tomar algo? kye·res en·*trar* a to·*mar al*·go

false friend

To say you like something you use the expression *me gusta* me *goos*·ta (lit: me it-pleases). Beware of using this expression about people though, as to say *me gustas* (lit: me you-please) has erotic overtones. So, to say that you enjoy someone's company, a less risqué expression is *me caes bien* me *ka*·es byen which equates to the English 'I like you'.

sex

el sexo

I want to make love to you.
Quiero hacerte el amor. kye·ro a·*ser*·te el a·*mor*

Do you have a condom?
¿Tienes un condón? tye·nes oon kon·*don*

I won't do it without protection.
No lo haré sin preservativos. no lo a·*re* seen pre·ser·va·*tee*·vos

I think we should stop now.
Pienso que deberíamos parar. pyen·so ke de·be·*ree*·a·mos pa·*rar*

Let's go to bed!
¡Vamos a la cama! va·mos a la *ka*·ma

Kiss me!	¡Bésame!	be·sa·me
I want you.	Te deseo.	te de·se·o
Take this off.	Sácate esto.	sa·ka·te es·to
Touch me here.	Tócame aquí.	to·ka·me a·kee
Do you like this?	¿Esto te gusta?	es·to te goos·ta
I (don't) like that.	Esto (no) me gusta.	es·to (no) me goos·ta
Please stop!	¡Para!	pa·ra
Please don't stop!	¡No pares!	no pa·res
Oh my god!	¡Ay dios qué rico!	ai dyos ke ree·ko
Oh yeah!	¡Así cariño, así!	a·see ka·ree·nyo a·see
That's great.	¡Eso, eso!	e·so e·so
Easy tiger!	¡Con calma!	kon kal·ma

faster	más rápido	mas ra·pee·do
harder	más fuerte	mas fwer·te
slower	más despacio	mas des·pa·syo
softer	más suave	mas swa·ve

That was amazing.
Eso fue increíble.　　　　e·so fwe een·kre·ee·ble

It's my first time.
Es mi primera vez.　　　　es mee pree·me·ra ves

I can't get it up – sorry.
Lo siento, no puedo levantarla.　lo syen·to no pwe·do le·van·tar·la

Don't worry, I'll do it myself.
No te preocupes, lo hago yo.　no te pre·o·koo·pes lo a·go yo

It helps to have a sense of humour.
Ayuda tener un　　　　　　a·yoo·da te·ner oon
sentido de humor.　　　　　sen·tee·do de oo·mor

Can I ...?	¿Puedo ...?	pwe·do ...
call you	llamarte	lya·mar·te
meet you tomorrow	verte mañana	ver·te ma·nya·na
stay over	quedarme	ke·dar·me

love

I'm in love with you.
Estoy enamorado/a de ti. m/f   es·*toy* e·na·mo·*ra*·do/a de ti

I love you.
Te quiero.   te *kye*·ro

Do you love me?
¿Me quieres?   me *kye*·res

I think we're good together.
Creo que estamos   *kre*·o ke es·*ta*·mos
bien juntos.   byen *khoon*·tos

problems

problemas

Are you seeing someone else?
¿Me estás engañando   me es·*tas* en·ga·*nyan*·do
con alguien?   kon *al*·gyen

He's just a friend.
Es un amigo nada más.   es oon a·*mee*·go *na*·da mas

She's just a friend.
Es una amiga nada más.   es *oo*·na a·*mee*·ga *na*·da mas

I don't think it's working out.
Creo que no está funcionando.   *kre*·o ke no es·*ta* foon·syo·*nan*·do

We'll work it out.
Lo resolveremos.   lo re·sol·ve·*re*·mos

I want to end the relationship.
Quiero que terminemos   *kye*·ro ke ter·mee·*ne*·mos
lo nuestro.   lo *nwes*·tro

I want to stay friends.
Me gustaría que   me goos·ta·*ree*·a ke
quedáramos como amigos.   ke·*da*·ra·mos *ko*·mo a·*mee*·gos

I never want to see you again.
No quiero volver a verte.   no *kye*·ro vol·*ver* a *ver*·te

religion

la religión

What's your religion?
¿Cuál es su/tu religión? pol/inf   kwal es soo/too re·lee·*khyon*

I'm (not) ...	*(No) Soy ...*	(no) soy ...
agnostic	*agnóstico/a* m/f	ag·*nos*·tee·ko/a
an atheist	*ateo/a* m/f	a·*te*·o/a
Buddhist	*budista*	boo·*dees*·ta
Catholic	*católico/a* m/f	ka·to·lee·ko/a
Christian	*cristiano/a* m/f	krees·*tya*·no/a
Hindu	*hindú*	een·*doo*
Jewish	*judío/a* m/f	khoo·*dee*·o/a
Muslim	*musulman/*	moo·sool·*man/*
	musulmana m/f	moo·sool·*ma*·na
practising	*practicante*	prak·tee·*kan*·te
religious	*religioso/a* m/f	re·lee·*khyo*·so/a

I (don't) believe in ...	*(No) Creo en ...*	(no) *kre*·o en ...
fate	*el destino*	el des·*tee*·no
God	*Dios*	dyos
I'd like to go to (the) ...	*Quisiera ir ...*	kee·*sye*·ra eer ...
church	*a la iglesia*	a la ee·*gle*·sya
mosque	*a la mezquita*	a la mes·*kee*·ta
synagogue	*a la sinagoga*	a la see·na·*go*·ga
temple	*al templo*	al *tem*·plo

indigenous languages

Latin America is a fascinating part of the world for anyone with more than a passing interest in languages. Although Spanish is the most widely spoken language, there are literally hundreds of distinct indigenous languages spoken throughout the Americas. In Central America alone there are some 250 indigenous languages, some of which have several dialects. This amazing linguistic diversity has its origins in migration patterns to the continent that began some 12,000 years ago when Latin America's original inhabitants are believed to have brought a number of languages across the Bering Strait from Asia.

In Latin America today, indigenous languages are spoken by at least 17 million people. Some are limited to small tribal communities in remote areas, while others have millions of speakers spread over large geographical areas. Below are some of the most widely-spoken languages:

Language	Where Spoken	Number of Speakers
Aymara	Bol, Chi, Per	3.5 million
Goajiro	Col, Ven	300,000
Guaraní	Arg, Brazil, Par,	5 million
Garifuna	Gua, Hon, Nic	200,000
Mapudungun	Arg, Chi	400,000
Quechua	Arg, Bol, Chi Col, Ecu, Per	8-10 million

While some languages continue to thrive, much of Latin America's rich linguistic heritage has already been lost. The extinction of a number of languages coincided with European settlement, as introduced diseases and slavery decimated entire tribes. Missionaries often contributed to this decline by prohibiting the use of native languages. It's estimated that as many as 2000 separate languages may have been spoken in South America prior to European settlement. Even today, the rate of language extinction continues apace as traditional lifestyles are eroded by development, and

Spanish eclipses native tongues. Their loss is catastrophic as each of these languages embodies the cultural identity and unique world view of its community of speakers. Today only a few hundred languages are spoken on the South American continent and most of these are endangered.

Latin American Spanish has borrowed many words from indigenous languages to describe some of the wonders of the New World. Many of these words spread into English via Latin American Spanish. Here are some of these borrowed words and the languages they come from:

Latin American Spanish	Indigenous Language	English
aguacate	ahuacatl (Nahuatl)	avocado
ananá(s)	ananas (Quechua)	pineapple
barbacoa	barbakoa (Taino)	barbecue
canoa	canaoua (Carib)	canoe
caníbal	caniba (Arawak)	cannibal
chicle	chictli (Nahuatl)	chewing gum
chile	chilli (Nahuatl)	chilli
chocolate	xocolatl (Aztec)	chocolate
coca	kúka (Quechua)	coca leaf
coyote	coyotl (Nahuatl)	coyote
hamaca	hamaca (Taino)	hammock
huracán	hurakán (Taino)	hurricane
jitomate/tomate	xitomatl (Nahuatl)	tomato
llama	llama (Quechua)	llama
maíz	mahiz (Taino)	maize/corn
papaya	ababai (Carib)	paw paw
patata/papa	batata (Taino)	potato
poncho	pantho (Araucanian)	poncho
quina	kina (Quechua)	quinine
tabaco	tabaco (Taino)	tobacco

For travellers to the Andes, Lonely Planet also has a Quechua phrasebook.

beliefs & cultural differences

Can I ... here?	¿Puedo ... aquí?	pwe·do ... a·kee
Where can I ...?	¿Dónde puedo ...?	don·de pwe·do ...
attend mass	asistir a la misa	a·sees·teer a la mee·sa
make confession	confesarme	kon·fe·sar·me
(in English)	(en inglés)	(en een·gles)
pray	rezar	re·sar
receive communion	comulgar	ko·mool·gar

cultural differences

las diferencias culturales

Is this a local or national custom?

¿Esto es una costumbre	es·to es oo·na kos·toom·bre
local o nacional?	lo·kal o na·syo·nal

I'm not used to this.

No estoy acostumbrado/a	no es·toy a·kos·toom·bra·do/a
a esto. m/f	a es·to

I don't mind watching, but I'd rather not join in.

No me importa mirar,	no me eem·por·ta mee·rar
pero prefiero no participar.	pe·ro pre·fye·ro no par·tee·see·par

I'll try it.

Lo probaré.	lo pro·ba·re

Sorry, I didn't mean to say/do anything wrong.

Lo siento, lo dice/hice	lo syen·to lo dee·se/ee·se
sin querer.	seen ke·rer

This is (very) ...	Esto es (muy) ...	es·to es (mooy) ...
different	diferente	dee·fe·ren·te
fun	divertido	dee·ver·tee·do
interesting	interesante	een·te·re·san·te

I'm sorry, it's against my ...	Lo siento, eso va en contra de ...	lo syen·to e·so va en kon·tra de ...
beliefs	mis creencias	mees kre·en·syas
religion	mi religión	mee re·lee·khyon

When's the gallery open?
¿A qué hora abre la galería? a ke *o*·ra *a*·bre la ga·le·*ree*·a

When's the museum open?
¿A qué hora abre el museo? a ke *o*·ra *a*·bre el moo·*se*·o

What kind of art are you interested in?
¿Qué tipo de arte le/te ke *tee*·po de *ar*·te le/te
interesa? pol/inf een·te·*re*·sa

What's in the collection?
¿Qué hay en la colección? ke ai en la ko·lek·*syon*

What do you think of …?
¿Qué piensa/piensas de …? pol/inf ke *pyen*·sa/*pyen*·sas de …

It's an exhibition of (pottery).
Hay una exposición de ai *oo*·na ek·spo·see·*syon* de
(alfarería). (al·fa·re·*ree*·a)

I like the works of (Fernando Botero).
Me gusta la obra de me *goos*·ta la *o*·bra de
(Fernando Botero). (fer·*nan*·do bo·*te*·ro)

It reminds me of (pre-Columbian art).
Me recuerda (el arte me re·*kwer*·da (el *ar*·te
precolombino). pre·ko·lom·*bee*·no)

I'm interested in … art.	*Me interesa el arte …*	me een·te·*re*·sa el *ar*·te …
Aztec	*azteca*	as·*te*·ka
baroque	*barroco*	ba·*ro*·ko
graphic	*gráfico*	*gra*·fee·ko
impressionist	*impresionista*	eem·pre·syo·*nees*·ta
Inca	*inca*	*een*·ka
Mayan	*maya*	*ma*·ya
pre-Columbian	*precolombino*	pre·ko·lom·*bee*·no
Renaissance	*renacentista*	re·na·sen·*tees*·ta

artwork	*material* m *gráfico*	ma·te·*ryal gra*·fee·ko
ceramics	*cerámica* f	se·*ra*·mee·ka
curator	*conservador/*	kon·ser·va·*dor/*
	conservadora m/f	kon·ser·va·*do*·ra
design	*diseño* m	dee·*se*·nyo
etching	*grabado* m	gra·*ba*·do
exhibition hall	*salón* m *de*	sa·*lon* de
	exhibiciones	ek·see·bee·*syo*·nes
installation	*instalación* f	een·sta·la·*syon*
opening	*apertura* f	a·per·*too*·ra
painter	*pintor/pintora* m/f	peen·*tor*/peen·*to*·ra
painting (artform)	*pintura* f	peen·*too*·ra
painting (canvas)	*cuadro* m	*kwa*·dro
period	*período* m	pe·*ree*·o·do
permanent	*colección* f	ko·lek·*syon*
collection	*permanente*	per·ma·*nen*·te
pottery	*alfarería* f	al·fa·re·*ree*·a
print	*reproducción* f	re·pro·dook·*syon*
sculptor	*escultor/*	es·kool·*tor/*
	escultora m/f	es·kool·*to*·ra
sculpture	*escultura* f	es·kool·*too*·ra
statue	*estatua* f	es·*ta*·twa
studio	*estudio* m	es·*too*·dyo
style	*estilo* m	es·*tee*·lo
technique	*técnica* f	*tek*·nee·ka
weaving	*tejido* m	te·*khee*·do

social niceities

Latin Americans are generally gregarious and don't easily take offence. At the same time they're very polite, almost to the point of ceremoniousness, in their public behaviour. Before getting to the point of a conversation it's customary to exchange pleasantries. Not to do so, in fact, is the mark of an ill-bred person. When approaching people for information, never do so without first using the appropriate greeting. It's also polite to greet the assembled company when entering a public place such as a shop or cafe.

For greetings and pleasantries, see **meeting people,** page 89.

sporting interests

los intereses deportivos

Do you like (sport)?
¿Te gustan (los deportes)?
te *goos*·tan (los de·*por*·tes)

Yes, very much.
Sí, mucho.
see *moo*·cho

Not really.
En realidad, no mucho.
en re·a·lee·*da* no *moo*·cho

I like watching it.
Me gusta mirar.
me *goos*·ta mee·*rar*

What sport do you play?
¿Qué deporte practicas?
ke de·*por*·te prak·*tee*·kas

I play (tennis).
Practico (el tenis).
prak·*tee*·ko (el *te*·nees)

What sport do you follow?
¿A qué deporte eres aficionado/a? m/f
a *ke* de·*por*·te *e*·res a·fee·syo·*na*·do/a

I follow (cycling).
Soy aficionado/a al (ciclismo). m/f
soy a·fee·syo·*na*·do/a al (see·*klees*·mo)

Who's your favourite sportsman?
¿Quién es tu deportista favorito?
kyen es too de·por·*tees*·ta fa·vo·*ree*·to

Who's your favourite sportswoman?
¿Quién es tu deportista favorita?
kyen es too de·por·*tees*·ta fa·vo·*ree*·ta

Who's your favourite team?
¿Cuál es tu equipo favorito?
kwal es too e·*kee*·po fa·vo·*ree*·to

For more sports, see the **dictionary**.

going to a game

Would you like to go to a (football) game?
¿Te gustaría ir a un   te goos·ta·*ree*·a eer a oon
partido (de fútbol)?   par·*tee*·do (de *foot*·bol)

Who are you supporting?
¿Con qué equipo vas?   kon ke e·*kee*·po vas

Who's playing?
¿Quién juega?   kyen *khwe*·ga

Who's winning?
¿Quién va ganando?   kyen va ga·*nan*·do

How much time is left?
¿Cuánto tiempo queda?   *kwan*·to *tyem*·po *ke*·da

What's the score?
¿Cómo van?   *ko*·mo van

It's a draw.
Empatados.   em·pa·*ta*·dos

That was a …	*¡Ese partido*	e·se par·*tee*·do
game!	*fue …!*	fwe …
bad	*malo*	*ma*·lo
boring	*aburrido*	a·boo·*ree*·do
great	*fabuloso*	fa·boo·*lo*·so
	(Arg) *bárbaro*	*bar*·ba·ro

sports talk

What a …!	*¡Qué …!*	ke …
goal	*golazo*	go·*la*·so
header	*cabezazo*	ka·be·*sa*·so
hit	*tiro*	*tee*·ro
kick/shot	*chute*	*choo*·te
pass	*pase*	*pa*·se
save	*atajada*	a·ta·*kha*·da

playing sport

Do you want to play?
¿Quieres jugar?   kye·res khoo·gar

Can I join in?
¿Puedo jugar?   pwe·do khoo·gar

Yes, that'd be great.
Sí, me encantaría.   see me en·kan·ta·ree·a

Not at the moment, thanks.
Ahora mismo no, gracias.   a·o·ra mees·mo no gra·syas

I have an injury.
Tengo una lesion.   ten·go oo·na le·syon

Where's the best place to jog around here?
¿Cuál es el mejor sitio   kwal es el me·khor see·tyo
para hacer footing por   pa·ra a·ser foo·teen por
aquí cerca?   a·kee ser·ka

Where's the nearest ...?	*¿Dónde está ...?*	don·de es·ta ...
gym	*el gimnasio*	el kheem·na·syo
	más cercano	mas ser·ka·no
swimming pool	*la piscina más*	la pee·see·na mas
	cercana	ser·ka·na
	(Arg) *la pileta más*	la pee·le·ta mas
	cercana	ser·ka·na
tennis court	*la cancha de tenis*	la kan·cha de te·nees
	más cercana	mas ser·ka·na

What's the charge per ...?	*¿Cúanto cobran por ...?*	kwan·to ko·bran por ...
day	*día*	dee·a
game	*partido*	par·tee·do
hour	*hora*	o·ra
visit	*visita*	vee·see·ta

Can I hire a …?	¿Es posible alquilar una …?	es po·see·ble al·kee·lar oo·na …
ball	pelota	pe·lo·ta
bicycle	bicicleta	bee·see·kle·ta
court	cancha	kan·cha
racquet	raqueta	ra·ke·ta

listen for …

too/mee poon·to	Tu/Mi punto.	Your/My point.
pa·sa·me·lo	¡Pásamelo!	Kick/Pass it to me!
khwe·gas byen	Juegas bien.	You're a good player.
gra·syas por el par·tee·do	Gracias por el partido.	Thanks for the game.

Do I have to be a member to attend?
¿Hay que ser socio/a para entrar? m/f
ai ke ser so·syo/a pa·ra en·trar

Is there a women-only session?
¿Hay alguna sesión sólo para mujeres?
ai al·goo·na se·syon so·lo pa·ra moo·khe·res

Where are the changing rooms?
¿Dónde están los vestuarios?
don·de es·tan los ves·twa·ryos

Can I have a locker?
¿Puedo usar una lócker?
pwe·do oo·sar oo·na lo·ker

cycling

el ciclismo

Where does the race pass through?
¿Por dónde pasa la carrera?
por don·de pa·sa la ka·re·ra

Where does the race finish?
¿Dónde termina la carrera?
don·de ter·mee·na la ka·re·ra

Who's winning?
¿Quién va ganando?
kyen va ga·nan·do

How many kilometres is today's (stage)?
  ¿Cuántos kilómetros tiene   kwan·tos kee·lo·me·tros tye·ne
  (la etapa) de hoy?   (la e·ta·pa) de oy

My favourite cyclist is (Santiago Botero).
  Mi ciclista favorito   mee see·klees·ta fa·vo·ree·to
  es (Santiago Botero).   es (san·tee·a·go bo·te·ro)

For phrases on getting around by bike, see **transport**, page 48.

diving

el buceo

I'd like to …	*Me gustaría …*	me goos·ta·ree·a …
explore wrecks	*explorar*	ek·splo·rar
	naufragios	now·fra·khyos
go scuba diving	*hacer*	a·ser
	submarinismo	soob·ma·ree·nees·mo
go snorkelling	*bucear con tubo*	boo·se·ar kon too·bo
	respiratorio	res·pee·ra·to·ryo
hire diving gear	*alquilar equipo*	al·kee·lar e·kee·po
	de buceo	de boo·se·o
hire snorkelling	*alquilar equipo*	al·kee·lar e·kee·po
gear	*de buceo con*	de boo·se·o kon
	tubo	too·bo
	respiratorio	res·pee·ra·to·ryo
learn to dive	*aprender a bucear*	a·pren·der a boo·se·ar

Where are some good diving sites?
  ¿Dónde hay buenos lugares   don·de ai bwe·nos loo·ga·res
  para bucear?   pa·ra boo·se·ar

Are there jellyfish?
  ¿Hay medusas?   ai me·doo·sas

Where can we hire (flippers)?
  ¿Dónde se puede alquilar   don·de se pwe·de al·kee·lar
  (aletas)?   (a·le·tas)

dive	*bucear*	boo·se·*ar*
diving boat	*barca* f *de buceo*	*bar*·ka de boo·*se*·o
diving course	*curso* m *de buceo*	*koor*·so de boo·*se*·o
diving equipment	*equipo* m *de buceo*	e·*kee*·po de boo·*se*·o
flippers	*aletas* f pl	a·*le*·tas
mask	*máscara* f	*mas*·ka·ra
snorkel	*tubo* m	*too*·bo
	respiratorio	res·pee·ra·*to*·ryo
wetsuit	*traje* m	*tra*·khe
	isotérmico	ee·so·*ter*·mee·ko

¡Olé!

Although some locals consider it a cruel and uncivilized activity, bullfighting is still popular in many Latin American countries. Here's some terminology that you may come across in connection with this controversial form of entertainment:

capote m	ka·*po*·te	bullfighter's cloak
corrida f	ko·*ree*·da	bullfight
espada f	es·*pa*·da	sword
plaza f *de toros*	*pla*·sa de *to*·ros	bullring
torero m	to·*re*·ro	bullfighter
toro m *bravo*	*to*·ro *bra*·vo	fighting bull
traje m *de luces*	*tra*·khe de *loo*·ses	bullfighter's highly decorated suit (lit: suit of lights)

extreme sports

los deportes extremos

Are you sure this is safe?
¿De verdad que esto es seguro?   de ver·*da* ke *es*·to es se·*goo*·ro

Is the equipment secure?
¿Está seguro el equipo?   es·*ta* se·*goo*·ro el e·*kee*·po

This is insane!
Esto es una locura!   *es*·to es *oo*·na lo·*koo*·ra

abseiling	*rappel* m	ra·*pel*
bungy-jumping	*banyi* m	ban·*yee*
canoeing	*piragüismo*	pee·ra·*gwees*·mo
canyoning	*canyoning* m	ka·nyo·*neen*
caving	*espeleología* f	es·pe·lyo·lo·*khee*·a
game fishing	*pesca* f *deportiva*	*pes*·ka de·por·*tee*·va
hiking	*excursionismo* m	ek·skoor·syo·*nees*·mo
kayaking	*kayakismo* m	ka·ya·*kees*·mo
mountain biking	*ciclismo* m de *montaña*	see·*klees*·mo de mon·*ta*·nya
mountaineering	*alpinismo* m	al·pee·*nees*·mo
paragliding	*parapente* m	pa·ra·*pen*·te
parasailing	*esquí* m *acuático con paracaídas*	es·*kee* a·*kwa*·tee·ko kon pa·ra·ka·*ee*·das
rock-climbing	*escalada* f de *roca*	es·ka·*la*·da de *ro*·ka
skydiving	*paracaidismo* m	pa·ra·kai·*dees*·mo
trekking	*trekking* m	*tre*·keen
white-water rafting	*descenso* m en *aguas bravas*	de·*sen*·so en *a*·gwas *bra*·vas

For words and phrases you might need while hiking, trekking or mountaineering, see **outdoors**, page 135 and **camping**, page 60.

horse riding

la equitación

Is there a horse-riding school around here?
¿Hay alguna escuela de equitación por aquí?
ai al·*goo*·na es·*kwe*·la de e·kee·ta·*syon* por a·*kee*

Are there rides available?
¿Es posible dar un paseo a caballo?
es po·*see*·ble dar oon pa·*se*·o a ka·*ba*·lyo

How long is the ride?
¿Cuánto dura el paseo?
kwan·to *doo*·ra el pa·*se*·o

skiing

What are the skiing conditions like at (Bariloche)?
¿Cuáles son las condiciones kwa·les son las kon·dee·syo·nes
de las pistas de esquí en de las pees·tas de es·kee en
(Bariloche)? (ba·ree·lo·che)

Is it possible to go cross-country skiing at (Portillo)?
¿Es posible hacer esquí de es po·see·ble a·ser es·kee de
fondo en (Portillo)? fon·do en (por·tee·lyo)

I'd like to hire (ski equipment).
Quisiera alquilar kee·sye·ra al·kee·lar
(equipo de esquí). (e·kee·po de es·kee)

How much is a pass for these slopes?
¿Cuánto cuesta el forfait kwan·to kwes·ta el for·fet
para estas pistas? pa·ra es·tas pees·tas

What level is that slope?
¿De qué nivel es esa pista? de ke nee·vel es e·sa pees·ta

Can I take lessons?
¿Puedo tomar clases? pwe·do to·mar kla·ses

soccer

Who plays for (River Plate)?
¿Quién juega para el kyen khwe·ga pa·ra el
(River Plate)? (ree·ver pla·te)

Which team is at the top of the league?
¿Qué equipo está en primera ke e·kee·po es·ta en pree·me·ra
posición en la tabla de po·see·syon en la ta·bla de
clasificaciones? kla·see·fee·ka·syo·nes

He's a great (player).
Es un (jugador) bárbaro. es oon (khoo·ga·dor) bar·ba·ro

He played brilliantly in the match against (Brazil).

Jugó fenomenal en el partido contra (Brasil).

khoo·*go* fe·no·me·*nal* en el par·*tee*·do *kon*·tra (bra·*seel*)

What a terrible team!

¡Qué equipo más malo!

ke e·*kee*·po mas *ma*·lo

ball	*balón* m	ba·*lon*
coach	*entrenador/*	en·tre·na·*dor/*
	entrenadora m/f	en·tre·na·*do*·ra
corner kick	*córner* m	*kor*·ner
cup	*copa* f	*ko*·pa
defensive player	*jugador/*	khoo·ga·*dor/*
	jugadora m/f	khoo·ga·*dor*·a
	de defensa	de de·*fen*·sa
expulsion	*expulsión* f	ek·spool·*syon*
foul	*faul* m	fowl
free kick	*tiro* m *libre*	*tee*·ro *lee*·bre
goal	*gol* m	gol
goalkeeper	*portero/a* m/f	por·*te*·ro/a
(Arg)	*arquero/a* m/f	ar·*ke*·ro/a
goal-scorer	*goleador/*	go·le·a·*dor/*
	goleadora m/f	go·le·a·*do*·ra
kickoff	*saque* m	*sa*·ke
league	*liga* f	*lee*·ga
offside	*offside*	of·sai
penalty (kick)	*penalty* m	pe·nal·*tee*
(Arg, CAm)	*penal* m	pe·*nal*
player	*jugador/*	khoo·ga·*dor/*
	jugadora m/f	khoo·ga·*do*·ra
red card	*tarjeta* f *roja*	tar·*khe*·ta *ro*·kha
score (a goal)	*marcar*	mar·*kar*
striker	*delantero/a* m/f	de·lan·*te*·ro/a
supporters	*hinchas* f pl	*een*·chas
(Arg)	*hinchadas* f pl	een·*cha*·das
throw-in	*saque* m *de banda*	*sa*·ke de *ban*·da
warning	*amonestación* f	a·mo·ne·sta·*syon*
yellow card	*tarjeta* f *amarilla*	tar·*khe*·ta a·ma·*ree*·lya

tennis

el tenis

Would you like to play tennis?
¿Quieres jugar al tenis? kye·res khoo·gar al te·nees

Can we play at night?
¿Se puede jugar de noche? se pwe·de khoo·gar de no·che

Game, set, match.
Juego, set y partido. khwe·go set ee par·tee·do

ace	*ace* m	a·se
advantage	*ventaja* f	ven·ta·kha
fault	*falta* f	fal·ta
play doubles (against)	*jugar dobles (contra)*	khoo·gar do·bles (kon·tra)
serve	*saque* m	sa·ke
set	*set* m	set

gringo lingo

One word you're bound to become well acquainted with in Latin America is *gringo* (or its feminine form *gringa*). In English usage it's a pejorative word meaning roughly 'English-speaking visitor to Latin America' but in Latin American Spanish the term has subtler nuances.

It can be a neutral term meaning simply 'foreign' (as an adjective) or 'foreigner', so if you're addressed, or referred to in this way, it's more than likely that there's no malice intended. *Gringo* is intended as pejorative only in certain contexts or when it's married with an unflattering descriptive word such as *pinche* ('goddam') or said in an unfriendly tone of voice. You'd no doubt pick up on the cues which might signal such intent. It's probably best to take the term with a grain of salt.

But who exactly is a *gringo*? The term can be used to refer to North Americans but, also, in a broader sense to visitors of European heritage. Blonde or fair-haired people are sometimes called *gringos* perhaps because their physical appearance marks them out as obviously foreign. The word is thought to have originated from the Spanish word *griego* meaning 'Greek'.

hiking & mountaineering

el excursionismo & el alpinismo

Where can I ...?	¿Dónde se puede ...?	don·de se pwe·de ...
buy supplies	comprar víveres	kom·prar vee·ve·res
find someone who knows this area	encontrar a alguien que conozca el área	en·kon·trar a al·gyen ke ko·nos·ka el a·re·a
get a map	obtener un mapa	ob·te·ner oon ma·pa
hire hiking gear	alquilar equipo para ir de excursión	al·kee·lar e·kee·po pa·ra eer de ek·skoor·syon
hire mountaineering gear	alquilar equipo de alpinismo	al·kee·lar e·kee·po de al·pee·nees·mo

Where can I find out about hiking trails?
¿Dónde hay información
sobre caminos rurales de
la zona?
don·de ai een·for·ma·syon
so·bre ka·mee·nos roo·ra·les
de la so·na

How long is the trail?
¿Cómo es de largo
el camino?
ko·mo es de lar·go
el ka·mee·no

How high is the climb?
¿A qué altura se escala?
a ke al·too·ra se es·ka·la

Is the path open (all year)?
¿Está la ruta abierta
(todo el año)?
es·ta la roo·ta a·byer·ta
(to·do el a·nyo)

Is it safe?
¿Es seguro?
es se·goo·ro

Is there a hut there?
¿Hay una cabaña allí?
ai oo·na ka·ba·nya a·lyee

When does it get dark?
¿A qué hora oscurece?
a ke o·ra os·koo·re·se

Do we need a guide?
¿Se necesita un guía? se ne·se·*see*·ta oon *gee*·a

Are there guided treks?
¿Se organizan se or·ga·*nee*·san
excursiones guiadas? ek·skoor·*syo*·nes gee·*a*·das

Are there guided climbs?
¿Se organizan escaladas se or·ga·*nee*·san es·ka·*la*·das
guiadas? gee·*a*·das

Do we need	*¿Se necesita*	se ne·se·*see*·ta
to take …?	*llevar …?*	lye·*var* …
bedding	*algo en que*	*al*·go en ke
	dormir	dor·*meer*
food	*comida*	ko·*mee*·da
water	*agua*	*a*·gwa
Is the track …?	*¿Es … el sendero?*	es … el sen·*de*·ro
(well-)marked	*(bien) marcado*	(byen) mar·*ka*·do
scenic	*pintoresco*	peen·to·*res*·ko
Which is the	*¿Cuál es el camino*	kwal es el ka·*mee*·no
… route?	*más …?*	mas …
easiest	*fácil*	*fa*·seel
shortest	*corto*	*kor*·to
Where's …?	*¿Dónde hay …?*	*don*·de ai …
a camping site	*un lugar de*	oon loo·*gar* de
	cámping	*kam*·peen
the nearest	*el pueblo*	el *pwe*·blo
village	*más cercano*	mas ser·*ka*·no
Where are the …	*¿Dónde hay …?*	*don*·de ai …
showers	*duchas*	*doo*·chas
toilets	*baños*	*ba*·nyos

Where have you come from?
¿De dónde vienes?
de *don*·de *vye*·nes

How long did it take?
¿Cuánto has tardado?
kwan·to as tar·*da*·do

Does this path go to (Huayna Picchu)?
¿Este camino va a
(Huayna Picchu)?
es·te ka·*mee*·no va a
(*wai*·na *pee*·choo)

Can we go through here?
¿Se puede pasar por aquí?
se *pwe*·de pa·*sar* por a·*kee*

Is the water OK to drink?
¿Se puede beber el agua?
se *pwe*·de be·*ber* el *a*·gwa

Where are we on this map?
¿Dónde estamos aquí
en el mapa?
don·de es·*ta*·mos a·*kee*
en el *ma*·pa

I'm lost.
Estoy perdido/a. m/f
es·*toy* per·*dee*·do/a

altitude	*altura* f	al·*too*·ra
binoculars	*prismáticos* m pl	prees·*ma*·tee·kos
cliff	*acantilado* m	a·kan·tee·*la*·do
crampon	*crampón* m	kram·*pon*
glacier	*glaciar* m	gla·*syar*
gloves	*guantes* m pl	*gwan*·tes
harness	*arnés* m	ar·*nes*
hiking boots	*botas* f pl *de montaña*	*bo*·tas de mon·*ta*·nya
ice	*hielo* m	*ye*·lo
ice-climbing	*subir de hielo*	soo·*beer* de *ye*·lo
mountain	*montaña* f	mon·*ta*·nya
mountain hut	*refugio* m *de montaña*	re·foo·*khyo* de mon·*ta*·nya
pass	*paso* m	*pa*·so
peak	*cumbre* f	*koom*·bre
pick	*piqueta* f	pee·*ke*·ta
steep	*escarpado/a* m/f	es·kar·*pa*·do/a
scale (climb)	*trepar*	tre·*par*

at the beach

Where's the ... beach?	¿Dónde está la playa ...?	don·de es·ta la pla·ya ...
nearest	más cercana	mas ser·ka·na
nicest	más bonita	mas bo·nee·ta
nudist	nudista	noo·dees·ta

signs

Prohibido Nadar	pro·ee·bee·do na·dar	No Swimming

Are there any ...?	¿Hay ...?	ai ...
reefs	arrecifes	a·re·see·fes
rips	corrientes	ko·ryen·tes
water hazards	peligros en el agua	pe·lee·gros en el a·gwa

Is it safe to ... here?	¿Es seguro ... aquí?	es se·goo·ro ... a·kee
dive	bucear	boo·se·ar
swim	nadar	na·dar

What time is ... tide?	¿A qué hora es la marea ...?	a ke o·ra es la ma·re·a ...
high	alta	al·ta
low	baja	ba·kha

listen for ...

kwee·da·do kon la ko·ryen·te *Cuidado con la corriente.*	Be careful of the undertow.
es pe·lee·gro·so ¡Es peligroso!	It's dangerous!
e·res mo·de·lo ¿Eres modelo?	Are you a model?

weather

What's the weather like?
  ¿Qué tiempo hace?   ke *tyem*·po *a*·se

(Today) It's raining.
  (Hoy) Llueve.   (oy) *lywe*·ve

(Tomorrow) It will rain.
  (Mañana) Lloverá.   (ma·*nya*·na) lyo·ve·*ra*

(Today) It's snowing.
  (Hoy) Nieva.   (oy) *nye*·va

(Tomorrow) It will snow.
  (Mañana) Nevará.   (ma·*nya*·na) ne·va·*ra*

Today it's …	*Hoy hace …*	oy *a*·se …
Will it be … tomorrow?	*¿Mañana hará …?*	ma·*nya*·na a·*ra* …
cold	*frío*	*free*·o
freezing	*un frío que pela*	oon *free*·o ke *pe*·la
hot	*calor*	ka·*lor*
sunny	*sol*	sol
warm	*calor*	ka·*lor*
windy	*viento*	*vyen*·to

Where can I buy a/an …?	*¿Dónde puedo comprar …?*	*don*·de *pwe*·do kom·*prar* …
rain jacket	*un impermeable*	oon eem·per·me·*a*·ble
sunblock	*crema solar*	*kre*·ma so·*lar*
umbrella	*un paraguas*	oon pa·*ra*·gwas

dry season	*época* f *seca*	*e*·po·ka *se*·ka
rainy season	*época* f *de lluvias*	*e*·po·ka de *lyoo*·vyas
snow	*nieve* f	*nye*·ve
storm	*tormenta* f	tor·*men*·ta
sun	*sol* m	sol

flora & fauna

What ... is that?	¿Qué ... es ése/ésa? m/f	ke ... es e·se/e·sa
animal	animal m	a·nee·mal
flower	flor f	flor
plant	planta f	plan·ta
tree	árbol m	ar·bol

Is it ...?	¿Es ...?	es ...
common	común	ko·moon
dangerous	peligroso/a m/f	pe·lee·gro·so/a
poisonous	venenoso/a m/f	ve·ne·no·so/a
protected	protegido/a m/f	pro·te·khee·do/a

What's it used for?
¿Para qué se usa?　　　　pa·ra ke se oo·sa

Can you eat it?
¿Se puede comerlo?　　　se pwe·de ko·mer·lo

Is it endangered?
¿Está en peligro de　　　es·ta en pe·lee·gro de
extinción?　　　　　　　ek·steen·syon

key language

lenguage clave

breakfast	*desayuno* m	de·sa·*yoo*·no
lunch	*comida* f	ko·*mee*·da
dinner	*cena* f	*se*·na
drink	*beber*	be·*ber*
eat	*comer*	ko·*mer*
snack	*tentempié* m	ten·tem·*pye*

wining & dining

You'll find there's no shortage of eateries where you can snack on the run or dine out at in Latin America. Here are some of the typical establishments you may come across:

bar bar
many offer cheap light meals

chifa *chee*·fa
term for Chinese restaurant in Chile, Bolivia and Peru

churrasquería choo·ras·ke·*ree*·a
restaurant serving mainly barbecued meat

fuente de soda fwen·te de *so*·da
cafe-style establishment serving snacks in addition to ice creams and soft drinks (lit: fountain of soda)

lonchería lon·che·*ree*·a
cheap snack bar/diner

parrillada pa·ree·*lya*·da
Argentinian steakhouse – a carnivore's delight!

restaurante chino res·tow·*ran*·te *chee*·no
popular and cheap Chinese restaurants serving bowls of *tallarines* (noodles) with chopped meat

finding a place to eat

Can you recommend a ...?	¿Puede recomendar ...?	pwe·de re·ko·men·dar ...
cafe	una cafetería	oo·na ka·fe·te·ree·a
restaurant	un restaurante	oon res·tow·ran·te

Where would you go for ...?	¿Adónde se va para ...?	a·don·de se va pa·ra ...
a business lunch	una comida de negocios	oo·na ko·mee·da de ne·go·syos
a celebration	festejar	fes·te·khar
a cheap meal	comer una comida barata	ko·mer oo·na ko·mee·da ba·ra·ta
local specialities	comer comida típica	ko·mer ko·mee·da tee·pee·ka

I'd like to reserve a table for ...	Quisiera reservar una mesa para ...	kee·sye·ra re·ser·var oo·na me·sa pa·ra ...
(two) people	(dos) personas	(dos) per·so·nas
(eight) o'clock	las (ocho)	las (o·cho)

I'd like ..., please.	Quisiera ..., por favor.	kee·sye·ra ... por fa·vor
a table for (five)	una mesa para (cinco)	oo·na me·sa pa·ra (seen·ko)
the menu	el menú	el me·noo
the drink list	la lista de bebidas	la lees·ta de be·bee·das
the (non-) smoking section	(no) fumadores	(no) foo·ma·do·res

Do you have ...? ¿Tienen ...? *tye*·nen ...
  children's meals *comidas para niños* ko·*mee*·das *pa*·ra *nee*·nyos
  a menu in English *un menú en inglés* oon me·*noo* en een·*gles*

Are you still serving food?
  ¿Siguen sirviendo comida? *see*·gen seer·*vyen*·do ko·*mee*·da

How long is the wait?
  ¿Cuánto hay que esperar? *kwan*·to ai ke es·pe·*rar*

eating out

143

at the restaurant

I'd like the menu, please.
Quisiera el menú, por favor.   kee·sye·ra el me·noo por fa·vor

Is it self-serve?
¿Es de autoservicio?   es de ow·to·ser·vee·syo

What would you recommend?
¿Qué me recomienda?   ke me re·ko·myen·da

I'll have what they're having.
Tomaré lo mismo que ellos.   to·ma·re lo mees·mo ke e·lyos

I'd like a local speciality.
Quisiera un plato típico.   kee·sye·ra oon pla·to tee·pee·ko

What's in that dish?
¿De qué es ese plato?   de ke es e·se pla·to

Does it take long to prepare?
¿Se tarda mucho en prepararlo?   se tar·da moo·cho en pre·pa·rar·lo

Is service included in the bill?
¿La cuenta incluye el servicio?   la kwen·ta een·kloo·ye el ser·vee·syo

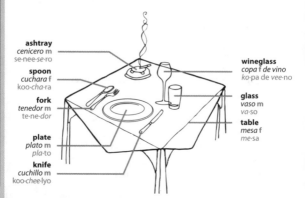

ashtray
cenicero m
se·nee·se·ro

spoon
cuchara f
koo·cha·ra

fork
tenedor m
te·ne·dor

plate
plato m
pla·to

knife
cuchillo m
koo·chee·lyo

wineglass
copa f *de vino*
ko·pa de vee·no

glass
vaso m
va·so

table
mesa f
me·sa

Are these complimentary?
¿*Éstos son gratis?*   es·tos son *gra*·tees

Is there (any tomato sauce)?
¿*Hay (salsa de tomate)?*   ai (*sal*·sa de to·*ma*·te)

Please bring …	*Por favor nos* *trae …*	por fa·*vor* nos *tra*·e …
the bill	*la cuenta*	la *kwen*·ta
a cloth	*un trapo*	oon *tra*·po
a glass	*un vaso*	oon *va*·so
a serviette	*una servilleta*	*oo*·na ser·vee·*lye*·ta
a wineglass	*una copa* *de vino*	*oo*·na *ko*·pa de vee·*no*

look for …

abrebocas	a·bre·*bo*·kas	appetisers
sopas	*so*·pas	soups
de entrada	de en·*tra*·da	starters
ensaladas	en·sa·*la*·das	salads
comidas ligeras	ko·*mee*·das lee·*khe*·ras	light meals
segundos platos	se·*goon*·dos *pla*·tos	main courses
postres	*pos*·tres	desserts
bebidas	be·*bee*·das	drinks
aperitivos	a·pe·ree·*tee*·vos	aperitifs
licores	lee·*ko*·res	spirits
cervezas	ser·*ve*·sas	beers
gaseosas	ga·se·*o*·sas	soft drinks
vinos blancos	*vee*·nos *blan*·kos	white wines
vinos de la casa	*vee*·nos de la *ka*·sa	house wines
vinos del lugar	*vee*·nos del loo·*gar*	local wines
vinos espumosos	*vee*·nos es·poo·*mo*·sos	sparkling wines
vinos rosados	*vee*·nos ro·*sa*·dos	roses
vinos tintos	*vee*·nos *teen*·tos	red wines
vinos dulces	*vee*·nos *dool*·ses	dessert wine
digestivos	dee·khes·*tee*·vos	digestifs

For more words you might see on a menu, see the **culinary reader**, page 159.

talking food

That was delicious!
¡Estaba buenísimo!   es·*ta*·ba bwe·*nee*·see·mo

My compliments to the chef.
Felicitaciones al   fe·lee·see·ta·*syo*·nes al
cocinero.   ko·see·*ne*·ro

I'm full.
Estoy satisfecho/a. m/f   es·*toy* sa·tees·*fe*·cho/a

I love …	*Me encanta …*	me en·*kan*·ta …
this dish	*este plato*	es·te *pla*·to
the local	*la comida*	la ko·*mee*·da
cuisine	*típica de*	*tee*·pee·ka de
	la zona	la *so*·na

---

lunch lingo

The main meal of the day in Latin America is lunch, known as *el almuerzo* or *la comida*. Many restaurants in Latin America provide a set menu for lunch, usually consisting of soup, a main course and a drink. This cheap and popular option goes under the following guises:

In Argentina, Central America and Chile:
almuerzo m *completo* or   al·*mwer*·so kom·*ple*·to
comida f *corrida*   ko·*mee*·da ko·*ree*·da

In Colombia:
almuerzo m *corriente*   al·*mwer*·so ko·*ryen*·te

In Costa Rica:
casado m   ka·*sa*·do

In Peru:
menú m   me·*noo*

This is …	Esto está …	es·to es·ta …
(too) cold	(demasiado) frío	(de·ma·sya·do) free·o
(too) hot	(demasiado)	(de·ma·sya·do)
	caliente	ka·lyen·te
burnt	quemado	ke·ma·do
(too) spicy	(demasiado)	(de·ma·sya·do)
	picante	pee·kan·te
superb	exquisito	ek·skee·see·to

breakfast

What's a typical (Chilean) breakfast?

¿Cómo es un típico	ko·mo es oon tee·pee·ko
desayuno (chileno)?	de·sa·yoo·no (chee·le·no)

bacon	tocino m	to·see·no
bread	pan m	pan
beans	frijoles m pl	free·kho·les
butter	mantequilla f	man·te·kee·lya
(SAm)	manteca f	man·te·ka
cereal	cereales m pl	se·re·a·les
cheese	queso m	ke·so
corn tamales	humitas f pl	oo·mee·tas
croissants	medialunas f pl	me·dya·loo·nas
eggs	huevos m pl	we·vos
jam	mermelada f	mer·me·la·da
omelette	tortilla f	tor·tee·lya
milk	leche f	le·che
muesli	muesli m	moo·es·lee
toast	tostadas f pl	tos·ta·das

See **self-catering**, page 153, and the **culinary reader**, page 159
for other breakfast items.

methods of preparation

I'd like it …	*Lo quisiera …*	lo kee·*sye*·ra …
I don't want it …	*No lo quiero …*	no lo *kye*·ro …
boiled	*hervido*	er·*vee*·do
deep-fried	*frito en*	*free*·to en
	aceite	a·*say*·te
	abundante	a·boon·*dan*·te
fried	*frito*	*free*·to
grilled	*a la parilla*	a la pa·*ree*·lya
medium	*no muy hecho*	no mooy e·cho
rare	*vuelta y vuelta*	*vwel*·ta ee *vwel*·ta
re-heated	*recalentado*	re·ka·len·*ta*·do
steamed	*al vapor*	al va·*por*
well-done	*muy hecho*	mooy e·cho
with the	*con el aliño*	kon el a·*lee*·nyo
dressing on	*aparte*	a·*par*·te
the side		
without (chilli)	*sin (chile)*	seen (*chee*·le)

in the bar

Excuse me!
¡Oiga!　　　　　　　　　　*oy*·ga

I'm next.
¡Ahora voy yo!　　　　　　a·*o*·ra voy yo

I'll have (a glass of red wine).
Para mí, (una copa de　　*pa*·ra mee (*oo*·na *ko*·pa de
vino tinto).　　　　　　　*vee*·no *teen*·to)

Same again, please.
Otra de lo mismo.　　　　*o*·tra de lo *mees*·mo

No ice, thanks.
Sin hielo, gracias.   seen *ye*·lo *gra*·syas

I'd like it straight, please.
Solo, por favor.   *so*·lo por fa·*vor*

I'll buy you a drink.
Te invito a una copa.   te een·*vee*·to a *oo*·na *ko*·pa

What would you like?
¿Qué quieres tomar?   ke *kye*·res to·*mar*

It's my round.
Es mi ronda.   es mee *ron*·da

You can get the next one.
La próxima la pagas tú.   la *prok*·see·ma la *pa*·gas too

Do you serve meals here?
¿Sirven comidas aquí?   *seer*·ven ko·*mee*·das a·*kee*

nonalcoholic drinks

Latin Americans drink prodigious quantities of sweet, fizzy drinks. The general term for soft drink is *gaseosa* but in Chile they are *bebidas*, in Panama *refrescos* or *sodas* and in Ecuador *colas*.

soft drink	*gaseosa* f	ga·se·*o*·sa
(orange) juice	*jugo* m *(de naranja)*	*khoo*·go (de na·*ran*·kha)
(fruit) milkshake	*licuado* m *(de frutas)*	lee·*kwa*·do (de *froo*·tas)
(cup of) tea	*(taza de) té*	(*ta*·sa de) te
(cup of) coffee	*(taza de) café*	(*ta*·sa de) ka·*fe*
... with milk	... *con leche*	... kon *le*·che
... without sugar	... *sin azúcar*	... seen a·*soo*·kar
... water	*agua* f ...	*a*·gwa ...
boiled	*hervida*	er·*vee*·da
sparkling mineral	*mineral con gas*	mee·ne·*ral* kon gas
still mineral	*mineral sin gas*	mee·ne·*ral* seen gas

¡necesito cafecito!

Visitors to Latin America who are expecting out-of-this-world coffee might be surprised to learn that the best beans are shipped overseas to earn export dollars. It's still a popular drink though and here's some vocabulary to help you order what you want:

black coffee		un café negro	oon ka·fe ne·gro
	(Col)	un café tinto	oon ka·fe teen·to
instant coffee		un nescafé	oon nes·ka·fe
milk coffee		un café con leche	oon ka·fe kon le·che
	(Col)	un perico	oon pe·ree·ko
small cup of coffee		un cafecito	oon ka·fe·see·to
	(Arg)	un café chico	oon ka·fe chee·ko
coffee with milk		un café con leche	oon ka·fe kon le·che
	(Arg)	un cortado	oon kor·ta·do

alcoholic drinks

bebidas alcohólicas

beer	cerveza f	ser·ve·sa
brandy	coñac m	ko·nyak
champagne	champán m	cham·pan
cocktail	combinado m	kom·bee·na·do
draught beer	cerveza f de baril	ser·ve·sa de ba·reel
wine	vino m	vee·no
a shot of ...	un trago de ...	oon tra·go de ...
gin	ginebra	khee·ne·bra
pisco (grape brandy)	pisco	pees·ko
rum	ron	ron
tequila	tequila	te·kee·la
vodka	vodka	vod·ka
whisky	güisqui	gwees·kee

a bottle/glass	una botella/copa	oo·na bo·te·lya/ko·pa
of ... wine	de vino ...	de vee·no ...
dessert	dulce	dool·se
red	tinto	teen·to
rose	rosado	ro·sa·do
sparkling	espumoso	es·poo·mo·so
white	blanco	blan·ko
a ... of beer	... de cerveza	... de ser·ve·sa
glass	un vaso	oon va·so
pint	una pinta	oo·na peen·ta
small bottle	un botellín	oon bo·te·lyeen
large bottle	una litrona	oo·na lee·tro·na
jug	una jarra	oo·na kha·ra
(SAm) un chop		oon chop

one too many?

¿una de más?

Cheers!
¡Salud! sa·loo

Thanks, but I don't feel like it.
Lo siento, pero no lo syen·to pe·ro no
me apetece. me a·pe·te·se

I don't drink alcohol.
No bebo alcohol. no be·bo al·kol

I'm tired, I'd better go home.
Estoy cansado/a, mejor es·toy kan·sa·do/a me·khor
me voy a casa. **m/f** me voy a ka·sa

Where's the toilet?
¿Dónde está el baño? don·de es·ta el ba·nyo

This is hitting the spot.
Me lo estoy pasando me lo es·toy pa·san·do
muy bien. mooy byen

I'm feeling drunk.
Esto me está es·to me es·ta
subiendo mucho. soo·byen·do moo·cho

The most common term for 'toilets' in Latin America is *baños* but *servicios sanitarios* or just *servicios* is a frequent alternative. When nature calls, make sure you avoid embarrassing incursions into the wrong territory by correctly interpreting the following nomenclature:

Men's toilets:

Caballeros	ka·ba·*lye*·ros	(lit: 'knights' but equivalent to 'gentlemen')
Hombres	*om*·bres	(lit: men)
Varones	va·*ro*·nes	(lit: men)

Women's toilets:

Damas	*da*·mas	(lit: ladies)
Señoras	se·*nyo*·ras	(lit: women)

I feel fantastic!
¡Me siento fenomenal!   me *syen*·to fe·no·me·*nal*

I really, really love you.
Te quiero muchísimo.   te *kye*·ro moo·*chee*·see·mo

I think I've had one too many.
Creo que he tomado   *kre*·o ke e to·*ma*·do
una de más.   *oo*·na de mas

Can you call a taxi for me?
¿Me puedes pedir un taxi?   me *pwe*·des pe·*deer* oon *tak*·see

I don't think you should drive.
No creo que deberías   no *kre*·o ke de·be·*ree*·as
conducir.   kon·doo·*seer*

I'm pissed.
Estoy borracho/a. m/f   es·toy bo·*ra*·cho/a

I feel ill.
Me siento mal.   me *syen*·to mal

I think you've had enough.
Me parece que has tomado   me pa·*re*·se ke as to·*ma*·do
bastante.   bas·*tan*·te

key language

lenguage clave

cooked	*cocido/a* m/f	ko·*see*·do/a
dried	*seco/a* m/f	*se*·ko/a
fresh	*fresco/a* m/f	*fres*·ko/a
frozen	*congelado/a* m/f	kon·khe·*la*·do/a
powdered	*en polvo*	en *pol*·vo
raw	*crudo/a* m/f	*kroo*·do/a
vacuum-packed	*envasado/a* m/f	en·va·*sa*·do/a
	al vacío	al va·*see*·o

shop talk

carnicería	kar·nee·se·*ree*·a	butcher
fiambrería	fyam·bre·*ree*·a	delicatessen
frutería	froo·te·*ree*·a	fruit shop
heladería	he·la·de·*ree*·a	ice-cream parlour
lechería	le·che·*ree*·a	dairy shop
mercado	mer·*ka*·do	market
panadería	pa·na·de·*ree*·a	baker
pastelería	pas·te·le·*ree*·a	cake shop
pescadería	pes·ka·de·*ree*·a	fish shop
pollería	po·lye·*ree*·a	poultry shop
supermercado	soo·per·mer·*ka*·do	supermarket
tabaquero	ta·ba·*ke*·ro	tobacconist
verdulería	ver·doo·le·*ree*·a	greengrocer

buying food

How much?
¿Cuánto?   kwan·to

How much is (a kilo of cheese)?
¿Cuánto vale (un kilo   kwan·to va·le (oon kee·lo
de queso)?   de ke·so)

What's the local speciality?
¿Cuál es la especialidad   kwal es la es·pe·sya·lee·da
de la zona?   de la so·na

What's that?
¿Qué es eso?   ke es e·so

What's that called?
¿Cómo se llama eso?   ko·mo se lya·ma e·so

Can I taste it?
¿Puedo probarlo/a? m/f   pwe·do pro·bar·lo/a

Can I have a bag, please?
¿Me da una bolsa, por favor?   me da oo·na bol·sa por fa·vor

look for ...

apropriado/a m/f **para cocinar en microondas**	a·pro·prya·do/a pa·ra ko·see·nar en mee·kro·on·das	microwaveable
consúmase dentro de (cuatro) días de abierto	kon·soo·ma·se den·tro de (kwa·tro) dee·as de a·byer·to	consume within (four) days of opening
consúmase antes del ...	kon·soo·ma·se an·tes del ...	use by ...
manténgase en el refrigerador	man·ten·ga·se en el re·free·khe·ra·dor	keep refrigerated

Where can I find the ... section?	¿Dónde está la sección de ...?	don·de es·ta la sek·syon de ...
dairy	productos lácteos	pro·dook·tos lak·te·os
frozen goods	productos congelados	pro·dook·tos kon·khe·la·dos
fruit and vegetable	frutas y verduras	froo·tas ee ver·doo·ras
meat	carne	kar·ne
poultry	aves	a·ves

I'd like ...	Déme ...	de·me ...
(200) grams	(doscientos) gramos	(do·syen·tos) gra·mos
a bottle	una botella	oo·na bo·te·lya
a dozen	una docena	oo·na do·se·na
a jar	una jarra	oo·na kha·ra
a kilo	un kilo	oon kee·lo
(two) kilos	(dos) kilos	(dos) kee·los
a packet	un paquete	oon pa·ke·te
a piece	un trozo	oon tro·so
(three) pieces	(tres) trozos	(tres) tro·sos
a slice	una loncha	oo·na lon·cha
(six) slices	(seis) lonchas	(says) lon·chas
a tin	una lata	oo·na la·ta
some ...	unos/unas ...	oo·nos/oo·nas ...
that one	ése/ésa m/f	e·se/e·sa
this one	esto/esta m/f	es·to/es·ta

Enough.	Ya.	ya
A bit more.	Un poco más.	oon po·ko mas
Less.	Menos.	me·nos

Do you have …?	¿Tiene …?	tye·ne …
anything cheaper	algo más barato	al·go mas ba·ra·to
other kinds	otros tipos	ot·ros tee·pos

cooking utensils

utensilios de cocina

Could I please borrow (a bottle opener)?
¿Me puede prestar (un abrebotellas)? — me pwe·de pres·tar (oon a·bre·bo·te·lyas)

Where's (a can opener)?
¿Dónde hay (un abrelatas)? — don·de ai (oon a·bre·la·tas)

For more cooking implements, see the **dictionary**.

ordering food

Is there a … restaurant near here?	*¿Hay un restaurante … por aquí?*	ai oon res·tow·*ran*·te … por a·*kee*
halal	*halal*	a·*lal*
kosher	*kosher*	ko·sher
vegetarian	*vegetariano*	ve·khe·ta·*rya*·no

I'm vegan.
Soy vegetariano/a soy ve·khe·ta·*rya*·no/a
estricto/a. m/f es·*treek*·to/a

Do you have (vegetarian) food?
¿Tienen comida *tye*·nen ko·*mee*·da
(vegetariana)? (ve·khe·ta·*rya*·na)

I don't eat (red meat).
No como (carne roja). no *ko*·mo (*kar*·ne *ro*·kha)

Is it cooked in/with (butter)?
¿Está cocinado en/con es·*ta* ko·see·*na*·do en/kon
(mantequilla)? (man·te·*kee*·lya)

Is this …?	*¿Esto es …?*	*es*·to es …
cholesterol-free	*sin colesterol*	seen ko·les·te·*rol*
decaffeinated	*sin cafeína*	seen ka·fe·*ee*·na
free of animal produce	*sin productos de animales*	seen pro·*dook*·tos de a·nee·*ma*·les
free-range	*de corral*	de ko·*ral*
genetically modified	*transgénico/a* m/f	trans·*khe*·nee·ko/a
gluten-free	*sin gluten*	seen *gloo*·ten
low-fat	*bajo/a* m/f *en grasas*	*ba*·kho/a en *gra*·sas
low in sugar	*bajo/a* m/f *en azúcar*	*ba*·kho/a en a·*soo*·kar
organic	*orgánico/a* m/f	or·*ga*·nee·ko/a
salt-free	*sin sal*	seen sal

Could you prepare a meal without …?	¿Me puede preparar una comida sin …?	me *pwe*·de pre·pa·*rar* oo·na ko·*mee*·da seen …
butter	mantequilla	man·te·*kee*·lya
eggs	huevos	*we*·vos
fish	pescado	pes·*ka*·do
meat/fish stock	caldo de carne/ pescado	*kal*·do de *kar*·ne/ pes·*ka*·do
pork	cerdo	*ser*·do
poultry	aves	*a*·ves
red meat	carne roja	*kar*·ne *ro*·kha

listen for …

le pre·goon·ta·*re* al ko·see·*ne*·ro
Le preguntaré al cocinero. **I'll check with the cook.**

to·do *lye*·va (kar·ne)
Todo lleva (carne). **It all has (meat) in it.**

pwe·de ko·*mer* …
¿Puede comer …? **Can you eat …?**

special diets & allergies

dietas especiales & alergias

I'm on a special diet.
Estoy a dieta especial. es·*toy* a *dye*·ta es·pe·*syal*

I'm allergic to …	Soy alérgico/a … m/f	soy a·*ler*·khee·ko/a …
dairy produce	a los productos lácteos	a los pro·*dook*·tos *lak*·te·os
eggs	a los huevos	a los *we*·vos
fish	al pescado	al pes·*ka*·do
gelatin	a la gelatina	a la khe·la·*tee*·na
gluten	al gluten	al *gloo*·ten
honey	a la miel	a la myel
MSG	al glutamato monosódico	al gloo·ta·*ma*·to mo·no·*so*·dee·ko
nuts	a las nueces	a las *nwe*·ses
peanuts	al maní	al ma·*nee*
seafood	al marisco	al ma·*rees*·ko

A

a la plancha a la *plan*·cha *grilled*
al vapor ⓜ al va·*por steamed*
a punto a *poon*·to *medium (steak)*
aceite ⓜ a·*say*·te *oil*
aceitunas ⓕ pl a·*say*·too·nas *olives*
— **alinadas (Cub)** a·lee·*na*·das *olives marinated in cummin, hot pepper, lemon, garlic & vinegar*
— **rellenas** re·*lye*·nas *stuffed olives*
achicoria ⓕ a·chee·*ko*·rya *chicory • endive*
achuras ⓕ pl a·*choo*·ras *offal*
adobo ⓜ a·*do*·bo *paste of garlic, oregano, paprika, peppercorn, salt, olive, lime juice & vinegar for seasoning meat*
agua ⓕ a·gwa *water*
— **de canilla** de ka·*nee*·lya *tap water*
— **de jamaica (CAm)** de kha·*mai*·ka *sweet, red, iced tea made from hibiscus flowers*
— **de la llave** de la *lya*·ve *tap water*
— **del tubo** del *too*·bo *tap water*
— **de vertiente** de ver·*tyen*·te *spring water*
— **de panel (Col)** de pa·*nel unrefined sugar melted in hot water*
— **mineral** mee·ne·*ral mineral water*
aguacate ⓜ a·gwa·*ka*·te *avocado*
— **salsa (Cub)** *sal*·sa *avocado sauce containing tomato, capsicum, olive, tomato & white rum*
aguardiente ⓜ **(Col)** a·gwar·*dyen*·te *spirit flavoured with aniseed*
ahumado/a ⓜ/ⓕ a·oo·*ma*·do/a *smoked*
ají ⓜ a·*khee red chilli • chilli sauce*

ajiaco ⓜ a·*khya*·ko *spicy potato stew • in Colombia, soup with chicken & three varieties of potato, served with corn & capers*
ajili-mójili ⓜ **(Pue)** a·khee·lee·*mo*·khee·lee *tangy garlic sauce*
ajillo, al a·*khee*·lyo, al *in garlic*
ajo ⓜ a·kho *garlic*
ajoporro ⓜ a·kho·*po*·ro *leek*
al ajillo al a·*khee*·lyo *in garlic*
al horno al *or*·no *baked*
albahaca ⓕ al·*ba*·ka *basil*
albóndigas ⓕ pl al·*bon*·dee·gas *meatballs*
alcachofa ⓕ al·ka·*cho*·fa *artichoke*
alcaparra ⓕ al·ka·*pa*·ra *caper*
alcaucil ⓜ **(SAm)** al·*kow*·seel *artichoke*
alcohol ⓜ al·*kol alcohol*
aliado ⓜ **(Chi)** a·*lya*·do *sandwich with cold ham & cheese*
alita ⓕ a·*lee*·ta *wing (bird or poultry)*
allioli ⓕ a·*lyo*·lee *garlic sauce*
almejas ⓕ pl al·*me*·khas *clams*
almendra ⓕ al·*men*·dra *almond*
almuerzo ⓜ al·*mwer*·so *lunch*
alubias ⓕ pl a·*loo*·byas *kidney beans*
amarillos ⓜ pl **(Pue)** a·ma·*ree*·lyos *fried ripe plantains coated with cinnamon, sugar & wine sauce*
ananá(s) ⓜ a·na·*na(s) pineapple*
anca ⓕ an·ka *haunch*
anchoas ⓕ pl an·*cho*·as *anchovies*
anguila ⓕ an·*gee*·la *eel*
anís ⓜ a·nees *anise • aniseed*
anticucho ⓜ **(Chi, Per, Bol)** an·tee·*koo*·cho *kebab*
apio ⓜ a·pyo *celery*
arenque ⓜ a·*ren*·ke *herring*

arepa ① **(Ven)** a·re·pa *small toasted or fried maize pancake sometimes stuffed*

areperas ① **(Ven)** a·re·pe·ras *snack bars selling* **arepas**

arreglados ⓜ pl **(Cos)** a·re·gla·dos *savoury filled puff pastries*

arrollado ⓜ a·ro·lya·do *rolled pork*

arroz ⓜ a·ros *rice*
— **con habichuelas (Pue)** kon a·bee·chwe·las *main course of rice & beans*
— **con leche** kon le·che *rice pudding*
— **con pollo** kon po·lyo *dish of rice & chicken*

arveja ① **(Ecu)** ar·ve·kha *pea stew*
— **seca** se·ka *split pea*

arvejas ① pl ar·ve·khas *peas*

asado ⓜ **(SAm)** a·sa·do *mixed grill*
— **al espiedo** al es·pye·do *spit roast*

asado/a ⓜ/① a·sa·do/a *roasted*
— **al horno** al or·no *oven roasted*

asopao ⓜ **de pollo (Pue)** a·so·pa·o de po·lyo *chicken stew with* **adobo** *seasoning*

atún ⓜ a·toon *tuna*
— **con ron (Cub)** kon ron *tuna with a rum sauce*

auyama ① **(Col, Ven)** ow·ya·ma *pumpkin*

ave ⓜ a·ve *fowl • poultry*

avellana ① a·ve·lya·na *hazelnut*

azafran ⓜ a·sa·fran *saffron*

azucar ⓜ a·soo·kar *sugar*

B

bacalao ⓜ ba·ka·la·o *(salted) cod*

baho ⓜ **(Nic)** ba·o *stew of beef, various types of plantains &* **yuca**

baleadas ① pl **(Hon)** ba·le·a·das *white flour tortillas filled with refried beans, cream & crumbled cheese*

banana ① **(Arg, Peru)** ba·na·na *banana*

banano ⓜ **(CAm,Col)** ba·na·no *banana*

bandeja ① **(Col)** ban·de·kha *main course*
— **paisa (Col)** pai·sa *traditional dish consisting of ground beef, sausage, red beans, rice, green banana, egg, salt pork & avocado*

baracoa ⓜ **special (Cub)** ba·ra·ko·a spe·syal *cocktail of rum, coconut cream, grapefruit juice & limejuice*

Barros Jarpa ⓜ **(Chi)** ba·ros khar·pa *sandwich with cold ham & melted cheese – named after a Chilean painter*

Barros Luco ⓜ **(Chi)** ba·ros loo·ko *steak sandwich with melted cheese – named after a Chilean president*

batata ① ba·ta·ta *sweet potato*

bebida ① be·bee·da *drink (beverage)*

beicon **con queso** bay·kon kon ke·so *cold bacon with cheese*

berberechos ⓜ pl ber·be·re·chos *cockles*

berenjena ① be·ren·khe·na *eggplant • aubergine*

berro be·ro *watercress*

besugo ⓜ be·soo·go *bream*

betarraga ① **(Chi, Bol)** ba·ta·ra·ga *beetroot*

bien asado/a ⓜ/① byen a·sa·do/a *well-done*

bien hecho/a ⓜ/① byen e·cho/a *well-done*

bife ⓜ **(Arg, Par, Uru)** bee·fe *steak*
— **a caballo** a ka·ba·lyo *steak served with two eggs & chips*
— **asado** a·sa·do *roast beef*
— **de chorizo** de cho·ree·so *rump steak*
— **de costilla** de kos·tee·lya *T-bone steak – also called* **chuleta**
— **de lomo** ⓜ de lo·mo *tenderloin*

bistec ⓜ bees·tek *steak*
— **con patatas** kon pa·ta·tas *steak & chips*

blanco ⓜ blan·ko *white (wine)*

bocadillo ⓜ **(Cub)** bo·ka·dee·lyo
sandwich filled with ham or cheese

bocaditos ⓜ pl **(Cub)** bo·ka·*dee*·tos
substantial snack dishes

bocas ⓕ pl **(Cos, Pan)** bo·kas *savoury
side dishes served at bars*

bollos ⓜ pl bo·lyos *bread rolls*

boniatillo ⓜ **(Cub)** bo·nya·*tee*·lyo
*dessert made from sweet potato, sugar,
cinnamon, lime, egg yolks & sherry*

boniato ⓜ **(Arg)** bo·*nya*·to
sweet potato

bori-bori ⓜ **(Par)** bo·ree·*bo*·ree
chicken soup with corn meal balls

botella ⓕ bo·*te*·lya *bottle*

breva ⓕ *bre*·va *fig*

brócoli ⓜ bro·ko·lee *broccoli*

budín ⓜ boo·*deen* *pudding*

buey ⓜ bway *ox*

C

caballa ⓕ ka·*ba*·lya *mackerel*

cabeza ⓕ ka·*be*·sa *head*

cabra ⓕ *ka*·bra *goat*

cacao ⓜ ka·*ka*·o *cocoa*

cachapa ⓕ **(Ven)** ka·*cha*·pa *large
round corn pancake often served
with cheese ham or both*

cachito ⓜ **(Ven)** ka·*chee*·to
*a type of hot croissant filled with
chopped ham*

café ⓜ ka·*fe* *coffee*
— **doble** *do*·ble *long black coffee*
— **marrón (Ven)** ma·*ron* *coffee
consisting of half coffee & half milk*
— **negro** *ne*·gro *black coffee*
— **tinto (Col)** *teen*·to *black coffee*
— **chico (Arg)** *chee*·ko *small cup of
coffee*
— **solo** *so*·lo *black coffee*

cafecito ⓜ ka·fe·*see*·to *small cup of
coffee*

cajeta ⓕ **(Cos)** ka·*khe*·ta *similar to
dulce de leche*

calabacín ⓜ ka·la·ba·*seen* *zucchini ·
courgette*

calabaza ⓕ ka·la·*ba*·sa *pumpkin ·
gourd · marrow*

calamares ⓜ pl ka·la·*ma*·res *calamari ·
squid*

caldereta ⓕ kal·de·*re*·ta *stew*

caldillo ⓜ **cubano (Cub)** kal·*dee*·lyo
koo·*ba*·no *hotpot made with steak,
onions, tomatoes, potatoes, hot
pepper, garlic, brown sugar & cumin*

caldo ⓜ *kal*·do *broth · stock*
— **de gallina** de ga·*lyee*·na
chicken soup
— **de patas (Ecu)** de pa·tas
soup made of boiled cattle hooves

caliente ka·*lyen*·te *hot*

callampas ⓕ **(Chi)** ka·*lyam*·pas
mushrooms

camarón ⓜ ka·ma·*ron*
shrimp · small prawn

cambur ⓜ **(Ven)** kam·*boor* *banana*

camomila ⓕ ka·mo·*mee*·la
camomile tea

camote ⓜ ka·*mo*·te *sweet potato*

caña ⓕ ka·nya *cane alcohol ·
aguardiente*
— **de azúcar** de a·*soo*·kar *sugar cane*

canela ⓕ ka·*ne*·la *cinnamon*

canelones ⓜ pl ka·ne·*lo*·nes
cannelloni

cangrejo ⓜ kan·*gre*·kho *crab*
— **de río** de *ree*·o *crayfish*

cañita ⓕ **(Pue)** ka·*nyee*·ta *homemade,
illegal rum*

capitàn ⓜ **(Chi)** ka·pee·*tan* *vermouth*

capón (SAm) ⓜ ka·*pon* *mutton*

carabinero ⓜ ka·ra·bee·*ne*·ro
large prawn

caracol ⓜ ka·ra·*kol* *snail*

carbonada ⓕ **(Arg)** kar·bo·*na*·da
*beef stew of rice, potatoes, maize,
squash, apples & peaches*

carimañola ⓕ **(Pan)** ka·ree·ma·*nyo*·la
*deep-fried roll filled with meat, made
from ground & boiled* **yuca**

carne ⓕ *kar*·ne meat
— **de caballo** de ka·*ba*·lyo *horsemeat*
— **de vaca** de *va*·ka *beef*
— **fría** *free*·a *cold meat*
— **mechada (Pue)** me·*cha*·da
roast beef
— **molida** mo·*lee*·da *minced meat*
carnicería ⓕ kar·nee·se·*ree*·a
butcher's shop
carpa ⓕ *kar*·pa *carp*
casado ⓜ **(Cos)** ka·*sa*·do *platter of rice, black beans, plantain, meat or fish, cabbage, an egg or avocado*
— **vegetariano (Cos)**
ve·khe·ta·*rya*·no *vegetarian version of casado*
casamiento ⓜ **(Sal)** ka·sa·*myen*·to *rice & beans mixed together*
castaña ⓕ kas·*ta*·nya *chestnut*
— **de Pará** de pa·*ra* *brazil nut*
cave ⓜ **(Hon)** *ka*·ve
a type of coffee liqueur
caza ⓕ *ka*·sa *game (meat)*
— **de temporada** de tem·po·*ra*·da *game in season*
cazuela ⓕ ka·*swe*·la *casserole • fish stew (Arg)*
— **de mariscos (Chi)** de ma·*rees*·kos *shellfish soup*
cebada ⓕ se·*ba*·da *barley*
cebolla ⓕ se·*bo*·lya *onion*
cerdo ⓜ *ser*·do *pig • pork*
cereales ⓜ pl se·re·*a*·les *cereal*
cereza ⓕ se·*re*·sa *cherry*
cerveza ⓕ ser·*ve*·sa *beer*
— **de barril** de ba·*reel*
draught beer • beer on tap
— **de malta** de *mal*·ta *dark beer*
— **lager** *la*·ger *lager beer*
— **negra** *ne*·gra *stout*
ceviche ⓜ se·*vee*·che *raw fish marinated in lemon juice, chilli or onions or both*
chacarero ⓜ **(Chi)** cha·ka·*re*·ro *beefsteak with tomato & vegetables*

chairo ⓜ **(Bol)** *chai*·ro *mutton or beef soup served with* **chuños**, *fresh potato & dried maize*
chajchu ⓜ **(Bol)** *chakh*·choo *beef with freeze-dried potatoes, hard-boiled egg, cheese & hot red pepper sauce*
chalote ⓜ cha·*lo*·te *spring onion • shallot*
champán ⓜ cham·*pan* *champagne*
champiñones ⓜ pl cham·pee·*nyo*·nes *mushrooms*
— **al ajillo** al a·*khee*·lyo
garlic mushrooms
chapalele ⓜ **(Chi)** cha·pa·*le*·le *boiled potato & flour bread*
chaque ⓜ **(Bol)** *cha*·ke *similar to* **chupe** *but much thicker & with more grain*
charque ⓜ **(Bol)** *char*·ke *dried beef, llama or other red meat*
— **kan** kan **charque** *served with mashed hominy*
chauchas ⓕ pl *chow*·chas *string beans*
chicha ⓕ **(Per, Bol)** *chee*·cha *maize beer associated with ceremonial & ritual occasions in Peru*
chicharrón ⓜ chee·cha·*ron* *fried pork fat*
chifa ⓕ **(Bol, CAm, Per)** *chee*·fa *chinese restaurant*
chilcano ⓜ **(Chi, Per)** cheel·*ka*·no *ginger ale – may be served with* **pisco**
chile ⓜ *chee*·le *pimento, (small red pepper)*
chimichurri ⓜ **(Arg, Uru)**
chee·mee·*choo*·ree *strong olive oil, parsley & garlic barbecue sauce*
chinchulines ⓜ pl cheen·choo·*lee*·nes *small intestines – a common* **asado** *dish*
chipa ⓕ **de almidón (Par)** *chee*·pa de al·mee·*don* *like* **chipa guazú** *but made with manioc flour rather than corn meal*
chipa ⓕ **guazú (Par)** *chee*·pa gwa·*soo* *dish resembling a cheese souffle containing corn meal*

chipirón ⓜ chee-pee-*ron* small squid

chirimoya ⓕ chee-ree-*mo*-ya custard apple

chispa tren ⓕ **(Cub)** *chees*-pa tren 'train sparks' – Cuban firewater

chivito ⓜ **(Uru)** chee-*vee*-to tasty & filling steak sandwich with a variety of additions including cheese, lettuce, tomato & bacon
— **al plato** al *pla*-to steak served with a fried egg, potato salad, green salad & french fries

chivo ⓜ *chee*-vo kid • baby goat

choclo ⓜ *cho*-klo maize • corn on the cob

choco ⓜ *cho*-ko cuttlefish

chocolate ⓜ cho-ko-*la*-te chocolate
— **caliente** ka-*lyen*-te hot chocolate drink
— **santafereño (Col)** san-ta-fe-re-*nyo* cup of hot chocolate accompanied by a piece of cheese & bread

chola ⓕ **(Bol)** *cho*-la bread roll filled with meat, onion, tomato & escabeche

chop ⓜ chop draught beer

choripán ⓜ **(Arg)** cho-ree-*pan* spicy sausage sandwich

chorizo ⓜ cho-*ree*-so spicy pork sausage
— **al horno** al *or*-no spicy baked sausage

chorlito ⓜ chor-*lee*-to plover (small game bird)

chuleta ⓕ choo-*le*-ta chop • cutlet • T-bone steak **(Arg)**
— **de puerco** de *pwer*-ko pork chop

chuños ⓜ pl **(Bol)** choo-*nyos* freeze-dried potatoes made by leaving potatoes out in the winter cold

chupe ⓜ *choo*-pe stew • soup • in Bolivia, a vegetable, meat & grain soup with a clear broth flavoured with ají, tomato, cumin or onion
— **de camarones (Per)** de ka-ma-*ro*-nes prawn soup
— **de cóngrio (Chi)** de *kon*-gryo conger eel stew
— **de locos (Chi)** de *lo*-kos abalone stew

churrasco ⓜ choo-*ras*-ko rib steak • in Ecuador, a hearty dish of rice, fried beef, fried eggs, vegetables, fried potatoes, a slice of avocado, tomato & rice

ciruela ⓕ see-*rwe*-la plum
— **seca** *se*-ka prune

ckocko ⓜ **(Bol)** *ko*-ko spicy chicken cooked in wine or **chicha** & served with maize, olives, raisins & aromatic condiments

clericó ⓜ **(Uru)** kle-ree-*ko* usually a mixture of white wine, fruit juice, a liqueur, fruit salad, ice & a carbonated soft drink or cider

cocina ⓕ ko-*see*-na kitchen • cuisine

cocinado/a ⓜ/ⓕ ko-see-*na*-do/a cooked

cocinar ko-see-*nar* to cook

cocinero/a ⓜ/ⓕ ko-see-*ne*-ro/a chef

coco ⓜ *ko*-ko coconut

codorniz ⓕ ko-dor-*nees* quail

coles ⓜ pl **de Bruselas** *ko*-les de broo-*se*-las Brussels sprouts

coliflor ⓕ ko-lee-*flor* cauliflower

combinado ⓜ kom-bee-*na*-do cocktail

completo ⓜ **(Chi)** kom-*ple*-to a hot dog with the lot

con gas ⓜ&ⓕ kon gas fizzy

con leche ⓜ kon *le*-che with milk

coñac ⓜ ko-*nyak* brandy

conejo ⓜ ko-*ne*-kho rabbit

confitería ⓕ kon-fee-te-*ree*-a sweet shop • candy store

confites ⓜ pl **(Bol)** kon·*fee*·tes *festive candies consisting of coloured sugar syrup, nuts, aniseed, fruits, biscuit or coconut*

copa ⓕ *ko*·pa *glass*

corazón ⓜ ko·ra·*son heart*

cordero ⓜ kor·*de*·ro *lamb*

cortado ⓜ **(Arg)** kor·*ta*·do *coffee with a little milk*

costilla ⓕ kos·*tee*·lya *loin • spare rib*
— **de cerdo** de *ser*·do *pork chop*

costillar ⓜ **de cordero** kos·tee·*lyar* de kor·*de*·ro *rack of lamb*

crema ⓕ *kre*·ma *cream*
— **batida** ba·*tee*·da *whipped cream*

croquetas (Cub) ⓕ pl kro·*ke*·tas *popular fried ham or chicken croquettes*

crudo/a ⓜ/ⓕ *kroo*·do/a *raw*

crustáceos ⓜ pl kroos·*ta*·se·os *shellfish*

cuadril ⓜ *kwa*·dreel *rump steak*

cubierto ⓜ koo·*byer*·to *cover charge*

cubo ⓜ **de hielo** *koo*·bo de *ye*·lo *ice cube*

cucharita ⓕ koo·cha·*ree*·ta *teaspoon*

cuenta ⓕ *kwen*·ta *bill • check*

curanto ⓜ **(Chi)** koo·*ran*·to *hearty stew of fish, shellfish, chicken, pork, lamb, beef & potato*

curtido ⓜ **(Sal)** koor·*tee*·do *mixture of pickled beets, cabbage & carrots served with* **pupusas**

cuy ⓜ kooy *grilled or roasted guinea pig*

D

damasco ⓜ da·*mas*·ko *apricot*

dátil ⓜ *da*·teel *date*

descafeinado/a ⓜ/ⓕ des·ka·fay·*na*·do/a *decaffeinated*

desnatado/a ⓜ/ⓕ des·na·*ta*·do/a *low-fat*

digestivo ⓜ dee·khes·*tee*·vo *digestif*

dorado/a ⓜ/ⓕ do·*ra*·do/a *browned*

dulce ⓜ **de leche (Arg)** *dool*·se de *le*·che *caramelised condensed milk • a filling in sweet pastries*

dulce *dool*·se *sweet*

dulces ⓜ pl *dool*·ses *confectionery • sweets*

E

(de) elaboración ⓕ **propia** (de) e·la·bo·ra·*syon* pro·pya *made on the premises*

elote ⓜ **(CAm)** e·*lo*·te *corn • corn on the cob*

empanada ⓕ em·pa·*na*·da *stuffed meat & vegetable turnover*

empanadilla ⓕ **(Pue)** em·pa·na·*dee*·lya *pocket of plantain or* **yuca** *dough stuffed with meat*

empanadillas ⓕ pl **de jueyes (Pue)** em·pa·na·*dee*·lyas de *khwe*·yes *highly seasoned land crab meat baked into an* **empanadilla** *of cassava paste*

empana (Cub) ⓕ em·*pa*·na *meat or vegetable pattie*

en escabeche ⓜ **(Pue)** en es·ka·*be*·che *way of preparing seafood by frying then chilling & pickling it*

en rodajas en ro·*da*·khas *sliced*

enchiladas ⓕ pl **(Hon)** en·chee·*lya*·das *crisp fried tortilla topped with spicy meat, salad & crumbled cheese*

endulzado/a ⓜ/ⓕ en·dool·*sa*·do/a *sweetened*

eneldo ⓜ e·*nel*·do *dill*

ensalada ⓕ en·sa·*la*·da *salad • in El Salvador, a mixed fruit juice served with fruit salad floating on top*
— **mixta** *meeks*·ta *mixed salad*
— **rusa** *roo*·sa *vegetable salad with mayonnaise*
— **verde** *ver*·de *green salad*

entremeses ⓕ pl en·tre·*me*·ses *hors-d'oeuvres*

erizos ⓜ pl **(Chi)** e·*ree*·sos *sea urchins*

escabeche ⓜ **(Bol)** es·ka·*be*·che *vegetables, onion & peppers preserved in vinegar*

espagueti ⓜ es·pa·*ge*·tee *spaghetti*

espárragos ⓜ pl es·*pa*·ra·gos *asparagus*

especialidad ⓕ es·pe·sya·lee·*da* *speciality*
— **de la casa** de la *ka*·sa *speciality of the house*
— **del día** del *dee*·a *speciality of the day*

espinacas ⓜ pl es·pee·*na*·kas *spinach*

espumoso/a ⓜ/ⓕ es·poo·*mo*·so/a *sparkling*

estofado ⓜ es·to·*fa*·do *stew*

estofado/a ⓜ/ⓕ es·to·*fa*·do/a *braised*

estragón ⓜ es·tra·*gon* *tarragon*

F

faba ⓜ *fa*·ba *type of dried bean*

facturas ⓕ pl **(Arg)** fak·*too*·ras *buns, cakes*

faisán ⓜ fai·*san* *pheasant*

falso conejo ⓜ **(Bol)** *fal*·so ko·*ne*·kho *'false rabbit' – greasy, glutinous meat-based dish*

fideos ⓜ pl fee·*de*·os *noodles*

filete ⓜ fee·*le*·te *fillet of meat or fish*
— **de bife** de *bee*·fe *beef fillet*

flan ⓜ flan *egg custard • creme caramel*

frambuesa ⓕ fram·*bwe*·sa *raspberry*

fresa ⓕ *fre*·sa *strawberry*

fresco/a ⓜ/ⓕ *fres*·ko/a *fresh*

frescos ⓜ pl **(Hon)** *fres*·kos *fruit drinks blended with water & sugar*

fricasés ⓜ **(Bol)** free·ka·*ses* *pork or chicken stew with maize grits*

frijol ⓜ free·*khol* *bean*
— **blanco** *blan*·ko *large butter bean*

frijoles ⓜ pl free·*kho*·les *beans*
— **con arroz (Gua)** kon *a*·ros *beans & rice*

frío/a ⓜ/ⓕ *free*·o/a *cold*

fritada ⓕ free·*ta*·da *scraps of fried or roast pork*

fritanga ⓕ free·*tan*·ga *hotpot or stew • in Bolivia, spicy hot pork with mint & hominy*

frito/a ⓜ/ⓕ *free*·to/a *fried*
— **a la sartén** a la sar·*ten* *pan-fried*

fruta ⓕ *froo*·ta *fruit*

frutilla ⓕ froo·*tee*·lya *strawberry*

fuerte *fwer*·te *strong*

G

galleta ⓕ ga·*lye*·ta *biscuit • cookie*

gallina ⓕ ga·*lyee*·na *chicken*

gallito ⓜ ga·*lyee*·to *cockerel*

gallo ⓜ *ga*·yo *rooster*

gallo ⓜ **pinto (Cos, Nic, Pan)** *ga*·lyo *peen*·to *lightly spiced mixture of rice & black beans traditionally served for breakfast, sometimes with **natilla** or fried eggs*

gallos ⓜ pl **(Cos)** *ga*·lyos *tortilla sandwiches containing meat, beans or cheese*

gambas ⓕ pl **rebozadas** *gam*·bas rebo·*sa*·das *batter-fried scampi (large prawns)*

ganso ⓜ *gan*·so *goose*

garbanzo ⓜ gar·*ban*·so *chickpea • garbanzo*

gaseoso/a ⓜ/ⓕ ga·se·o·*so*/a *fizzy*

gazpacho ⓜ ga·*spa*·cho *cold tomato & vegetable soup*

ginebra ⓕ **bols (Arg)** khee·*ne*·bra bols *alcoholic drink similar to gin*

girasol ⓜ khee·ra·*sol* *sunflower*

glaseado/a ⓜ/ⓕ gla·se·a·*do*/a *glazed • iced*

gol ⓜ **(Chi)** gol *translucent alcoholic mixture of butter, sugar & milk*

granada ⓕ gra·*na*·da *pomegranate*

grande *gran*·de *large • big*

grasa ⓕ *gra*·sa *grease • fat*

gratinado/a ⓜ/ⓕ gra·tee·*na*·do/a *au gratin*

grosella ① gro·se·lya *redcurrant*
— **espinosa** es·pee·no·sa *gooseberry*
— **negra** ne·gra *blackcurrant*

güífiti ⓜ **(Hon)** gi·fee·tee *mix of aguardiente with aromatic & marine plants – a Garífuna specialty*

guinda ① **(Per)** geen·da *sweet cherry brandy*

guindado ⓜ **(Chi)** geen·da·do *fermented alcoholic drink made from a cherry-like fruit, brandy, cinnamon & cloves*

guindilla ① geen·dee·lya *hot chilli*

guisantes ⓜ pl gee·san·tes *peas*

guiso ⓜ **(Cos)** gee·so *stew*

güisqui ⓜ gwees·kee *whisky*

H

haba ① a·ba *broad bean · Lima bean*

hallaca ① **(Ven)** a·lya·ka *chopped pork, beef or chicken or both with vegetables & olives, all folded in a maize dough, wrapped in banana leaves & steamed*

hamburguesa ① am·boor·ge·sa *hamburger*

harina ① a·ree·na *flour*

hecho/a ⓜ/① e·cho/a *made · prepared*

heladería ① e·la·de·ree·a *ice-cream parlour*

helado/a ⓜ/① e·la·do/a *chilled · iced*

helado ⓜ e·la·do *ice cream*

hervido/a ⓜ/① er·vee·do/a *boiled*
— **a fuego lento** a fwe·go len·to *simmered*

hervir er·veer *boil*

hierba ① yer·ba *herb*

hierbabuena ① yer·ba·bwe·na *mint*

hígado ⓜ ee·ga·do *liver*

higo ⓜ ee·go *fig*

hocico ⓜ o·see·ko *snout*

hongo ⓜ on·go *button mushroom*

horchata ① **(Cos)** or·cha·ta *rice-based drink flavoured with cinnamon*
— **de cebada (Sal)** de se·ba·da *sweet barley-based beverage spiced with cinnamon*

hormiga ① **culona (Col)** or·mee·ga koo·lo·na *large fried ants – unique to Santander*

horneado/a ⓜ/① or·ne·a·do/a *baked*

hornear or·ne·ar *bake*

horno ⓜ or·no *oven*

horno, al or·no, al *oven baked*

hortalizas ① pl or·ta·lee·sas *vegetables*

hueso ⓜ we·so *bone*

huevos ⓜ pl we·vos *eggs*
— **cocidos** ko·see·dos *boiled eggs*
— **de paslama** de pas·la·ma *turtle eggs – a popular dish in Nicaragua though ecologically suspect*
— **duros** doo·ros *hard-boiled eggs*
— **estrellados** es·tre·lya·dos *fried eggs*
— **fritos** free·tos *fried eggs*
— **pericos** pe·ree·kos *scrambled eggs with fried onions*
— **revueltos** re·vwel·tos *scrambled eggs*

humitas ① pl **(Bol)** oo·mee·tas *corn tamales filled with spiced beef, vegetables & potatoes*
— **en chala (Chi)** en cha·la *popular & tasty snack of steamed tamales wrapped in corn husks*

húngaros ⓜ pl **(Uru)** oon·ga·ros *spicy sausages on a hot dog roll*

I

infusión ⓜ een·foo·syon *herbal tea*

J

jabalí ⓜ kha·ba·lee *wild boar*

jamón ⓜ kha·mon *ham*
— **dulce** dool·se *boiled ham*
— **serrano** se·ra·no *cured ham*

jengibre ⓜ khen·khee·bre *ginger*

jochi ⓜ kho-chee agouti (a rodent prized for its meat)

jolque ⓜ (Bol) khol-ke kidney soup

jueyes ⓟl (Pue) khwe-yes land crabs – an island staple

jugo ⓜ khoo-go juice
— **exprimido** ⓜ ek-spree-mee-do freshly-squeezed juice

jugoso/a ⓜ/ⓕ khoo-go-so/a succulent

K

kala purkha ⓕ (Bol) ka-la poor-ka soup made from maize cooked in a ceramic dish by adding a steaming chunk of heavy pumice

kosher ko-sher kosher

kuchen ⓜ (Chi) koo-chen pastries filled with local fruit baked by Chileans of German descent

L

lager la-ger light-coloured or pale beer · lager

langosta ⓕ lan-gos-ta spiny lobster

langostino ⓜ lan-gos-tee-no prawn · lobster

lawa ⓕ (Bol) la-wa soup made from a broth thickened with corn starch or wheat flour

leche ⓕ le-che milk
— **desnatada** des-na-ta-da skimmed milk

lechón ⓜ le-chon suckling pig – a speciality of Cochabamba in Bolivia & found elsewhere as a fiesta dish

lechona ⓕ (Col) le-cho-na pig carcass stuffed with its own meat, rice & dried peas, then baked in an oven

lechuga ⓕ le-choo-ga lettuce

legumbre ⓕ le-goom-bre pulse

lengua ⓕ len-gwa tongue

lenguado ⓜ len-gwa-do lemon sole · dab

lenteja ⓕ len-te-kha lentil · in Ecuador, a lentil stew

lentejas ⓕ pl len-te-khas lentils

licuados ⓜ pl lee-kwa-dos milk-blended fruit drinks

lima ⓕ lee-ma lime

limón ⓜ lee-mon lemon

limonadas ⓕ pl lee-mo-na-das lemonade made with lime or lemon juice, water & sugar

lista ⓕ **de vinos** lees-ta de vee-nos wine list

llajhua ⓕ (Bol) lya-khwa hot salsa made from tomatoes & hot pepper pods

llano/a lya-no/a plain

llapingachos ⓜ pl (Ecu) lya-peen-ga-chos fried mashed-potato-&-cheese pancakes often served with fritada

llaucha ⓕ pl **paceña (Bol)** lyow-cha pa-se-nya doughy cheese bread

locotos ⓜ pl (Bol) lo-ko-tos small hot pepper pods

locro ⓜ lo-kro in Argentina & Paraguay, a maize stew · in Ecuador, potato soup with corn & avocado or cheese topping

lomo ⓜ lo-mo loin
— **a lo pobre (Chi)** a lo po-bre enormous slab of beef topped with two fried eggs & served with french fries
— **con pimientos** kon pee-myen-tos pork sausage with peppers
— **de cerdo** de ser-do pork loin · sausage
— **saltado (Per)** sal-ta-do chopped steak fried with onions, tomatoes, potatoes & served with rice

longaniza ⓕ lon-ga-nee-sa dark pork sausage

M

macarrones ⓜ pl ma-ka-ro-nes macaroni

maíz ⓜ ma-ees corn · maize · sweet corn

mallorca ⓕ (Pue) ma-lyor-ka sweet pastry covered with powdered sugar

malta ① **(Pue)** *mal·*ta *nonalcoholic, vitamin-fortified malt beverage*

mandarina ① *man·da·ree·*na *tangerine*

mango ⓜ *man·*go *mango*

maní ⓜ *ma·nee peanut*

mantequilla ① *man·te·kee·*lya *butter*

manzana ① *man·sa·*na *apple*

maracuyá ① *ma·ra·koo·*ya *passionfruit*

marinado/a ⓜ/① *ma·ree·na·*do/a *marinated*

mariscos ⓜ pl *ma·rees·*kos *seafood · shellfish*

masaco ⓜ **(Bol)** *ma·sa·*ko *llama charque served with mashed plantain or yuca*

matambre ⓜ **relleno (Arg)** *ma·ta·am·*bre *re·lye·*no *stuffed & rolled flank steak, baked or eaten cold as an appetiser*

mate ⓜ *ma·*te *tea prepared from yerba mate – the most popular hot beverage in Argentina, Paraguay & Uruguay* — **de coca (Bol, Per)** de *ko·*ka *coca-leaf tea*

mavi ⓜ **(Pue)** *ma·*vee *a root-beer-like drink made from the bark of the ironwood tree*

mayonesa ① *ma·yo·ne·*sa *mayonnaise*

mazamorro ⓜ *ma·sa·mo·*ro *in Costa Rica, a pudding made from corn starch · in Paraguay, corn mush*

mazapan ⓜ *ma·sa·*pan *marzipan · almond paste*

mazorca ① *ma·sor·*ka *corn on the cob*

mbaipy heé ⓜ **(Par)** *mba·ee·*pee e·*e dessert of corn, milk & molasses*

mbaipy soó ⓜ **(Par)** *mba·ee·*pee so·*o hot maize pudding with meat chunks*

mbeyú ⓜ **(Par)** *mbe·*yoo *grilled manioc pancake*

medialunas ① pl *me·dya·loo·*nas *'half moons' – small croissants which are a popular breakfast food in Argentinian cafes*

mediana ① *me·dya·*na *bottle (third of a litre)*

medianoche ⓜ **(Pue)** *me·dya·no·*che *ham, pork & cheese sandwich*

medio y medio ⓜ **(Uru)** *me·*dyo ee *me·*dyo *mixture of sparkling wine & white wine*

mejilla ① *me·khee·*lya *cheek*

mejillones ⓜ pl *me·khee·lyo·*nes *mussels* — **al vapor** al va·*por steamed mussels*

melocotón ⓜ *me·lo·ko·*ton *peach*

melón ⓜ *me·*lon *melon*

membrillo ⓜ *mem·bree·*lyo *quince*

menta ① *men·*ta *mint*

menú ⓜ *me·*noo *menu*

menudencias ① pl **(SAm)** *me·noo·den·*syas *giblets*

menudo ⓜ **de pollo** *me·noo·*do de *po·*lyo *gizzard · poultry entrails*

mercado ⓜ *mer·ka·*do *market*

merengadas ① pl **(Ven)** *me·ren·ga·*das *milkshake containing juice*

merluza ① pl *mer·loo·*sa *hake – in Argentina, it's served batter-fried with mashed potatoes* — **a la plancha** ① a la *plan·*cha *grilled hake*

mermelada ① *mer·me·la·*da *jam*

miel ① myel *honey*

migas ① pl *mee·*gas *fried breadcrumb dish*

milhojas ① pl **(Pue)** meel o·*khas 'a thousand leaves' – layers of thin pastry filled with almond & honey paste*

milanesa ① *mee·la·ne·*sa *schnitzel*

milcao ⓜ **(Chi)** meel·*kow potato bread*

mojama ① *mo·kha·*ma *cured tuna*

mojo ⓜ **isleño (Pue)** *mo·*kho ees·*le·*nyo *piquant sauce of vinegar, tomato sauce, olive oil, onions, capers, pimentos, olives, bay leaves & garlic – often served with fried fish*

molleja ① *mo·lye·*kha *sweetbread*

mondongo ⓜ **(Ven)** mon·*don*·go *seasoned tripe cooked in bouillon with maize, potatoes & other vegetables*

montado ⓜ mon·*ta*·do *tiny sandwich served as an appetiser*

mora ⓕ *mo*·ra *blackberry*

morcilla ⓕ mor·*see*·lya *blood sausage – a common* **asado** *dish*

moros y cristianos ⓜ pl **(Cub)** *mo*·ros ee krees·*tya*·nos *'Moors & Christians' – dish of black beans & rice*

mostaza ⓕ mos·*ta*·sa *mustard*

mosto ⓜ **(Par)** *mos*·to *sugar-cane juice*

mote ⓜ **con huesillo (Chi)** *mo*·te kon we·*see*·lyo *peach nectar with barley kernels*

muchacho ⓜ **(Ven)** moo·*cha*·cho *'boy' – roast loin of beef served in sauce*

muslo ⓜ *moos*·lo *thigh*

muy hecho/a ⓜ&ⓕ mooy e·cho/a *well-done*

N

nabo ⓜ *na*·bo *turnip*

nacatamales ⓜ pl **(Nic)** na·ka·ta·*ma*·les *cornmeal, meat, vegetables & herbs wrapped in banana leaves*

naranja ⓕ na·*ran*·kha *orange*

naranjadas ⓕ pl na·ran·*kha*·das *lemonades made with orange juice*

nata ⓕ *na*·ta *cream*

natilla ⓕ **(Cos)** na·*tee*·lya *sour cream*

natillas ⓕ pl na·*tee*·lyas *custard* • *creamy milk dessert*

nuez ⓕ nwes *nut* • *walnut*

O

ocas ⓕ pl **(Bol)** *o*·kas *tough, purple, potato-like tubers*

ojo ⓜ **de bife** *o*·kho de *bee*·fe *eye of round steak*

olímpicos ⓜ pl **(Uru)** o·*leem*·pee·kos *club sandwiches*

oporto ⓜ o·*por*·to *port*

orejón ⓜ o·re·*khon* *dried apricot*

orgánico/a ⓜ or·*ga*·nee·ko/a *organic*

ostión ⓜ os·*tyon* *scallop*

ostiones ⓜ pl **(Cub)** os·tyo·nes *drink or appetiser containing mussels or oysters, rum, lime juice, salt & pepper*

ostras ⓕ pl *os*·tras *oysters*

oveja ⓕ o·*ve*·kha *ewe*

P

pabellón ⓜ **(Ven)** pa·be·*lyon* *main course consisting of shredded beef, rice, beans & fried plantain – Venezuela's national dish*

pacumutas ⓕ pl **(Bol)** pa·koo·*moo*·tas *enormous chunks of grilled meat accompanied by* **yuca**, *onions & other trimmings*

paila ⓕ **marina (Chi)** *pai*·la ma·*ree*·na *fish & shellfish chowder*

pajarito ⓜ pa·kha·*ree*·to *small bird*

paleta ⓕ pa·*le*·ta *shoulder*

palillo ⓜ pa·*lee*·lyo *toothpick*

palmitos ⓜ pl **(Cos)** pal·*mee*·tos *hearts of palm – usually served in a vinegar dressing*

paloma ⓕ pa·*lo*·ma *pigeon*

palta ⓕ **(SAm)** *pal*·ta *avocado*

— **a la jardinera (Per)** a la khar·dee·*ne*·ra *avocado stuffed with cold vegetables & mayonnaise*

— **a la reina (Per)** a la *ray*·na *avocado stuffed with chicken salad*

pan ⓜ pan *bread*

— **de coco (Hon)** de *ko*·ko *coconut bread*

panapen ⓜ **(Pue)** pa·*na*·pen *breadfruit*

panchos ⓜ pl **(Uru, Arg)** *pan*·chos *mild sausages on a hot dog roll*

panes ⓜ pl **(Sal)** *pa*·nes *French breads sliced open & stuffed with chicken or turkey*

papas ① pl *pa·*pas *potatoes*
— **fritas** *free·*tas *chips • French fries*
— **rellenas (Bol)** re·*lye·*nas *stuffed potatoes – a speciality from the central highlands*

papitas ① pl pa·*pee·*tas *crisps • potato chips*

parrilla ① pa·*ree·*lya *grill*

parrillada ① pa·*ree·*lya·da *mixed grill – huge slabs of grilled meat prepared over hot coals served with spicy sauces & vegetables • steak house – an institution in Argentina*

pasa ⓜ *pa·*sa *raisin*

pasankalla ⓜ **(Bol)** pa·san·*ka·*lya *puffed maize with caramel – very sticky & chewy concoction*

pasta ① *pas·*ta *pasta*

pastel ⓜ *pas·*tel *pastry • cake • in Puerto Rico, a sweeter version of an* **empanadilla** *with a stuffing of raisins, beans, fish or pork*
— **de choclo (Chi)** de *cho·*klo *maize casserole filled with vegetables, chicken & beef*

pastelillos ⓜ pl **(Pue)** pas·te·*lee·*lyos *smaller version of a* **pastel** *stuffed with meat & cheese*

patacones ⓜ pl **(Pan, Cos)** pa·ta·*ko·*nes *fried green plantains cut into thin pieces, salted & then pressed & fried*

patisería ① pa·tee·se·*ree·*a *cake shop*

patita ① **de cerdo** pa·*tee·*ta de *ser·*do *pig's trotter*

pato ⓜ *pa·*to *duck*

pavo ⓜ *pa·*vo *turkey*

pebre ⓜ **(Chi)** *pe·*bre *tasty condiment made from chopped tomatoes, onion, garlic, chilli peppers, coriander & parsley*

pechuga ① pe·*choo·*ga *breast meat*

pedido ⓜ pe·*dee·*do *order*

pejibaye ⓜ **(Cos)** pe·khee·*ba·*ye *starchy palm fruit also eaten as a salad*

pepinillo ⓜ pe·pee·*nee·*lyo *gherkin*

pepino ⓜ pe·*pee·*no *cucumber*

pera ① *pe·*ra *pear*

perca ① *per·*ka *perch*

perdiz ① per·*dees *partridge*

perejil ⓜ pe·re·*kheel *parsley*

perico ⓜ **(Col)** pe·*ree·*ko *small milk coffee*

pescadería ① pes·ka·de·*ree·*a *fish shop*

pescadilla ① pes·ka·*dee·*lya *whiting*

pescado ⓜ pes·*ka·*do *fish*
— **de agua dulce** de *a·*gwa *dool·*se *freshwater fish*
— **de mar** de mar *saltwater fish*

pescaíto ⓜ pes·ka·*ee·*to *tiny fried fish*

pez ⓜ **espada** pes es·*pa·*da *swordfish*

picada ① **(Arg)** pee·*ka·*da *snack*

picadillo ⓜ pee·ka·*dee·*lyo *minced meat • in Cuba, ground beef hash with capsicum, raisins, ham, spices, olives & rice*

picante pee·*kan·*te *spicy*

pierna ① *pyer·*na *leg*

pil pil ⓜ peel peel *often spicy garlic sauce*

pimentón ⓜ pee·men·*ton *paprika*

pimienta ① pee·*myen·*ta *pepper*

pimiento ⓜ pee·*myen·*to *capsicum • bell pepper*

piña ① *pee·*nya *pineapple*

pinchita ① **(Pue)** peen·*chee·*ta *homemade, illegal rum*

pincho ⓜ *peen·*cho *kebab*

piñón ⓜ pee·*nyon *pine nut*

pintado ⓜ **(Col)** peen·*ta·*do *small milk coffee*

piononos ⓜ pl **(Pue)** pyo·*no·*nos *deep-fried cones made from plantains stuffed with cheese (or meat) & coated with egg batter*

pipas ① pl *pee·*pas *green coconuts with a straw to drink the milk*

pique ⓜ **a lo macho (Bol)** *pee·*ke a lo *ma·*cho *chunked grilled beef & sausage served with french fries, lettuce, tomatoes, onions, capsicum &* **locotos**

pisco ⓜ **(Chi, Per)** *pees·ko grape brandy – often served as a* **pisco sauer** *with egg white, lemon juice & powdered sugar*

pistacho ⓜ *pees·ta·cho pistachio*

plancha ⓕ *plan·cha grill*

plátano ⓜ *pla·ta·no banana • plantain*

— **maduro (Pan)** *ma·doo·ro slices of ripe plantains baked or broiled with butter, brown sugar & cinnamon*

platija ⓕ *pla·tee·kha flounder*

plato ⓜ *pla·to plate • dish*

poché *po·che poached*

poco hecho/a ⓜ/ⓕ *po·ko e·cho/a rare*

pollo ⓜ *po·lyo chicken*

— **a la canasta (Bol)** *a la ka·nas·ta 'chicken in a basket' – chicken served with mustard, fries or* **yuca** *&* **ají**

polvo ⓜ *pol·vo powder*

pomelo ⓜ *po·me·lo grapefruit*

porotos ⓜ pl *po·ro·tos beans*

porrón ⓜ **de cerveza** *po·ron de ser·ve·sa bottled beer*

postre ⓜ *pos·tre dessert*

potaje ⓜ *po·ta·khe stew*

primer plato *pree·mer pla·to first course • entree*

puchero ⓜ **(Arg)** *poo·che·ro casserole with beef, chicken, bacon, sausage, blood sausage, maize, peppers, tomatoes, onions, cabbage, sweet potatoes & squash*

puerros ⓜ pl *pwe·ros leek*

pukacapa ⓕ **(Bol)** *poo·ka·ka·pa circular* **empanada** *filled with cheese, olives, onions & hot pepper sauce*

pulpo ⓜ *pool·po octopus*

— **a la gallega** *a la ga·lye·ga octopus in sauce*

punto ⓜ *a* **poon·to**, *a medium (steak)*

pupusas ⓕ pl **(Sal)** *poo·poo·sas cornmeal pastry stuffed with farmer's cheese, refried beans,* **chicharrón,** *or all three (called* **revuelta**)

Q

queque ⓜ *ke·ke cake*

— **seco** *se·ko pound cake*

quesillos ⓜ pl **(Nic)** *ke·see·lyos soft cheese & onions folded in a* **tortilla**

quesito ⓜ **(Pue)** *ke·see·to sweet baked shell stuffed with cheese & topped with honey*

queso ⓜ *ke·so cheese*

— **fruta bomba (Cub)** *froo·ta bom·ba appetiser of warm papaya & cheese*

quinoa ⓕ **(Bol)** *kee·no·a nutritious indigenous grain high in protein & used to thicken stews*

quinto ⓜ *keen·to very small bottle*

R

rábano ⓜ *ra·ba·no radish*

rabo ⓜ *ra·bo tail*

ración ⓕ *ra·syon small tapas plate or dish*

rancio/a ⓜ/ⓕ *ran·syo/a stale*

ranga ⓕ **(Bol)** *ran·ga potato soup with chopped liver*

rape ⓜ *ra·pe monkfish*

raspados ⓜ pl **(Pan)** *ras·pa·dos cones made of shaved ice topped with fruit syrup & sweetened condensed milk*

refresco ⓜ **(Bol)** *re·fres·ko fruit-based juice with a dried peach in it*

refrescos ⓜ pl *re·fres·kos soft drinks*

relleno ⓜ *re·lye·no stuffing • in Bolivia, a stuffed corn fritter similar to* **humitas**

relleno/a ⓜ/ⓕ *re·lye·no/a stuffed*

remolacha ⓕ *re·mo·la·cha beetroot*

repollo ⓜ *re·po·lyo cabbage*

revoltijo ⓜ *re·vol·tee·kho scrambled egg*

revuelta ⓕ **(Sal)** *re·vwel·ta cornmeal pastry stuffed with farmer's cheese, refried beans and fried pork fat*

riñón ⓜ *ree·nyon kidney*

rodaja ① ro·da·kha *slice*

romero ⓜ ro·me·ro *rosemary*

ron ⓜ ron *rum*

rondón ⓜ **(Cos)** ron·don *thick seafood-based soup blended with coconut milk*

ropa ① **vieja (Pan)** ro·pa vye·kha *'old clothes' – spicy shredded beef combination served over rice*

rosado ⓜ ro·sa·do *rosé*

rostro ⓜ **asado (Bol)** ros·tro a·sa·do *roasted sheep's head*

ruibarbo ⓜ roo·ee·bar·bo *rhubarb*

S

sal ① sal *salt*

salado/a ⓜ/① sa·la·do *salted · salty*

salchichas ① pl sal·chee·chas *sausages similar to hot dogs*

salmón ⓜ sal·mon *salmon*

salpicón ⓜ **(Cub)** sal·pee·kon *salad made from cold meat, potatoes, olives, capers, onion, lettuce, pineapple, capsicum & vinegar*

salsa ① sal·sa *sauce*
— **de carne** de kar·ne *gravy*

salteado/a ⓜ/① sal·te·a·do/a *sauteed*

salteñas ① pl **(Bol)** sal·te·nyas *delicious rugby-ball shaped meat & vegetable pasties that originated in Salta (Argentina)*

salvaje sal·va·khe *wild*

sancocho ⓜ san·ko·cho *In Panama, a spicy chicken & vegetable stew · in Puerto Rico, vegetable soup containing plantains, tomatoes, green pepper, chilli pepper, cilantro leaves, onion & corn kernels · in Venezuela, vegetable stew with meat, fish or chicken*

sandía ① san·dee·a *watermelon*

sangre ① san·gre *blood*

sangría ① san·gree·a *sangria (red wine punch)*

sardina ① sar·dee·na *sardine*

seco ⓜ **(Ecu)** se·ko *'dry' – meat stew served with rice*

seco/a ⓜ/① se·ko/a *dry · dried*

segundo ⓜ **plato** se·goon·do pla·to *main course*

sémola ① se·mo·la *semolina*

sepia ① se·pya *cuttlefish*

servilleta ① ser·vee·lye·ta *serviette · napkin*

sésamo ⓜ se·sa·mo *sesame*

sesos ⓜ pl se·sos *brains*

sidra ① see·dra *cider*

silpancho ⓜ **(Bol)** seel·pan·cho *a thin greasy schnitzel*

sin cubierto ⓜ seen koo·byer·to *no cover charge*

sin gas ⓜ seen gas *still*

sin grasa seen gra·sa *lean*

sobrasada ① so·bra·sa·da *soft pork sausage*

sofrito ⓜ **(Pue)** so·free·to *seasoning consisting of garlic, onions & pepper browned in olive oil then flavoured with annatto seeds*

soja ① so·kha *soya*

solomillo ⓜ so·lo·mee·lyo *sirloin*

sooyo sopy ⓜ **(Par)** soo·yo so·pee *thick soup of ground meat, accompanied by rice or noodles*

sopa ① so·pa *soup*
— **a la criolla (Per)** a la kryo·lya *lightly spiced noodle soup with beef, egg, milk & vegetables*
— **de caracol (Hon)** de ka·ra·kol *conch soup made with coconut*
— **de mariscos (Chi)** de ma·rees·kos *shellfish soup*
— **de mondongo (Hon)** de mon·don·go *tripe soup – reputed to be a good hangover remedy*
— **de pescado** de pes·ka·do *fish soup*
— **paraguaya (Par)** ① pa·ra·gwa·ya *corn bread with cheese & onion*

sopaipa ① **(Chi)** so·pai·pa *dark-brown unbaked wheat & flour bread*

sopaipillas ① **(Bol)** so·pai·*pee*·lyas
sweet fried breads

sopón ⓜ **de pescado (Pue)** so·*pon* de
pes·*ka*·do *fish soup flavoured with
garlic, onions & sherry*

submarino ⓜ **(Arg)** soob·ma·*ree*·no
*breakfast beverage consisting of a
semisweet chocolate bar dissolved in
steamed milk*

suflé ⓜ soo·*fle* *souffle*

T

tajadas ① pl **(Nic, Pan, Ven)**
ta·*kha*·das *sliced plantains served as a
base for grilled meat & cabbage salad*

tajaditas ① pl **(Hon)** ta·kha·*dee*·tas
crispy, fried banana chips

tallarines ⓜ pl ta·lya·*ree*·nes *noodles
mixed with pork, chicken, beef or
vegetables sold at* **chifas**

tamales ⓜ pl ta·*ma*·les *cornmeal
dough filled with spiced beef,
vegetables & potatoes & wrapped in a
maize husk & fried, grilled or baked ·
in Colombia, chopped pork with
rice & vegetables folded in a maize
dough, wrapped in banana leaves &
steamed*
— **asados (Cos)** a·*sa*·dos *sweet
cornmeal cakes*

tarta ① *tar*·ta *cake*

tasajo **(Pan)** ta·*sa*·kho *dried meat
cooked with vegetables*

tatú ⓜ ta·*too* *armadillo*

tawa-tawas ⓜ **(Bol)** ta·wa·*ta*·was *type
of donut*

té ⓜ te *tea*
— **con leche** kon *le*·che *tea with
milk*
— **con limón** kon lee·*mon* *tea with
lemon*
— **de menta** de *men*·ta *mint tea*
— **sin leche** seen *le*·che *black tea*

tembleque ⓜ **(Pue)** tem·*ble*·ke
*pudding-like concoction of coconut
milk & cinnamon*

tereré ⓜ **(Par)** te·re·*re* *ice-cold mate*

ternera ① ter·*ne*·ra *veal*

thimpu ⓜ **(Bol)** teem·poo *spicy lamb
& vegetable stew*

tibio/a ⓜ/① *tee*·bee·o/a *warm*

timochenko ⓜ **(Hon)**
tee·mo·*chen*·ko **aguardiente**
*mixed with aromatic plants of the
region*

tinto ⓜ *teen*·to *red (wine) · in Colombia, a small cup of black coffee*

tira ① **de asado** *tee*·ra de a·*sa*·do
a narrow strip of rib roast

tocino ⓜ to·*see*·no *bacon*
— **ahumado** a·oo·*ma*·do *smoked
bacon*
— **con queso** kon *ke*·so *cold bacon
with cheese*

tojorí ⓜ **(Bol)** to·kho·*ree* *oatmeal-like
concoction of mashed corn,
cinnamon & sugar*

tomatada ① **de cordero (Bol)**
to·ma·*ta*·da de kor·*de*·ro *lamb stew
with tomato sauce*

tomate ⓜ to·*ma*·te *tomato*

torta ① *tor*·ta *tart · cake · flan*

tortilla ① tor·*tee*·lya *omelette*
— **de maíz (Pan, Ecu)** de ma·*ees*
thick, fried cornmeal tortilla

tortillas ① pl **con quesillo (Hon)**
tor·*tee*·lyas kon ke·*see*·lyo *two crisp
fried tortillas with melted white
cheese between them*

tortuga ① tor·*too*·ga *turtle*

tostada ① tos·*ta*·da *toast*

tostones ⓜ pl **(Pue)** tos·*to*·nes *fried
green plantains*

trigo ⓜ *tree*·go *wheat*

tripa ① *tree*·pa *tripe*
— **gorda** *gor*·da *large intestine – a
common* **asado** *dish*

tripas ① pl *tree*·pas *offal*

trozo ⓜ *tro*·so *slice · piece*

trucha ① *troo*·cha *trout*

trufa ① *troo*·fa *truffle*

tubo ⓜ *too·bo* tall glass (quarter of a litre)

tucumana ⓕ **(Bol)** *too·koo·ma·na* tasty, heavily spiced puff-pastry shell packed with egg, potatoes, chicken & onions

tuétano ⓜ *twe·ta·no* bone marrow

turrón ⓜ *too·ron* almond nougat

U

ubre ⓕ *oo·bre* udder

uva ⓕ *oo·va* grape

V

vaca ⓕ *va·ka* beef

vacío ⓜ *va·see·o* flank steak – textured & chewy, but tasty

vainilla ⓕ *vay·nee·lya* vanilla

vapor ⓜ *va·por* steam

vapor, al *va·por, al* steamed

vaso ⓜ *va·so* glass

vegetal ⓜ *ve·khe·tal* vegetable

vegetariano/a ⓜ/ⓕ *ve·khe·ta·rya·no/a* vegetarian

venado ⓜ *ve·na·do* venison

venera ⓕ *ve·ne·ra* scallop

verduras ⓕ pl *ver·doo·ras* green vegetables

vigorón ⓜ **(Nic)** *vee·go·ron* cassava steamed & topped with fried pork rind & cabbage salad, usually served on a banana leaf

vinagre ⓜ *vee·na·gre* vinegar

vino ⓜ *vee·no* wine
— **de la casa** de la *ka·sa* house wine
— **espumoso** es·poo·mo·so sparkling wine
— **muy seco** mooy *se·ko* very dry wine
— **seco** *se·ko* dry wine

W

wafle ⓜ *wa·fle* waffle

witu ⓜ **(Bol)** *gwee·to* beef stew with pureed tomatoes

Y

yaguarlocro ⓜ **(Ecu)** *ya·gwar·lo·kro* potato soup with chunks of barely congealed blood sausage floating in it

yerba ⓕ **mate** dried chopped leaf of Ilex Paraguayensis which is made into a tea in Argentina, Uruguay & Paraguay

yogur ⓜ *yo·goor* yogurt

yuca ⓕ *yoo·ka* cassava – a common staple in Latin American cuisine

Z

zanahoria ⓕ *sa·na·o·rya* carrot

zapallo ⓜ **(SAm)** *sa·pa·lyo* pumpkin

zarzuela ⓕ **de marisco** *sar·swe·la de ma·rees·ko* seafood stew

emergencies

emergencias

Help!	¡Socorro!	so·*ko*·ro
Stop!	¡Pare!	*pa*·re
Go away!	¡Váyase!	*va*·ya·se
Thief!	¡Ladrón!	la·*dron*
Fire!	¡Fuego!	*fwe*·go
Watch out!	¡Cuidado!	kwee·*da*·do

Call the police!
¡Llame a la policía! *lya*·me a la po·lee·*see*·a

Call a doctor!
¡Llame a un médico! *lya*·me a oon *me*·dee·ko

Call an ambulance!
¡Llame a una ambulancia! *lya*·me a *oo*·na am·boo·*lan*·sya

It's an emergency.
Es una emergencia. es *oo*·na e·mer·*khen*·sya

Could you help me, please?
¿Me puede ayudar, por favor? me *pwe*·de a·yoo·*dar* por fa·*vor*

I have to use the telephone.
Necesito usar el teléfono. ne·se·*see*·to oo·*sar* el te·*le*·fo·no

I'm lost.
Estoy perdido/a. **m/f** es·toy per·*dee*·do/a

Where are the toilets?
¿Dónde están los baños? *don*·de es·*tan* los *ba*·nyos

signs

Comisaría de Policía	ko·me·sa·*ree*·a de po·lee·*see*·a	**Police Station**
Policía	po·lee·*see*·a	**Police**
Urgencias	oor·*khen*·syas	**Casualty**

Is it safe …?	¿Es seguro …?	es se·goo·ro …
at night	por la noche	por la no·che
for foreigners	para los extranjeros	pa·ra los ek·stran·khe·ros
for gay travellers	para viajeros gay	pa·ra vya·khe·ros gay
for women travellers	para viajeras	pa·ra vya·khe·ras

police

la policía

As police in Latin America can wield considerable power, it's best to adopt a respectful and deferential attitude when dealing with them.

Where's the police station?
  ¿Dónde está la comisaría?   don·de es·ta la ko·mee·sa·ree·a

I want to report an offence.
  Quiero denunciar un   kye·ro de·noon·syar oon
  delito.   de·lee·to

(My bag) was stolen.
  (Mi bolso) fue robado.   (mee bol·so) fwe ro·ba·do

I've lost (my wallet).
  He perdido (mi cartera).   e per·dee·do (mee kar·te·ra)

I've been robbed.
  Me han robado.   me an ro·ba·do

He's/She's been assaulted.
  Le/La han asaltado. m/f   le/la an a·sal·ta·do

I've been raped.
  He sido violado/a. m/f   e see·do vyo·la·do/a

He's/She's been raped.
  Ha sido violado/a. m/f   a see·do vyo·la·do/a

He/She tried to … me.   *Él/Ella intentó …*   el/*e*·lya een·ten·*to* …

assault	*asaltarme*	a·sal·*tar*·me
rape	*violarme*	vyo·*lar*·me
rob	*robarme*	ro·*bar*·me

I want to contact my embassy/consulate.
Quiero ponerme en contacto con mi embajada/ consulado.
kye·ro po·*ner*·me en kon·*tak*·to kon mee em·ba·*kha*·da/ kon·soo·*la*·do

Can I call someone?
¿Puedo llamar a alguien?
pwe·do lya·*mar* a al·*gyen*

Can I call a lawyer?
¿Puedo llamar a un abogado?
pwe·do lya·*mar* a oon a·bo·*ga*·do

I need a lawyer who speaks English.
Necesito un abogado que hable inglés.
ne·se·*see*·to oon a·bo·*ga*·do ke *a*·ble een·*gles*

Can I pay an on-the-spot fine?
¿Puedo pagar una multa al contado?
pwe·do pa·*gar* oo·na *mool*·ta al kon·*ta*·do

This drug is for personal use.
Esta droga es para uso personal.
es·ta *dro*·ga es *pa*·ra oo·so per·so·*nal*

I have a prescription for this drug.
Tengo receta para este medicamento.
ten·go re·*se*·ta *pa*·ra es·te me·dee·ka·*men*·to

What am I accused of?
¿De qué me acusan?
de ke me a·*koo*·san

I apologise.
Lo siento.
lo *syen*·to

I didn't realise I was doing anything wrong.

No sabía que estaba   no sa·*bee*·a ke es·*ta*·ba
haciendo algo mal.   a·*syen*·do *al*·go mal

I'm innocent.

Soy inocente.   soy ee·no·*sen*·te

I (don't) understand.

(No) Entiendo.   (no) en·*tyen*·do

the police may say ...

You'll be charged with ...	*Será acusado/a de ... m/f*	se·*ra* a·koo·*sa*·do/a de ...
He'll/She'll be charged with ...	*Él/Ella será acusado/a de ... m/f*	el/e·lya se·*ra* a·koo·*sa*·do/a de ...
anti-government activities	*actividades contra el gobierno*	ak·tee·vee·*da*·des *kon*·tra el go·*byer*·no
assault	*asalto*	a·*sal*·to
disturbing the peace	*alterar el orden público*	al·te·*rar* el *or*·den *poo*·blee·ko
murder	*homicidio*	o·mee·*see*·dyo
overstaying your visa	*quedarse más tiempo de lo que permite el visado*	ke·*dar*·se mas *tyem*·po de lo ke per·*mee*·te el vee·*sa*·do
possession (of illegal substances)	*posesión (de sustancias ilegales)*	po·se·*syon* (de soos·*tan*·syas ee·le·*ga*·les)
rape	*violación*	vyo·la·*syon*
shoplifting	*ratería*	ra·te·*ree*·a
speeding	*exceso de velocidad*	ek·*se*·so de ve·lo·see·*da*
theft	*robo*	*ro*·bo

doctor

el médico

Where's the nearest ...?	¿Dónde está ... más cercano/a? m/f	don·de es·ta ... mas ser·ka·no/a
(night) chemist	la farmacia f (de guardia)	la far·ma·sya (de gwar·dya)
(Col)	la droguería f (de guardia)	la dro·ge·ree·a (de gwar·dya)
dentist	el dentista m	el den·tees·ta
doctor	el médico m	el me·dee·ko
hospital	el hospital m	el os·pee·tal
medical centre	el consultorio m	el kon·sool·to·ryo
optometrist	el oculista m	el o·koo·lees·ta

I need a doctor (who speaks English).
Necesito un médico
(que hable inglés).
ne·se·see·to oon me·dee·ko
(ke a·ble een·gles)

Could I see a female doctor?
¿Puede examinarme
una médica?
pwe·de ek·sa·mee·nar·me
oo·na me·dee·ka

Can the doctor come here?
¿Puede visitarme el
médico?
pwe·de vee·see·tar·me el
me·dee·ko

Can I see someone who practises (acupuncture)?
¿Puedo ver a alguien
que practique
(la acupuntura)?
pwe·do ver a al·gyen
ke prak·tee·ke
(la a·koo·poon·too·ra)

I've been vaccinated against ...	*Estoy vacunado/a contra ...* m/f	es·*toy* va·koo·*na*·do/a *kon*·tra ...
He's/She's been vaccinated against ...	*Está vacunado/a contra ...* m/f	es·*ta* va·koo·*na*·do/a *kon*·tra ...
(yellow) fever	*la fiebre (amarilla)*	la *fye*·bre (a·ma·*ree*·lya)
hepatitis A/B/C	*la hepatitis A/B/C*	la e·pa·*tee*·tees a/be/se
tetanus	*el tétano*	el *te*·ta·no
typhoid	*la tifus*	la *tee*·foos

I need new glasses.
Necesito anteojos nuevos. — ne·se·*see*·to an·te·o·khos *nwe*·vos

I need new contact lenses.
Necesito lentes de contacto nuevas. — ne·se·*see*·to *len*·tes de kon·*tak*·to *nwe*·vas

I've run out of my medication.
Se me terminaron los medicamentos. — se me ter·mee·*na*·ron los me·dee·ka·*men*·tos

Can I have a receipt for my insurance?
¿Puede darme un recibo para mi seguro médico? — *pwe*·de *dar*·me oon re·*see*·bo *pa*·ra mee se·*goo*·ro *me*·dee·ko

Please use a new syringe.
Por favor, use una jeringa nueva. — por fa·*vor* oo·se *oo*·na khe·*reen*·ga *nwe*·va

I have my own syringe.
Tengo mi propia jeringa. — *ten*·go mee *pro*·pya khe·*reen*·ga

I don't want a blood transfusion.
No quiero que me hagan una transfusión de sangre. — no *kye*·ro ke me *a*·gan *oo*·na trans·foo·*syon* de *san*·gre

I don't use Western medicine.
No uso la medicina occidental. — no *oo*·so la me·dee·*see*·na ok·see·den·*tal*

the doctor may say ...

What's the problem?
¿Qué le pasa? — ke le *pa*·sa

Where does it hurt?
¿Dónde le/la duele? m/f — *don*·de le/la *dwe*·le

Do you have a temperature?
¿Tiene fiebre? — *tye*·ne *fye*·bre

How long have you been like this?
¿Desde cuándo se siente así? — *des*·de *kwan*·do se *syen*·te a·*see*

Have you had this before?
¿Ha tenido esto antes? — a te·*nee*·do *es*·to *an*·tes

Are you sexually active?
¿Es usted sexualmente activo/a? m/f — es oos·*te* sek·swal·*men*·te ak·*tee*·vo/a

Have you had unprotected sex?
¿Ha tenido relaciones sexuales sin protección? — a te·*nee*·do re·la·*syo*·nes sek·*swa*·les seen pro·tek·*syon*

Are you allergic to anything?
¿Tiene usted alergias? — *tye*·ne oos·*te* a·*ler*·khyas

Are you on medication?
¿Se encuentra bajo medicación? — se en·*kwen*·tra *ba*·kho me·dee·ka·*syon*

Do you ...?	¿Usted ...?	oos·*te* ...
drink	*bebe*	*be*·be
smoke	*fuma*	*foo*·ma
take drugs	*toma drogas*	*to*·ma *dro*·gas

How long are you travelling for?
¿Por cuánto tiempo está viajando? — por *kwan*·to *tyem*·po es·*ta* vya·*khan*·do

You need to be admitted to hospital.
Necesita ingresar al hospital. — ne·se·*see*·ta een·gre·*sar* al os·pee·*tal*

You should return home for treatment.
Debería regresar a casa para obtener tratamiento. — de·be·*ree*·a re·gre·*sar* a *ka*·sa *pa*·ra ob·te·*ner* tra·ta·*myen*·to

symptoms & conditions

I'm sick.
Estoy enfermo/a. m/f

es·*toy* en·*fer*·mo/a

My friend is sick.
Mi amigo está enfermo. m
Mi amiga está enferma. f

mee a·*mee*·go es·*ta* en·*fer*·mo
mee a·*mee*·ga es·*ta* en·*fer*·ma

It hurts here.
Me duele aquí.

me *dwe*·le a·*kee*

I've been injured.
He sido herido.

e *see*·do e·*ree*·do

I've been vomiting.
He estado vomitando.

e es·*ta*·do vo·mee·*tan*·do

I'm dehydrated.
Estoy deshidratado/a. m/f

es·*toy* des·ee·dra·*ta*·do/a

I can't sleep.
No puedo dormir.

no *pwe*·do dor·*meer*

I feel ...	*Tengo ...*	*ten*·go ...
hot and cold	*escalofríos*	es·ka·lo·*free*·os
breathless	*falta de aliento*	*fal*·ta de a·*lyen*·to

I feel ...	*Me siento ...*	me *syen*·to ...
anxious	*ansioso/a* m/f	an·*syo*·so/a
better	*mejor*	me·*khor*
depressed	*deprimido/a* m/f	de·pree·*mee*·do/a
dizzy	*mareado/a* m/f	ma·re·*a*·do/a
nauseous	*con nauseas*	kon *now*·se·as
shivery	*destemplado/a* m/f	des·tem·*pla*·do/a
strange	*raro/a* m/f	*ra*·ro/a
weak	*débil*	*de*·beel
worse	*peor*	pe·*or*

I have (a) ...	Tengo ...	*ten*·go ...
altitude sickness	*soroche*	so·*ro*·che
cough	*tos*	tos
fever	*fiebre*	*fye*·bre
headache	*dolor de cabeza*	do·*lor* de ka·*be*·sa
migraine	*migraña*	mee·*gra*·nya

I'm ...	Soy ...	soy ...
asthmatic	*asmático/a* m/f	as·*ma*·tee·ko/a
diabetic	*diabético/a* m/f	dya·*be*·tee·ko/a
epileptic	*epiléptico/a* m/f	e·pee·*lep*·tee·ko/a

I have a cold.
Estoy resfriado/a. m/f — es·*toy* res·*frya*·do/a
Tengo un resfrío. **(SAm)** — *ten*·go oon res·*free*·o

I have a heart condition.
Sufro del corazón. — *soo*·fro del ko·ra·*son*

I've (recently) had ...
(Hace poco) He tenido ... — (*a*·se *po*·ko) e te·*nee*·do ...

He's/She's (recently) had ...
(Hace poco) Ha tenido ... — (*a*·se *po*·ko) a te·*nee*·do ...

I'm on medication for ...
Estoy bajo medicación para ... — es·*toy ba*·kho me·dee·ka·*syon pa*·ra ...

He's/She's on medication for ...
Está bajo medicación para ... — es·*ta ba*·kho me·dee·ka·*syon pa*·ra ...

This is my usual medicine.
Éste es mi medicamento habitual. — *es*·te es mee me·dee·ka·*men*·to a·bee·*twal*

I think it's the medication I'm on.
Me parece que son los medicamentos que estoy tomando. — me pa·*re*·se ke son los me·dee·ka·*men*·tos ke es·*toy* to·*man*·do

For more symptoms and conditions, see the **dictionary**.

women's health

I think I'm pregnant.
Creo que estoy embarazada. kre·o ke es·*toy* em·ba·ra·*sa*·da

I'm pregnant.
Estoy embarazada. es·*toy* em·ba·ra·*sa*·da

I'm on the Pill.
Tomo la píldora. *to*·mo la *peel*·do·ra

I haven't had my period for (five) days/weeks.
Hace (cinco) días/semanas *a*·se (*seen*·ko) *dee*·as/se·*ma*·nas
que no me viene la regla. ke no me *vye*·ne la *re*·gla

I've noticed a lump here.
Me he fijado que tengo un me e fee·*kha*·do ke *ten*·go oon
bulto aquí. *bool*·to a·*kee*

the doctor may say ...

Are you sexually active?
¿Es usted sexualmente es oos·*te* sek·swal·*men*·te
activa? ak·*tee*·va

Are you using contraception?
¿Usa anticonceptivos? *oo*·sa an·tee·kon·sep·*tee*·vos

Are you menstruating?
¿Tiene la menstruación? *tye*·ne la mens·trwa·*syon*

Are you pregnant?
¿Está embarazada? es·*ta* em·ba·ra·*sa*·da

When did you last have your period?
¿Cuándo le vino la regla *kwan*·do le *vee*·no la *re*·gla
por última vez? por *ool*·tee·ma ves

You're pregnant.
Está embarazada. es·*ta* em·ba·ra·*sa*·da

I need ...	Quisiera ...	kee·sye·ra ...
contraception	usar algún	oo·sar al·goon
	método	me·to·do
	anticonceptivo	an·tee·kon·sep·tee·vo
the morning-after pill	tomar la píldora	to·mar la peel·do·ra
	del día siguiente	del dee·a see·gyen·te
a pregnancy test	una prueba de	oo·na prwe·ba de
	embarazo	em·ba·ra·so

For more terms which relate to women's health, see the **dictionary**.

allergies

alergias

I'm allergic to ...	Soy alérgico/a ... m/f	soy a·ler·khee·ko/a ...
He's/She's allergic to ...	Es alérgico/a ... m/f	es a·ler·khee·ko/a ...
antibiotics	a los antibióticos	a los an·tee·byo·tee·kos
anti-inflammatories	a los anti-inflamatorios	a los an·tee·een·fla·ma·to·ryos
aspirin	a la aspirina	a la as·pee·ree·na
bees	a las abejas	a las a·be·khas
codeine	a la codeina	a la ko·de·ee·na
penicillin	a la penicilina	a la pe·nee·see·lee·na
pollen	al polen	al po·len

I have hay fever.
Tengo alergia al polen.   ten·go a·ler·khya al po·len

I have a skin allergy.
Tengo una alergia en la piel.   ten·go oo·na a·ler·khya en la pyel

For food-related allergies, see **vegetarian & special meals**, page 158.

parts of the body

las partes del cuerpo

My (knee) hurts.
 Me duele (la rodilla).
 me *dwe*·le (la ro·*dee*·lya)

I can't move (my ankle).
 No puedo mover (el tobillo).
 no *pwe*·do mo·*ver* (el to·*bee*·lyo)

I have a cramp (in my foot).
 Tengo calambres (en el pie).
 ten·go ka·*lam*·bres (en el pye)

(My arm) is swollen.
 Se me hinchó (el brazo).
 se me een·*cho* (el *bra*·so)

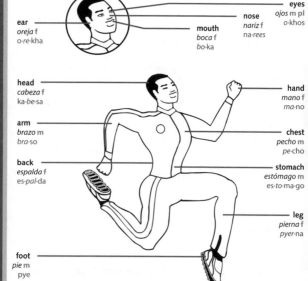

eyes
ojos m pl
o·khos

nose
nariz f
na·rees

ear
oreja f
o·re·kha

mouth
boca f
bo·ka

head
cabeza f
ka·be·sa

arm
brazo m
bra·so

back
espalda f
es·pal·da

foot
pie m
pye

hand
mano f
ma·no

chest
pecho m
pe·cho

stomach
estómago m
es·to·ma·go

leg
pierna f
pyer·na

chemist

la farmacia

I need something for (diarrhoea).
*Necesito algo para
(diarrea).*
ne·se·*see*·to al·go *pa*·ra
(dee·a·*re*·a)

Do I need a prescription for (antihistamines)?
*¿Necesito receta para
(antihistamínicos)?*
ne·se·*see*·to re·*se*·ta *pa*·ra
(an·tee·ees·ta·*mee*·nee·kos)

I have a prescription.
Tengo receta médica.
ten·go re·*se*·ta *me*·dee·ka

How many times a day?
¿Cuántas veces al día?
kwan·tas *ve*·ses al *dee*·a

Will it make me drowsy?
*¿Me producirá
somnolencia?*
me pro·doo·see·*ra*
som·no·*len*·sya

health

187

dentist

I have a broken tooth.
Se me ha roto un diente. — se me a *ro*·to oon *dyen*·te

I have a cavity.
Tengo una caries. — *ten*·go oo·na *ka*·ryes

I have a toothache.
Me duele una muela. — me *dwe*·le *oo*·na *mwe*·la

I've lost a filling.
Se me ha caído un empaste. — se me a ka·*ee*·do oon em·*pas*·te

I need a filling.
Necesito un empaste. — ne·se·*see*·to oon em·*pas*·te

My dentures are broken.
Se me han roto los dientes postizos. — se me an *ro*·to los *dyen*·tes pos·*tee*·sos

My gums hurt.
Me duelen las encías. — me *dwe*·len las en·*see*·as

I don't want it extracted.
No quiero que me lo arranque. — no *kye*·ro ke me lo a·*ran*·ke

I need an anaesthetic.
Necesito anestesia. — ne·se·*see*·to a·nes·*te*·sya

Ouch!
¡Ay! — ai

listen for ...

a·bra
Abra. — **Open wide.**

en·*khwa*·ge
Enjuague. — **Rinse.**

es·to le/la *pwe*·de do·*ler* oon *po*·ko
Esto le/la puede doler un poco. m/f — **This might hurt a little.**

es·to no le/la do·le·*ra*
Esto no le/la dolerá. m/f — **This won't hurt a bit.**

mwer·da *es*·to
Muerda esto. — **Bite down on this.**

SUSTAINABLE TRAVEL

As the climate change debate heats up, the matter of sustainability becomes an important part of the travel vernacular. In practical terms, this means assessing our impact on the environment and local cultures and economies – and acting to make that impact as positive as possible. Here are some basic phrases to get you on your way…

communication & cultural differences

I'd like to learn some of your local dialects.
Quisiera aprender algo   kee·sye·ra a·pren·der al·go
de su dialecto local.   de soo dya·lek·to lo·kal

Would you like me to teach you some English?
¿Le gustaría que le enseñe   le goo·sta·ree·a ke le en·se·nye
un poco de inglés?   oon po·ko de een·gles

Is this a local or national custom?
¿Es esta una costumbre   es es·ta oo·na kos·toom·bre
de la zona o es más bien   de la so·na o es mas byen
una costumbre nacional?   oo·na kos·toom·bre na·syo·nal

I respect your customs.
Respeto sus costumbres.   res·pe·to soos kos·toom·bres

community benefit & involvement

I'd like to volunteer my skills.
¿Podría contribuir   po·dree·a kon·tree·boo·eer
con mis conocimientos?   kon mees ko·no·see·myen·tos

Are there any volunteer programs available in the area?
¿Hay programas para   ai pro·gra·mas pa·ra
voluntarios en esta zona?   vo·loon·ta·ryos en es·ta so·na

What sorts of issues is this community facing?

¿Qué tipos de problemas ke *tee*·pos de pro·*ble*·mas
enfrenta esta comunidad? en·*fren*·ta es·ta ko·moo·nee·*dad*

armed conflict	*conflicto armado* m	kon·*fleek*·to ar·*ma*·do
armed drug traffickers	*narcotraficantes armados* m pl	nar·ko·tra·fee·*kan*·tes ar·*ma*·dos
armed guerrillas	*guerrilla armada* f	ge·*ree*·lya ar·*ma*·da
armed paramilitary groups	*grupos armados de paramilitares* m pl	*groo*·pos ar·*ma*·dos de pa·ra·mee·lee·*ta*·res
media control	*control mediático* m	kon·*trol* me·*dya*·tee·ko
poor living conditions	*condiciones míseras de vida* f pl	kon·dee·*syo*·nes *mee*·se·ras de *vee*·da
social and political unrest	*disturbios políticos y sociales* m pl	dees·*toor*·byos po·*lee*·tee·kos ee so·*sya*·les
violent youth gangs	*bandas de jóvenes violentos* m pl	*ban*·das de *kho*·ve·nes vyo·*len*·tos

environment

Where can I recycle this?

¿Dónde puedo reciclar esto? *don*·de *pwe*·do re·see·*klar* es·to

transport

Can we get there by public transport?

¿Podemos llegar allí po·*de*·mos lye·*gar* a·*lee*
en transporte público? en trans·*por*·te *poo*·blee·ko

Can we get there by bike?

¿Podemos llegar allí po·*de*·mos lye·*gar* a·*lee*
en bicicleta? en bee·see·*kle*·ta

I'd prefer to walk there.

Prefiero caminar pre·*fye*·ro ka·mee·*nar*
para ir allí. *pa*·ra eer a·*lee*

accommodation

I'd like to stay at a locally run hotel.
   Prefiero hospedarme en   pre·*fye*·ro os·pe·*dar*·me en
   un hotel de esta zona.   oon o·*tel* de *es*·ta *so*·na

Can I turn the air conditioning off and open the window?
   ¿Puedo apagar el aire   *pwe*·do a·pa·*gar* el *ai*·re
   acondicionado y abrir   a·kon·dee·syo·*na*·do ee a·*breer*
   la ventana?   la ven·*ta*·na

Are there any ecolodges here?
   ¿Hay algunas cabañas   ai al·*goo*·nas ka·*ba*·nyas
   ecológicas por aquí?   e·ko·*lo*·khee·kas por a·*kee*

There's no need to change my sheets.
   No hace falta cambiar   no *a*·se *fal*·ta kam·*byar*
   mis sábanas.   mees *sa*·ba·nas

shopping

Where can I buy locally produced goods/souvenirs?
   ¿Dónde puedo comprar   *don*·de *pwe*·do kom·*prar*
   productos/recuerdos   pro·*dook*·tos/re·*kwer*·dos
   de esta localidad?   de *es*·ta lo·ka·lee·*dad*

Is this made from animal skins?
   ¿Está hecho esto de   es·*ta e*·cho *es*·to de
   piel de animales?   pyel de a·nee·*ma*·les

Which forests are these products sourced from?
   ¿De qué bosque obtienen   de ke *bos*·ke ob·*tye*·nen
   estos productos?   *es*·tos pro·*dook*·tos

food

Do you sell ...?   *¿Vende ...?*   *ven*·de ...
   locally produced   *productos*   pro·*dook*·tos
     food   *locales*   lo·*ka*·les
   organic   *productos*   pro·*dook*·tos
     produce   *orgánicos*   or·*ga*·nee·kos

Can you tell me what traditional foods I should try?

¿Qué platos típicos me   ke *pla*·tos *tee*·pee·kos me
puede recomendar?   *pwe*·de re·ko·men·*dar*

sightseeing

Does your company …?	*¿Su empresa …?*	soo em·*pre*·sa …
donate money to charity	*hace donaciones a la caridad*	*a*·se do·na·*syo*·nes a la ka·ree·*dad*
hire local guides	*emplea guías de esta zona*	em·*ple*·a *gee*·as de *es*·ta *so*·na

Does the guide speak …?	*¿El guía habla …?*	el *gee*·a *a*·bla …
Aymara	*Aimara*	ai·*ma*·ra
Guaraní	*Guaraní*	gwa·ra·*nee*
Maya	*Maya*	*ma*·ya
Náhuatl	*Náhuatl*	*now*·atl
Quechua	*Quechua*	*ke*·chwa

Are cultural tours available?

¿Ofrecen tours culturales?   o·*fre*·sen toors kool·too·*ra*·les

Nouns in the dictionary have their gender indicated by ⓜ or ⓕ. If it's a plural noun, you'll also see pl. When a word that could be either a noun or a verb has no gender indicated, it's a verb.

A

(be) able *poder* po·*der*
aboard *a bordo* a bor·do
abortion *aborto* ⓜ a·*bor*·to
about *sobre* so·bre
above *arriba* a·*ree*·ba
abroad *en el extranjero* en el ek·stran·*khe*·ro
accept *aceptar* a·sep·*tar*
accident *accidente* ⓜ ak·see·*den*·te
accommodation *alojamiento* ⓜ a·lo·kha·*myen*·to
across *a través* a tra·*ves*
activist *activista* ⓜ&ⓕ ak·tee·*vees*·ta
acupuncture *acupuntura* ⓕ a·koo·poon·*too*·ra
adaptor *adaptador* ⓜ a·dap·ta·*dor*
addicted *adicto/a* ⓜ/ⓕ a·*deek*·to/a
address *dirección* ⓕ dee·rek·*syon*
administration *administración* ⓕ ad·mee·nees·tra·*syon*
admission price *precio de entrada* ⓜ *pre*·syo de en·*tra*·da
admit (accept) *admitir* ad·mee·*teer*
admit (acknowledge) *reconocer* re·ko·no·*ser*
admit (allow to enter) *dejar entrar* de·*khar* en·*trar*
adult *adulto/a* ⓜ/ⓕ a·*dool*·to/a
advertisement *anuncio* ⓜ a·*noon*·syo
advice *consejo* ⓜ kon·*se*·kho
advise *aconsejar* a·kon·se·*khar*
aerobics *aeróbic* ⓜ a·e·ro·beek
Africa *África* ⓕ *a*·free·ka
after *después de* des·*pwes* de

aftershave *loción para después del afeitado* ⓕ lo·*syon* pa·ra des·*pwes* del a·fay·ta·do
again *otra vez* o·tra ves
age *edad* ⓕ e·da
aggressive *agresivo/a* ⓜ/ⓕ a·gre·*see*·vo/a
agree *estar de acuerdo* es·*tar* de a·*kwer*·do
agriculture *agricultura* ⓕ a·gree·kool·*too*·ra
AIDS *SIDA* ⓜ *see*·da
air *aire* ⓜ *ai*·re
airmail *correo aéreo* ⓜ ko·*re*·o a·*e*·re·o
(by) airmail *por vía aérea* por *vee*·a a·*e*·re·a
air-conditioned *con aire acondicionado* kon *ai*·re a·kon·dee·syo·*na*·do
airline *aerolínea* ⓕ a·e·ro·*lee*·ne·a
airport *aeropuerto* ⓜ a·e·ro·*pwer*·to
airport tax *tasa del aeropuerto* ⓕ *ta*·sa del a·e·ro·*pwer*·to
aisle (plane, train) *pasillo* ⓜ pa·*see*·lyo
alarm clock *despertador* ⓜ des·per·ta·*dor*
alcohol *alcohol* ⓜ al·*kol*
all (singular) *todo/a* ⓜ/ⓕ sg *to*·do/a
all (plural) *todos/as* ⓜ/ⓕ pl *to*·dos/as
allergy *alergia* ⓕ a·*ler*·khya
allow *permitir* per·mee·*teer*
almond *almendra* ⓕ al·*men*·dra
almost *casi* ka·see
alone *solo/a* ⓜ/ⓕ *so*·lo/a
already *ya* ya
also *también* tam·*byen*

altar *altar* m al·tar
altitude *altura* ① al·too·ra
altitude sickness *soroche* m so·ro·che
always *siempre* syem·pre
amateur *amateur* m&① a·ma·toor
ambassador *embajador/*
embajadora m/① em·ba·kha·dor/
em·ba·kha·do·ra
ambulance *ambulancia* ①
am·boo·lan·sya
America *América* ① a·me·ree·ka
among *entre* en·tre
amount *cantidad* kan·tee·da
anarchist *anarquista* m&① a·nar·kees·ta
ancient *antiguo/a* m/① an·tee·gwo/a
and *y* ee
angry *enojado/a* m/① e·no·kha·do/a
animal *animal* m a·nee·mal
animal rights *derechos* m pl *de*
animales de·re·chos de a·nee·ma·les
ankle *tobillo* m to·bee·lyo
annoyed *fastidiado/a* m/①
fas·tee·dya·do/a
answer *respuesta* ① res·pwes·ta
answering machine *contestador* m
automático kon·tes·ta·dor
ow·to·ma·tee·ko
ant *hormiga* ① or·mee·ga
antibiotics *antibióticos* m pl
an·tee·byo·tee·kos
antihistamines *antihistaminicos* m pl
an·tee·ees·ta·mee·nee·kos
antimalarial tablets *pastillas* ① pl
antipalúdicas pas·tee·lyas
an·tee·pa·loo·dee·kas
antinuclear *antinuclear*
an·tee·noo·kle·ar
antique *antigüedad* ① an·tee·gwe·da
antiseptic *antiséptico* m
an·tee·sep·tee·ko
any (singular) *alguno/a* m/① sg
al·goo·no/a
any (plural) *algunos/as* m/① pl
al·goo·nos/as
appendix *apéndice* ① a·pen·dee·se
apple *manzana* ① man·sa·na
appointment *cita* ① see·ta

apricot m *damasco* da·mas·ko
archaeological *arqueológico/a* m/①
ar·ke·o·lo·khee·ko/a
architect *arquitecto/a* m/①
ar·kee·tek·to/a
architecture *arquitectura* ①
ar·kee·tek·too·ra
Argentina *Argentina* ① ar·khen·tee·na
argue *discutir* dees·koo·teer
arm *brazo* m bra·so
armadillo *armadillo* m ar·ma·dee·lyo
army *ejercito* m e·kher·see·to
arrest *detener* de·te·ner
arrivals *llegadas* ① pl lye·ga·das
arrive *llegar* lye·gar
art *arte* m ar·te
art gallery *museo* m *de arte* moo·se·o
de ar·te
artist *artista* m&① ar·tees·ta
ashtray *cenicero* ① se·nee·se·ro
Asia ① *Asia* a·sya
ask (a question) *preguntar* pre·goon·tar
ask (for something) *pedir* pe·deer
aspirin *aspirina* ① as·pee·ree·na
ass (bum) *culo* m koo·lo
asthma *asma* ① as·ma
athletics *atletismo* m at·le·tees·mo
atmosphere *atmósfera* ① at·mos·fe·ra
aubergine *berenjena* ① be·ren·khe·na
aunt *tía* ① tee·a
Australia *Australia* ① ows·tra·lya
automatic *automático/a* m/①
ow·to·ma·tee·ko/a
automatic teller machine *cajero* m
automático ka·khe·ro ow·to·ma·tee·ko
autumn *otoño* m o·to·nyo
avenue *avenida* ① a·ve·nee·da
avocado *palta* ① pal·ta

B

B&W (film) *blanco y negro* blan·ko
ee ne·gro
baby *bebé* m&① be·be
baby food *comida* ① *de bebé*
ko·mee·da de be·be
baby powder *talco* m tal·ko

babysitter *babysitter* ⓜ & ⓕ be·bee·*see*·ter

back (body) *espalda* ⓕ es·*pal*·da

backpack *mochila* ⓕ mo·*chee*·la

bacon *tocino* ⓜ to·*see*·no

bad *malo/a* ⓜ/ⓕ *ma*·lo/a

bag (general) *bolso* ⓜ *bol*·so

bag (shopping) *bolsa* ⓕ *(de compras)* *bol*·sa (de *kom*·pras)

baggage *equipaje* ⓜ e·kee·*pa*·khe

baggage allowance *límite* ⓜ *de equipaje* *lee*·mee·te de e·kee·*pa*·khe

baggage claim *recogida* ⓕ *de equipajes* re·ko·*khee*·da de e·kee·*pa*·khes

bakery *panadería* ⓕ pa·na·de·*ree*·a

balance (account) *saldo* ⓜ *sal*·do

balcony *balcón* ⓜ bal·*kon*

ball *pelota* ⓕ pe·*lo*·ta

ballet *ballet* ⓜ ba·*le*

ballpoint pen *bolígrafo* ⓜ bo·*lee*·gra·fo

banana (CAm) *plátano* ⓜ *pla*·ta·no

banana (SAm) *banana* ⓕ ba·*na*·na

banana (Ven) *cambur* ⓜ kam·*boor*

band (music) *grupo* ⓜ *groo*·po

bandage *vendaje* ⓜ ven·*da*·khe

Band-Aids *curitas* ⓕ pl koo·*ree*·tas

bank (money) *banco* ⓜ *ban*·ko

bank account *cuenta* ⓕ *bancaria* *kwen*·ta ban·*ka*·rya

banknotes *billetes* ⓜ pl *de banco* bee·*lye*·tes de *ban*·ko

baptism *bautizo* ⓜ bow·*tee*·so

bar *bar* ⓜ bar

barber *barbero* ⓜ bar·*be*·ro

baseball *béisbol* ⓜ *bays*·bol

basket *canasta* ⓕ ka·*nas*·ta

basketball *basquetbol* ⓜ *bas*·ket·bol

bath *baño* ⓜ *ba*·nyo

bath tub *bañera* ⓕ ba·*nye*·ra

bathing suit *traje* ⓜ *de baño* • *malla* ⓕ *de baño* *tra*·khe de *ba*·nyo • *ma*·lya de *ba*·nyo

bathroom *baño* ⓜ *ba*·nyo

battery (car) *batería* ⓕ ba·te·*ree*·a

battery (general) *pila* ⓕ *pee*·la

be *ser* • *estar* ser • es·*tar*

beach *playa* ⓕ *pla*·ya

beans *frijoles* ⓜ pl free·*kho*·les

beautician *esteticista* ⓜ & ⓕ es·te·tee·*sees*·ta

beautiful *bello/a* ⓜ/ⓕ be·*lyo*/a

beauty salon *salón* ⓜ *de belleza* sa·*lon* de be·*lye*·sa

because *porque* por·*ke*

bed *cama* ⓕ *ka*·ma

bedding *ropa* ⓕ *de cama* *ro*·pa de *ka*·ma

bedroom *habitación* ⓕ a·bee·ta·*syon*

bee *abeja* ⓕ a·*be*·kha

beef *carne* ⓕ *de vaca* *kar*·ne de *va*·ka

beer *cerveza* ⓕ ser·*ve*·sa

beetroot *remolacha* ⓕ re·mo·*la*·cha

before *antes* an·tes

beggar *mendigo/a* ⓜ/ⓕ men·*dee*·go/a

begin *comenzar* ko·men·*sar*

behind *detrás de* de·*tras* de

bell pepper *pimiento* ⓜ pee·*myen*·to

below *abajo* a·*ba*·kho

Belize *Belice* ⓕ be·*lee*·se

best *mejor* me·*khor*

bet *apuesta* ⓕ a·*pwes*·ta

better *mejor* me·*khor*

between *entre* en·tre

bible *biblia* ⓕ *bee*·blya

bicycle *bicicleta* ⓕ bee·see·*kle*·ta

big *grande* gran·de

bike *bici* ⓕ *bee*·see

bike chain *cadena* ⓕ *de bici* ka·*de*·na de *bee*·see

bike path *camino* ⓜ *de bici* ka·*mee*·no de *bee*·see

bill (account) *cuenta* ⓕ *kwen*·ta

biodegradable *biodegradable* byo·de·gra·*da*·ble

biography *biografía* ⓕ byo·gra·*fee*·a

bird *pájaro* ⓜ *pa*·kha·ro

birth certificate *partida* ⓕ *de nacimiento* par·*tee*·da de na·see·*myen*·to

birthday *cumpleaños* ⓜ koom·ple·*a*·nyos

biscuit *galleta* ⓕ ga·*lye*·ta

bite (dog) *mordedura* ⓕ mor·de·*doo*·ra

bite (insect) *picadura* ① pee·ka·*doo*·ra

black *negro/a* ⓜ/① *ne*·gro/a

blanket *frazada* ① fra·*sa*·da

blind *ciego/a* ⓜ/① *sye*·go/a

blister *ampolla* ① am·*po*·lya

blocked *atascado/a* ⓜ/① a·tas·*ka*·do/a

blood *sangre* ① *san*·gre

blood group *grupo* ⓜ *sanguíneo* *groo*·po san·*gee*·ne·o

blood pressure *presión* ① *arterial* pre·*syon* ar·te·*ryal*

blood test *análisis* ⓜ *de sangre* a·*na*·lee·sees de *san*·gre

blue *azul* a·*sool*

board (plane, ship) *embarcarse* em·bar·*kar*·se

boarding house *pensión* ① pen·*syon*

boarding pass *tarjeta* ① *de embarque* tar·*khe*·ta de em·*bar*·ke

boat *barco* ⓜ *bar*·ko

body *cuerpo* ⓜ *kwer*·po

Bolivia *Bolivia* ① bo·*lee*·vya

bomb *bomba* ① *bom*·ba

bone *hueso* ⓜ *we*·so

book *libro* ⓜ *lee*·bro

book (reserve) *reservar* re·ser·*var*

booked out *lleno/a* ⓜ/① *lye*·no/a

bookshop *librería* ① lee·bre·*ree*·a

boots *botas* ① pl *bo*·tas

border (frontier) *frontera* ① fron·*te*·ra

borders (photography) *marcos* ⓜ pl *mar*·kos

(be) bored (estar) *aburrido/a* ⓜ/① (es·*tar*) a·boo·*ree*·do/a

boring *aburrido/a* ⓜ/① a·boo·*ree*·do/a

borrow *pedir* pe·*deer*

botanic garden *jardín* ⓜ *botánico* khar·*deen* bo·ta·nee·ko

both *ambos* ⓜ/① pl *am*·bos

bottle *botella* ① bo·*te*·lya

bottle opener *abrebotellas* ⓜ a·bre·bo·*te*·lyas

(at the) bottom (al) fondo (de) (al) *fon*·do (de)

bowl *bol* ⓜ bol

box *caja* ① *ka*·kha

boxing *boxeo* ⓜ bok·*se*·o

boy *chico* ⓜ *chee*·ko

boyfriend *novio* ⓜ *no*·vyo

bra *corpiño* ⓜ kor·*pee*·nyo

Braille *Braille* ⓜ bray·*e*·le

brake *freno* ⓜ pl *fre*·no

brandy *coñac* ko·*nyak*

brave *valiente* va·*lyen*·te

Brazil *Brasil* ⓜ bra·*seel*

bread *pan* ⓜ pan

  rye bread *pan* ⓜ *de centeno* pan de sen·*te*·no

  sourdough bread *pan* ⓜ *de masa fermentada* pan de *ma*·sa fer·men·*ta*·da

  white bread *pan* ⓜ *blanco* pan *blan*·ko

  wholemeal bread *pan* ⓜ *integral* pan een·te·*gral*

bread rolls *bollos* ⓜ pl *bo*·lyos

break *romper* rom·*per*

break down *descomponerse* des·kom·po·*ner*·se

breakfast *desayuno* ⓜ de·sa·*yoo*·no

breast (poultry) *pechuga* ① pe·*choo*·ga

breasts *senos* ⓜ *se*·nos

breathe *respirar* res·pee·*rar*

bribe (CAm) *mordida* ① mor·*dee*·da

bribe (SAm) *coima* ① *koy*·ma

bribe *coimear* koy·me·*ar*

bridge *puente* ⓜ *pwen*·te

briefcase *maletín* ⓜ ma·le·*teen*

brilliant *briliante* bree·*lyan*·te

bring *traer* tra·*er*

broken *roto/a* ⓜ/① *ro*·to/a

broken down (machine) *averiado/a* ⓜ/① a·ve·*rya*·do/a

bronchitis *bronquitis* ① bron·*kee*·tees

brother *hermano* ⓜ er·*ma*·no

brown *marrón* ma·*ron*

bruise *moretón* ⓜ mo·re·*ton*

Brussels sprouts *coles* ⓜ pl *de Bruselas* ko·les de broo·*se*·las

bucket *balde* ⓜ *bal*·de

budget *presupuesto* ⓜ pre·soo·*pwes*·to

Buddhist *budista* ⓜ&① boo·*dees*·ta

buffet (meal) *buffet* ⓜ *boo*·fet

bug *bicho* ⓜ *bee*·cho

build *construir* kons·troo·*eer*
building *edificio* ⓜ e·dee·*fee*·syo
bulb *bombillo* ⓜ bom·*bee*·lyo
bulb (Ecu, Per) *foco* ⓜ *fo*·ko
bull *toro* ⓜ *to*·ro
bullfight *corrida* ⓕ ko·*ree*·da
bullring *plaza* ⓕ *de toros* *pla*·sa de *to*·ros
bum (ass) *culo* ⓜ *koo*·lo
burn *quemadura* ⓕ ke·ma·*doo*·ra
burn *quemar* ke·*mar*
bus (city) *autobús* ⓜ ow·to·*boos*
bus (intercity) *ómnibus* ⓜ *om*·nee·boos
bus station (city) *estación* ⓕ *de autobuses* es·ta·*syon* de ow·to·*boo*·ses
bus station (intercity) *estación* ⓕ *de ómnibuses* es·ta·*syon* de *om*·nee·boo·ses
bus stop (city) *parada* ⓕ *de autobús* pa·*ra*·da de ow·to·*boos*
bus stop (intercity) *parada* ⓕ *de ómnibus* pa·*ra*·da de *om*·nee·boos
business *negocio* ⓜ ne·*go*·syo
business class *clase* ⓕ *preferente* *kla*·se pre·fe·*ren*·te
business person *comerciante* ⓜ&ⓕ ko·mer·*syan*·te
busker *artista callejero/a* ⓜ/ⓕ ar·*tees*·ta ka·lye·*khe*·ro/a
busy *ocupado/a* ⓜ/ⓕ o·koo·*pa*·do/a
but *pero* *pe*·ro
butcher's shop *carnicería* ⓕ kar·nee·se·*ree*·a
butter *mantequilla* ⓕ man·te·*kee*·lya
butterfly *mariposa* ⓕ ma·ree·*po*·sa
button *botón* ⓜ bo·*ton*
buy *comprar* kom·*prar*
buzzard *gallinazo* ⓜ ga·lyee·*na*·so

C

cabbage *repollo* ⓜ re·*po*·lyo
cable *cable* ⓜ *ka*·ble
cable car *teleférico* ⓜ te·le·*fe*·ree·ko
cactus *cactus* ⓜ *kak*·toos
cafe *cafetería* ⓕ ka·fe·te·*ree*·a
cake *torta* ⓕ *tor*·ta
cake shop *pastelería* ⓕ pas·te·le·*ree*·a

calculator *calculadora* ⓕ kal·koo·la·*do*·ra
calendar *calendario* ⓜ ka·len·*da*·ryo
call *llamar* lya·*mar*
camera *cámara* ⓕ *(fotográfica)* *ka*·ma·ra (fo·to·*gra*·fee·ka)
camera shop *tienda* ⓕ *de fotografía* *tyen*·da de fo·to·gra·*fee*·a
camp *acampar* a·*kam*·par
campsite *cámping* ⓜ *kam*·peen
camping store *tienda* ⓕ *de provisiones de cámping* *tyen*·da de pro·vee·*syo*·nes de *kam*·peen
can (tin) *lata* ⓕ *la*·ta
can (be able) *poder* po·*der*
can opener *abrelatas* a·bre·*la*·tas
Canada *Canadá* ⓜ ka·na·*da*
cancel *cancelar* kan·se·*lar*
cancer *cáncer* ⓜ *kan*·ser
candle *vela* ⓕ *ve*·la
candy *dulces* ⓜ pl *dool*·ses
cantaloupe *cantalupo* ⓜ kan·ta·*loo*·po
capsicum *pimiento* ⓜ pee·*myen*·to
car *carro* ⓜ *ka*·ro
car hire *alquiler* ⓜ *de carro* al·kee·*ler* de *ka*·ro
car owner's title *papeles* ⓜ pl *del auto* pa·*pe*·les del *ow*·to
car park *parking* ⓜ *par*·keen
car registration *matrícula* ⓕ ma·*tree*·koo·la
caravan *caravana* ⓕ ka·ra·*va*·na
cards *cartas* ⓕ pl *kar*·tas
care (about something) *preocuparse por* pre·o·koo·*par*·se por
care (for someone) *cuidar de* kwee·*dar* de
caring *bondadoso/a* ⓜ/ⓕ bon·da·*do*·so/a
carriage (train) *vagón* ⓜ va·*gon*
carpenter *carpintero* ⓜ kar·peen·*te*·ro
carrot *zanahoria* ⓕ sa·na·o·rya
carry *llevar* lye·*var*
carton *cartón* ⓜ kar·*ton*
cash *dinero* ⓜ *en efectivo* dee·*ne*·ro en e·fek·*tee*·vo
cash (a cheque) *cobrar (un cheque)* ko·*brar* (oon *che*·ke)

cash register *caja* ① *registradora* ka·kha re·khees·tra·do·ra

cashew *castaña* ① *de cajú* kas·ta·nya de ka·khoo

cashier *cajero/a* ⓜ/① ka·khe·ro/a

casino *casino* ⓜ ka·see·no

cassette *casete* ⓜ ka·set

castle *castillo* ⓜ kas·tee·lyo

casual work *trabajo* ⓜ *eventual* tra·ba·kho e·ven·twal

cat *gato/a* ⓜ/① ga·to/a

cathedral *catedral* ① ka·te·dral

Catholic *católico/a* ⓜ/① ka·to·lee·ko/a

cauliflower *coliflor* ko·lee·flor

cave *cueva* ① kwe·va

cavity (tooth) *caries* ① ka·ryes

CD *cómpact* ⓜ kom·pak

celebration *celebración* ① se·le·bra·syon

cell phone *teléfono* ⓜ *móvil* te·le·fo·no mo·veel

cemetery *cementerio* ⓜ se·men·te·ryo

cent *centavo* ⓜ sen·ta·vo

centimetre *centímetro* ⓜ sen·tee·me·tro

Central America *Centroamérica* ① sen·tro·a·me·ree·ka

Central American *centroaméricano/a* ⓜ/① sen·tro·a·me·ree·ka·no/a

central heating *calefacción* ① *central* ka·le·fak·syon sen·tral

centre *centro* ⓜ sen·tro

ceramic *cerámica* ① se·ra·mee·ka

cereal *cereales* se·re·a·les

certificate *certificado* ⓜ ser·tee·fee·ka·do

chain *cadena* ① ka·de·na

chair *silla* ① see·lya

chance *oportunidad* ① o·por·too·nee·da

change (money) *cambio* ⓜ kam·byo

change *cambiar* kam·byar

changing room *vestuario* ⓜ ves·twa·ryo

charming *encantador/encantadora* ⓜ/① en·kan·ta·dor/en·kan·ta·do·ra

chat up *tratar de ligar* tra·tar de lee·gar

cheap *barato/a* ⓜ/① ba·ra·to/a

cheat *tramposo/a* ⓜ/① tram·po·so/a

check (bill) *cuenta* ① kwen·ta

check *revisar* re·vee·sar

check-in (airport) *facturación* ① fak·too·ra·syon

check-in (baggage) *facturación* ① *de equipaje* fak·too·ra·syon de e·kee·pa·khe

check-in (hotel) *registrar* re·khees·trar

checkpoint *control* ⓜ kon·trol

cheese *queso* ⓜ ke·so

chef *cocinero/a* ⓜ/① ko·see·ne·ro/a

chemist (shop) *farmacia* ① far·ma·sya

chemist (person) *farmacéutico/a* ⓜ/① far·ma·see·oo·tee·ko/a

cheque *cheque* ⓜ che·ke

chess *ajedrez* ⓜ a·khe·dres

chest *pecho* ⓜ pe·cho

chewing gum *chicle* ⓜ chee·kle

chicken *pollo* po·lyo

chickpeas *garbanzos* ⓜ pl gar·ban·sos

child *niño/a* ⓜ/① nee·nyo/a

child's car seat *asiento* ⓜ *de seguridad para bebés* a·syen·to de se·goo·ree·da pa·ra be·bes

childminding service *guardería* ① gwar·de·ree·a

Chile *Chile* ① chee·le

chilli *ají* ⓜ a·khee

chilli sauce *salsa* ① *de ají* sal·sa de a·khee

chocolate *chocolate* ⓜ cho·ko·la·te

cholera *cólera* ① ko·le·ra

choose *escoger* es·ko·kher

chopping board *tabla* ① *de cortar* ta·bla de kor·tar

Christian *cristiano/a* ⓜ/① krees·tya·no/a

Christmas *Navidad* ① na·vee·da

Christmas Eve *Nochebuena* ① no·che·bwe·na

church *iglesia* ① ee·gle·sya

cider *sidra* ① see·dra

cigar *cigarro* ⓜ see·ga·ro

cigarette *cigarillo* ⓜ see·ga·ree·lyo

cigarette lighter *mechero* ⓜ me·che·ro

cigarette paper *papel* ⓜ *de fumar* pa·pel de foo·mar

cinema *cine* ⓜ see·ne

circus *circo* ⓜ seer·ko

citizenship *ciudadanía* ① syoo·da·da·*nee*·a

city *ciudad* ① syoo·*da*

city centre *centro* ⓜ *de la ciudad* *sen*·tro de la syoo·*da*

civil rights *derechos* ⓜ pl *civiles* de·*re*·chos see·*vee*·les

classical *clásico/a* ⓜ/① *kla*·see·ko/a

clean *limpio/a* ⓜ/① *leem*·pyo/a

cleaning *limpieza* ① leem·*pye*·sa

client *cliente/a* ⓜ/① *klyen*·te/a

cliff *acantilado* ⓜ a·kan·tee·*la*·do

climb *subir* soo·*beer*

cloak *capote* ⓜ ka·*po*·te

cloakroom *guardarropa* ⓜ gwar·da·*ro*·pa

clock *reloj* ⓜ re·*lokh*

close (nearby) *cerca ser*·ka

close (shut) *cerrar* se·*rar*

closed *cerrado/a* ⓜ/① se·*ra*·do/a

clothes line *cuerda* ① *para tender la ropa kwer*·da *pa*·ra ten·*der* la *ro*·pa

clothing *ropa* ① *ro*·pa

clothing store *tienda* ① *de ropa tyen*·da de *ro*·pa

cloud *nube* ① *noo*·be

cloudy *nublado/a* ⓜ/① noo·*bla*·do/a

clutch *embrague* ⓜ em·*bra*·ge

coach (sport) *entrenador/entrenadora* ⓜ/① en·tre·na·*dor*/en·tre·na·*do*·ra

coast *costa* ① *kos*·ta

coat *saco* ⓜ *sa*·ko

coke (drug) *coca* ① *ko*·ka

cocaine *cocaína* ① ko·ka·*ee*·na

coca plant *coca* ① *ko*·ka

cockroach *cucaracha* ① koo·ka·*ra*·cha

cocoa *cacao* ⓜ ka·*kow*

coconut *coco* ⓜ *ko*·ko

coconut palm *palma* ① *de coco pal*·ma de ko·ko

codeine *codeína* ① ko·de·*ee*·na

coffee *café* ⓜ ka·*fe*

coins *monedas* ① pl mo·*ne*·das

coke (drug) *coca* ① *ko*·ka

cold *frío/a* ⓜ/① *free*·o/a

(have a) cold *(tener) resfrío* (te·*ner*) res·*free*·o

colleague *colega* ⓜ&① ko·*le*·ga

collect call *llamada* ① *a cobro revertido* lya·*ma*·da a *ko*·bro re·ver·*tee*·do

college (hall of residence) *residencia* ① *de estudiantes* re·see·*den*·sya de es·too·*dyan*·tes

college (school) *colegio* ⓜ ko·*le*·khyo

college (university) *universidad* ① oo·nee·ver·see·*da*

Colombia *Colombia* ① ko·*lom*·bya

colour *color* ⓜ ko·*lor*

comb *peine* ⓜ *pay*·ne

come *venir* ve·*neer*

comedy *comedia* ① ko·*me*·dya

comics *cómics* ⓜ pl *ko*·meeks

comfortable *cómodo/a* ⓜ/① *ko*·mo·do/a

communion *comunión* ① ko·moo·*nyon*

communist *comunista* ⓜ&① ko·moo·*nees*·ta

companion *compañero/a* ⓜ/① kom·pa·*nye*·ro/a

company *compañía* ① kom·pa·*nyee*·a

compass *brújula* ① *broo*·khoo·la

complain *quejarse* ke·*khar*·se

computer *computadora* ① kom·poo·ta·*do*·ra

computer game *juego* ⓜ *de computadora khwe*·go de kom·poo·ta·*do*·ra

concert *concierto* ⓜ kon·*syer*·to

conditioner *acondicionador* ⓜ a·kon·dee·syo·na·*dor*

condom *condón* ⓜ kon·*don*

condor *cóndor* ⓜ kon·*dor*

confession *confesión* ① kon·fe·*syon*

confirm *confirmar* kon·feer·*mar*

connection *conexión* ① ko·nek·*syon*

conservative *conservador/ conservadora* ⓜ/① kon·ser·va·*dor*/ kon·ser·va·*do*·ra

constipation *estreñimiento* ⓜ es·tre·nyee·*myen*·to

consulate *consulado* ⓜ kon·soo·*la*·do

contact lenses *lentes* ⓜ pl *de contacto len*·tes de kon·*tak*·to

contemporary *contemporáneo/a* ⓜ/ⓕ
kon·tem·po·*ra*·ne·o/a
contraceptive *anticonceptivo* ⓜ
an·tee·kon·sep·*tee*·vo
contract *contrato* ⓜ kon·*tra*·to
convenience store *tienda* ⓕ *de*
artículos básicos tyen·da de
ar·*tee*·koo·los ba·*see*·kos
convent *convento* ⓜ kon·*ven*·to
cook *cocinero/a* ⓜ/ⓕ ko·see·*ne*·ro/a
cook *cocinar* ko·see·*nar*
cookie *galleta* ⓕ ga·*lye*·ta
corkscrew *sacacorchos* ⓜ sa·ka·*kor*·chos
corn *maíz* ⓜ ma·*ees*
cornflakes *copos* ⓜ pl *de maíz*
ko·pos de ma·*ees*
corner *esquina* ⓕ es·*kee*·na
corrupt *corrupto/a* ⓜ/ⓕ ko·*roop*·to/a
cost ⓜ *coste* ⓜ *kos*·te
cost *costar* kos·*tar*
Costa Rica *Costa Rica* ⓕ *kos*·ta *ree*·ka
cottage cheese *requesón* ⓜ re·ke·*son*
cotton *algodón* ⓜ al·go·*don*
cotton balls *bolas* ⓕ pl *de algodón*
bo·las de al·go·*don*
cough *tos* ⓕ tos
cough medicine *jarabe* ⓜ kha·*ra*·be
count *contar* kon·*tar*
counter (shop) *mostrador* ⓜ
mos·tra·*dor*
country (nation) *país* ⓜ pa·*ees*
countryside *campo* ⓜ *kam*·po
coupon *cupón* ⓜ koo·*pon*
courgette *calabacín* ⓜ ka·la·ba·*seen*
court (legal) *tribunal* ⓜ tree·boo·*nal*
court (tennis) *cancha* ⓕ *kan*·cha
cousin *primo/a* ⓜ/ⓕ *pree*·mo/a
cover charge (restaurant) *precio* ⓜ
del cubierto *pre*·syo del koo·*byer*·to
cover charge (venue) *precio* ⓜ *de*
entrada *pre*·syo de en·*tra*·da
cow *vaca* ⓕ *va*·ka
craft market *mercado* ⓜ *de artesanía*
mer·*ka*·do de ar·te·sa·*nee*·a
craft *artesanía* ⓕ ar·te·sa·*nee*·a
crash (accident) *choque* ⓜ *cho*·ke
crazy *loco/a* ⓜ/ⓕ *lo*·ko/a

cream *crema* ⓕ *kre*·ma
cream cheese *queso* ⓜ *cremoso*
ke·so kre·*mo*·so
creche *guardería* ⓕ gwar·de·*ree*·a
credit card *tarjeta* ⓕ *de crédito*
tar·*khe*·ta de *kre*·dee·to
cricket (sport) *críquet* ⓜ *kree*·ket
crocodile *cocodrilo* ⓜ ko·ko·*dree*·lo
crop *cosecha* ⓕ ko·*se*·cha
crowded *abarrotado/a* ⓜ/ⓕ
a·ba·ro·*ta*·do/a
Cuba *Cuba* ⓕ *koo*·ba
cucumber *pepino* ⓜ pe·*pee*·no
cup *taza* ⓕ *ta*·sa
cupboard *armario* ⓜ ar·*ma*·ryo
currency exchange *cambio* ⓜ
(de dinero) *kam*·byo (de dee·*ne*·ro)
current *corriente* ⓕ ko·*ryen*·te
current affairs *informativo* ⓜ
een·for·ma·*tee*·vo
curry *curry* ⓜ *koo*·ree
curry powder *curry* ⓜ *en polvo* *koo*·ree
en *pol*·vo
customs *aduana* ⓕ a·*dwa*·na
cut *cortar* kor·*tar*
cutlery *cubiertos* ⓜ pl koo·*byer*·tos
CV *historial* ⓜ *profesional* ees·to·*ryal*
pro·fe·syo·*nal*
cycle *andar en bicicleta* an·*dar* en
bee·see·*kle*·ta
cycling *ciclismo* ⓜ see·*klees*·mo
cyclist *ciclista* ⓜ&ⓕ see·*klees*·ta
cystitis *cistitis* ⓕ sees·*tee*·tees

D

dad *papá* ⓜ pa·*pa*
daily *diariamente* dya·rya·*men*·te
dance *baile* ⓕ *bai*·le
dance *bailar* bai·*lar*
dangerous *peligroso/a* ⓜ/ⓕ
pe·lee·*gro*·so/a
dark *oscuro/a* ⓜ/ⓕ os·*koo*·ro/a
date (appointment) *cita* ⓕ *see*·ta
date (day) *fecha* ⓕ *fe*·cha
date (a person) *salir con* sa·*leer* kon

date of birth *fecha* ⓕ *de nacimiento* fe·cha de na·see·*myen*·to
daughter *hija* ⓕ *ee*·kha
dawn *alba* ⓕ *al*·ba
day *día* ⓜ *dee*·a
day after tomorrow *pasado mañana* pa·*sa*·do ma·*nya*·na
day before yesterday *anteayer* an·te·a·*yer*
dead *muerto/a* ⓜ/ⓕ *mwer*·to/a
deaf *sordo/a* ⓜ/ⓕ *sor*·do/a
decide *decidir* de·see·*deer*
deep *profundo/a* ⓜ/ⓕ pro·*foon*·do/a
deforestation *deforestación* ⓕ de·fo·res·ta·*syon*
delay *demora* ⓕ de·*mo*·ra
deliver *entregar* en·tre·*gar*
democracy *democracia* ⓕ de·mo·kra·*see*·a
demonstration (protest) *manifestación* ⓕ ma·nee·fes·ta·*syon*
dengue fever *fiebre* ⓕ *del dengue* fye·bre del *den*·ge
dental floss *hilo* ⓜ *dental* ee·lo den·*tal*
dentist *dentista* ⓜ&ⓕ den·*tees*·ta
deodorant *desodorante* ⓜ de·so·do·*ran*·te
depart (person) *partir* par·*teer*
depart (plane etc) *salir* sa·*leer*
department store *grande almacén* ⓜ *gran*·de al·ma·*sen*
departure (person) *partida* ⓕ par·*tee*·da
departure (plane etc) *salida* ⓕ sa·*lee*·da
deposit (bank) *depósito* ⓜ de·po·*see*·to
descendant *descendiente* ⓜ de·sen·*dyen*·te
desert *desierto* ⓜ de·*syer*·to
design *diseño* ⓜ dee·*se*·nyo
destination *destino* ⓜ des·*tee*·no
detail *detalle* ⓜ de·*ta*·lye
detective novel *novela* ⓕ *negra* no·*ve*·la *ne*·gra
diabetes *diabetes* ⓕ dya·*be*·tes
dial tone *tono* ⓜ *to*·no
diaper *pañal* ⓜ pa·*nyal*
diaphragm *diafragma* ⓜ dya·*frag*·ma

diarrhoea *diarrea* ⓕ dya·*re*·a
diary *agenda* ⓕ a·*khen*·da
dictionary *diccionario* ⓜ deek·syo·*na*·ryo
die *morir* mo·*reer*
diet (customary food) *dieta* ⓕ *dye*·ta
diet (slimming) *régimen* ⓜ re·khee·men
different *diferente* dee·fe·*ren*·te
difficult *difícil* dee·*fee*·seel
dining car *vagón* ⓜ *restaurante* va·*gon* res·tow·*ran*·te
digital camera *cámara* ⓕ *digital* ka·ma·ra *dee*·khee·*tal*
dinner *cena* ⓕ *se*·na
direct *directo/a* ⓜ/ⓕ dee·*rek*·to/a
direct-dial *servicio* ⓜ *telefónico automático* ser·*vee*·syo te·le·*fo*·nee·ko ow·to·ma·*tee*·ko
director *director/directora* ⓜ/ⓕ dee·rek·*tor*/dee·rek·*to*·ra
dirty *sucio/a* ⓜ/ⓕ *soo*·syo/a
disabled *minusválido/a* ⓜ/ⓕ mee·noos·*va*·lee·do/a
disco *discoteca* ⓕ dees·ko·te·ka
discount *descuento* ⓜ des·*kwen*·to
discover *descubrir* des·koo·*breer*
discrimination *discriminación* ⓕ dees·kree·mee·na·*syon*
disease *enfermedad* ⓕ en·fer·mee·*da*
disk *disco* ⓜ *dees*·ko
disposable camera *cámara* ⓕ *descartable* ka·ma·ra des·kar·*ta*·ble
diving *submarinismo* ⓜ soob·ma·ree·*nees*·mo
diving equipment *equipo* ⓜ *de inmersión* e·*kee*·po de een·mer·*syon*
dizzy *mareado/a* ⓜ/ⓕ ma·re·*a*·do/a
do *hacer* a·*ser*
doctor *médico/a* ⓜ/ⓕ *me*·dee·ko/a
dog *perro/a* ⓜ/ⓕ *pe*·ro/a
dole *subsidio* ⓜ *de desempleo* soob·*see*·dyo de des·em·*ple*·o
doll *muñeca* ⓕ moo·*nye*·ka
dollar *dólar* ⓜ *do*·lar
domestic (country) *nacional* na·syo·*nal*
domestic flight *vuelo* ⓜ *doméstico* *vwe*·lo do·mes·*tee*·ko

Dominican Republic *República* ⓕ
Dominicana re·poo·blee·ka
do·mee·nee·ka·na
donkey *burro* ⓜ boo·ro
door *puerta* ⓕ pwer·ta
dope *droga* ⓕ dro·ga
double *doble* do·ble
double bed *cama* ⓕ *de matrimonio*
ka·ma de ma·tree·mo·nyo
double copies (photos)
dos copias ⓕ pl dos ko·pyas
double room *habitación* ⓕ *doble*
a·bee·ta·syon do·ble
down *hacia abajo* a·see·a a·ba·kho
downhill *cuesta abajo* kwes·ta a·ba·kho
dozen *docena* ⓕ do·se·na
drama *drama* ⓜ dra·ma
draw *dibujar* dee·boo·khar
dream *soñar* so·nyar
dress *vestido* ⓜ ves·tee·do
drink *copa* ⓕ ko·pa
drink *tomar* to·mar
drinkable *potable* po·ta·ble
drive *conducir* kon·doo·seer
drivers licence *carnet* ⓜ kar·net
drug (medicinal) *medicina* ⓕ
me·dee·see·na
drug addiction *drogadicción* ⓕ
dro·ga·deek·syon
drug dealer *traficante* ⓜ *de drogas*
tra·fee·kan·te de dro·gas
drugs (illegal) *drogas* ⓕ pl dro·gas
drums *batería* ⓕ ba·te·ree·a
drunk *borracho/a* ⓜ/ⓕ bo·ra·cho/a
dry *seco/a* ⓜ/ⓕ se·ko/a
dry *secar* se·kar
duck *pato* ⓜ pa·to
dummy (pacifier) *chupete* ⓜ choo·pe·te
during *durante* doo·ran·te
DVD *DVD* de oo·ve de
dysentry *disentería* ⓕ dee·sen·te·ree·a

E

each *cada* ka·da
ear *oreja* ⓕ o·re·kha
early *temprano* tem·pra·no
earn *ganar* ga·nar

earplugs *tapones* ⓜ pl *para los oídos*
ta·po·nes pa·ra los o·ee·dos
earrings *aretes* ⓜ pl a·re·tes
Earth *Tierra* ⓕ tye·ra
earthquake *terremoto* ⓜ te·re·mo·to
east *este* ⓜ es·te
Easter *Pascua* ⓕ pas·kwa
easy *fácil* fa·seel
eat *comer* ko·mer
economy class *clase* ⓕ *turística* kla·se
too·rees·tee·ka
eczema *eczema* ⓕ ek·se·ma
Ecuador *Ecuador* ⓜ e·kwa·dor
education *educación* ⓕ e·doo·ka·syon
egg *huevo* ⓜ we·vo
eggplant *berenjena* ⓕ be·ren·khe·na
elections *elecciones* ⓕ pl e·lek·syo·nes
electrician *electricista* ⓜ&ⓕ
e·lek·tree·sees·ta
electricity *electricidad* ⓕ
e·lek·tree·see·da
elevator *ascensor* ⓜ a·sen·sor
El Salvador *El Salvador* ⓜ el sal·va·dor
embarrassed *avergonzado/a* ⓜ/ⓕ
a·ver·gon·sa·do/a
embassy *embajada* ⓕ em·ba·kha·da
emergency *emergencia* ⓕ
e·mer·khen·sya
emotional *emocional* e·mo·syo·nal
employee *empleado/a* ⓜ/ⓕ
em·ple·a·do/a
employer *patrón/patrona* ⓜ/ⓕ
pa·tron/pa·tro·na
empty *vacío/a* ⓜ/ⓕ va·see·o/a
end *fin* ⓜ feen
end *acabar* a·ka·bar
endangered species *especies* ⓕ pl
en peligro de extinción es·pe·syes en
pe·lee·gro de ek·steen·syon
engagement (marriage)
compromiso ⓜ kom·pro·mee·so
engine *motor* ⓜ mo·tor
engineer *ingeniero/a* ⓜ/ⓕ
een·khe·nye·ro/a
engineering *ingeniería* ⓕ
een·khe·nye·ree·a
England *Inglaterra* ⓕ een·gla·te·ra

English (language) inglés ⓜ een·*gles*

English inglés/inglésa ⓜ/ⓕ een·*gles*/een·*gle*·sa

enjoy (oneself) divertirse dee·ver·*teer*·se

enough suficiente soo·fee·*syen*·te

enter entrar en·*trar*

entertainment guide guía ⓕ de los espectáculos gee·a de los es·pek·*ta*·koo·los

envelope sobre ⓜ so·bre

environment medio ⓜ ambiente me·dyo am·*byen*·te

epilepsy epilepsia ⓕ e·pee·*lep*·sya

equality igualdad ⓕ ee·gwal·*da*

equipment equipo ⓜ e·*kee*·po

escalator escalera ⓕ mecánica es·ka·*le*·ra me·*ka*·nee·ka

euro euro ⓜ e·oo·ro

Europe Europa ⓕ e·oo·ro·pa

euthanasia eutanasia ⓕ e·oo·ta·*na*·sya

evening noche ⓕ no·che

everything todo to·do

example ejemplo ⓜ e·*khem*·plo

excellent excelente ek·se·*len*·te

excess baggage exceso ⓜ de equipaje ek·*se*·so de e·kee·*pa*·khe

exchange cambio ⓜ de dinero *kam*·byo de dee·*ne*·ro

exchange cambiar kam·*byar*

exchange rate tipo ⓜ de cambio *tee*·po de *kam*·byo

excluded no incluido/a ⓜ/ⓕ no een·kloo·*ee*·do/a

exhaust (car) escape ⓜ es·*ka*·pe

exhibition exposición ⓕ ek·spo·see·*syon*

exit salida ⓕ sa·*lee*·da

expensive caro/a ⓜ/ⓕ *ka*·ro/a

experience experiencia ⓕ ek·spe·*ryen*·sya

exploitation explotación ⓕ ek·splo·ta·*syon*

express expreso/a ⓜ/ⓕ ek·*spre*·so/a

express mail correo ⓜ urgente ko·*re*·o oor·*khen*·te

extension (visa) prolongación ⓕ pro·lon·ga·*syon*

eye ojo ⓜ o·kho

eye drops gotas ⓕ pl para los ojos *go*·tas *pa*·ra los o·khos

F

fabric tela ⓕ *te*·la

face cara ⓕ *ka*·ra

factory fábrica ⓕ *fa*·bree·ka

factory worker obrero/a ⓜ/ⓕ o·*bre*·ro/a

fall (tumble) caída ⓕ ka·*ee*·da

fall (season) otoño ⓜ o·*to*·nyo

family familia ⓕ fa·*mee*·lya

family name apellido ⓜ a·pe·*lyee*·do

famous conocido/a ⓜ/ⓕ ko·no·*see*·do/a

fan (person) hincha ⓜ&ⓕ *een*·cha

fan (machine) ventilador ⓜ ven·tee·la·*dor*

fan belt correa ⓕ del ventilador ko·*re*·a del ven·tee·la·*dor*

fantasy fantasía ⓕ fan·ta·*see*·a

far lejos le·khos

farm granja ⓕ *gran*·kha

farmer agricultor/agricultora ⓜ/ⓕ a·gree·kool·*tor*/a·gree·kool·*to*·ra

fast rápido/a ⓜ/ⓕ *ra*·pee·do/a

fat gordo/a ⓜ/ⓕ *gor*·do/a

father padre ⓜ *pa*·dre

father-in-law suegro ⓜ *swe*·gro

faucet grifo ⓜ *gree*·fo

fault (someone's) culpa ⓕ *kool*·pa

faulty defectuoso/a ⓜ/ⓕ de·fek·*two*·so/a

feel sentir sen·*teer*

feelings sentimientos ⓜ pl sen·tee·*myen*·tos

fence cerca ⓕ *ser*·ka

fencing (sport) esgrima ⓕ es·*gree*·ma

festival festival ⓜ fes·tee·*val*

fever fiebre ⓕ *fye*·bre

few pocos/as ⓜ/ⓕ pl po·kos/as

fiance(e) prometido/a ⓜ/ⓕ pro·me·*tee*·do/a

fiction (literature) (literatura de) ficción ⓕ (lee·te·ra·*too*·ra de) feek·*syon*

fig higo ⓜ ee·go

fight pelea ⓕ pe·*le*·a

film (cinema) film ⓜ feelm

film (roll for camera) *película* ①
pe-*lee*-koo-la

film speed *sensibilidad* ①
sen-see-bee-lee-*da*

filtered *con filtro* kon *feel*-tro

find *encontrar* en-kon-*trar*

fine *multa* ① *mool*-ta

finger *dedo* ⓜ *de*-do

finish *terminar* ter-mee-*nar*

fire *fuego* ⓜ *fwe*-go

firewood *leña* ① *le*-nya

first *primero/a* ⓜ/① pree-*me*-ro/a

first class *primera clase* ① pree-*me*-ra
kla-se

first-aid kit *maletín de primeros*
auxilios ma-le-*teen* de pree-*me*-ros
ow-*see*-lyos

fish *pez* ⓜ pes

fish (as food) *pescado* ⓜ pes-*ka*-do

fish shop *pescadería* ① pes-ka-de-*ree*-a

fishing *pesca* ① *pes*-ka

flag *bandera* ① ban-*de*-ra

flamingo *flamenco* ① fla-*men*-ko

flash (camera) *flash* flash

flashlight (torch) *linterna* ① leen-*ter*-na

flannel (wash cloth) *toallita* ①
to-a-*lyee*-ta

flat *llano/a* ⓜ/① *lya*-no/a

flea *pulga* ① *pool*-ga

flip-chart *flip chart* ⓜ fleep chart

flood *inundación* ① ee-noon-da-*syon*

floor (ground) *suelo* ⓜ *swe*-lo

floor (storey) *piso* ⓜ *pee*-so

florist *florista* ⓜ&① flo-*rees*-ta

flour *harina* ① a-*ree*-na

flower *flor* ① flor

flu *gripe* ① *gree*-pe

fly *mosca* ① *mos*-ka

fly *volar* vo-*lar*

foggy *brumoso/a* ⓜ/① broo-mo-*so*/a

follow *seguir* se-*geer*

food *comida* ① ko-*mee*-da

food poisoning *intoxicación* ①
alimenticia een-tok-see-ka-*syon*
a-lee-men-*tee*-sya

food supplies *víveres* ⓜ pl *vee*-ve-res

foot *pie* ⓜ pye

football (soccer) *fútbol* ⓜ *foot*-bol

footpath *acera* ① a-*se*-ra

footpath (CAm) *andén* ⓜ an-*den*

footpath (SAm) *vereda* ① ve-*re*-da

foreign *extranjero/a* ⓜ/①
ek-stran-*khe*-ro/a

foreigner *extranjero/a* ⓜ/①
ek-stran-*khe*-ro/a

forest *bosque* ⓜ *bos*-ke

forever *para siempre* pa-ra syem-*pre*

forget *olvidar* ol-vee-*dar*

forgive *perdonar* per-do-*nar*

fork *tenedor* ⓜ te-ne-*dor*

fortnight *quincena* ① keen-*se*-na

foyer *vestíbulo* ⓜ ves-*tee*-boo-lo

fragile *frágil* *fra*-kheel

France *Francia* ① *fran*-sya

free (gratis) *gratis* *gra*-tees

free (not bound) *libre* *lee*-bre

freeze *congelar* kon-khe-*lar*

fridge *refrigeradora* ①
re-free-khe-ra-*do*-ra

friend *amigo/a* ⓜ/① a-*mee*-go/a

frog *rana* ① *ra*-na

frost *escarcha* ① es-*kar*-cha

frostbite *congelación* ①
kon-khe-la-*syon*

frozen foods *productos* ⓜ pl
congelados pro-*dook*-tos
kon-khe-*la*-dos

fruit *fruta* ① *froo*-ta

fruit picking *recolección* ① *de fruta*
re-ko-lek-*syon* de *froo*-ta

fry *freír* fre-*eer*

frying pan *sartén* ① sar-*ten*

full *lleno/a* ⓜ/① *lye*-no/a

full-time *a tiempo completo* a tyem-*po*
kom-*ple*-to

fun *diversión* ① dee-ver-*syon*

funeral *funeral* ⓜ foo-ne-*ral*

funny *gracioso/a* ⓜ/① gra-syo-*so*/a

furniture *muebles* ⓜ pl *mwe*-bles

future *futuro* ⓜ foo-*too*-ro

G

game (play) *juego* ⓜ *khwe*-go

game (sport) *partido* ⓜ par-*tee*-do

garage (car repair) *taller* ⓜ ta-*lyer*

garage (car shelter) *garage* ⓜ ga·*ra*·khe

garden *jardín* ⓜ khar·*deen*

gardening *jardinería* ⓕ
khar·dee·ne·*ree*·a

garlic *ajo* ⓜ *a*·kho

gas (for cooking) *gas* ⓜ gas

gas (petrol) *gasolina* ⓕ ga·so·*lee*·na

gas cartridge *cartucho* ⓜ *de gas*
kar·*too*·cho de gas

gastroenteritis *gastroenteritis* ⓕ
gas·tro·en·te·*ree*·tees

gate *verja* ⓕ *ver*·kha

gay *gay* gay

gears *marchas* ⓕ pl *mar*·chas

general *general* khe·ne·*ral*

Germany ⓕ *Alemania* a·le·*ma*·nya

gift *regalo* ⓜ re·*ga*·lo

gig *actuación* ⓕ ak·twa·*syon*

ginger *jengibre* ⓜ khen·*khee*·bre

girl *chica* ⓕ *chee*·ka

girlfriend *novia* ⓕ *no*·vya

give *dar* dar

glandular fever *fiebre* ⓕ *glandular*
fye·bre glan·doo·*lar*

glass (drinking) *vaso* ⓜ *va*·so

glass (material) *vidrio* ⓜ *vee*·dryo

glasses *anteojos* ⓜ pl an·te·o·khos

glossy *brillante* bree·*lyan*·te

gloves *guantes* ⓜ pl *gwan*·tes

go *ir* eer

go out with *salir con* sa·*leer* kon

goat *cabra* ⓕ *ka*·bra

god *dios* dyos

goggles *anteojos* ⓜ pl an·te·o·khos

gold *oro* ⓜ *o*·ro

golf ball *pelota* ⓕ *de golf* pe·*lo*·ta
de golf

golf course *cancha* ⓕ *de golf* *kan*·cha
de golf

good *bueno/a* ⓜ/ⓕ *bwe*·no/a

government *gobierno* ⓜ go·*byer*·no

grams *gramos* ⓜ pl *gra*·mos

grandchild *nieto/a* ⓜ/ⓕ *nye*·to/a

grandfather *abuelo* ⓜ a·*bwe*·lo

grandmother *abuela* ⓕ a·*bwe*·la

grapefruit *pomelo* ⓜ po·*me*·lo

grapes *uvas* ⓕ pl *oo*·vas

grass *hierba* ⓕ *yer*·ba

grave *tumba* ⓕ *toom*·ba

great *fantástico/a* ⓜ/ⓕ fan·*tas*·tee·ko/a

green *verde* *ver*·de

greengrocer *verdulero/a* ⓜ/ⓕ
ver·doo·*le*·ro/a

grey *gris* grees

grocer's *almacén* ⓜ al·ma·*sen*

groundnut *maní* ⓜ ma·*nee*

group *grupo* ⓜ *groo*·po

grow *crecer* kre·*ser*

Guatemala *Guatemala* ⓕ gwa·te·*ma*·la

guess *adivinar* a·dee·vee·*nar*

guide (audio) *guía* ⓕ *audio* gee·a
ow·dyo

guide (person) *guía* ⓜ&ⓕ *gee*·a

guide dog *perro* ⓜ *guía* pe·ro gee·a

guidebook *guía* ⓕ *gee*·a

guided tour *recorrido* ⓜ *guiado*
re·ko·*ree*·do gee·a·do

guilty *culpable* kool·*pa*·ble

guinea pig *cuy* ⓜ kooy

guitar *guitarra* ⓕ gee·*ta*·ra

gum (chewing) *chicle* ⓜ *chee*·kle

gum (mouth) *encía* ⓕ en·*see*·a

gymnastics *gimnasia* ⓕ kheem·*na*·sya

gynaecologist *ginecólogo/a* ⓜ/ⓕ
khee·ne·*ko*·lo·go/a

H

hail *granizo* ⓜ gra·*nee*·so

hair *pelo* ⓜ *pe*·lo

haircut *corte* ⓜ *de pelo* kor·te de *pe*·lo

hairdresser *peluquero/a* ⓜ/ⓕ
pe·loo·*ke*·ro/a

halal *halal* a·*lal*

half *medio/a* ⓜ/ⓕ *me*·dyo/a

hallucinate *alucinar* a·loo·see·*nar*

ham *jamón* ⓜ kha·*mon*

hammer *martillo* ⓜ mar·*tee*·lyo

hammock *hamaca* ⓕ a·*ma*·ka

hand *mano* ⓕ *ma*·no

handbag *bolso* ⓜ *bol*·so

handicraft *artesanía* ⓕ ar·te·sa·*nee*·a

handkerchief *pañuelo* ⓜ pa·*nywe*·lo

handlebar *manillar* ⓜ ma·nee·*lyar*

handmade *hecho/a* ⓜ/ⓕ *a mano* e·cho/a a a ma·no

handsome *buen mozo/a* ⓜ/ⓕ bwen mo·so/a

happy *feliz* fe·lees

harassment *acoso* ⓜ a·ko·so

harbour *puerto* ⓜ pwer·to

hard (not easy) *difícil* dee·fee·seel

hard (not soft) *duro/a* ⓜ/ⓕ doo·ro/a

hardware store *ferretería* ⓕ fe·re·te·ree·a

hash *hachís* ⓜ a·chees

hat *sombrero* ⓜ som·bre·ro

have *tener* te·ner

hay fever *alergia* ⓕ *de polén* a·ler·khya de po·len

he *él* el

head *cabeza* ⓕ ka·be·sa

headache *dolor* ⓜ *de cabeza* do·lor de ka·be·sa

headlights *faros* ⓜ pl fa·ros

health *salud* ⓕ sa·loo

hear *oír* o·eer

hearing aid *audífono* ⓜ ow·dee·fo·no

heart *corazón* ⓜ ko·ra·son

heart condition *condición* ⓕ *cardíaca* kon·dee·syon kar·dee·a·ka

heat *calor* ⓜ ka·lor

heater *estufa* ⓕ es·too·fa

heating *calefacción* ⓕ ka·le·fak·syon

heavy *pesado/a* ⓜ/ⓕ pe·sa·do/a

helmet *casco* ⓜ kas·ko

help *ayudar* a·yoo·dar

her *su* soo

hepatitis *hepatitis* ⓕ e·pa·tee·tees

herbalist *herborista* ⓜ&ⓕ er·bo·rees·ta

herbs *hierbas* ⓕ pl yer·bas

here *aquí* a·kee

heroin *heroína* ⓕ e·ro·ee·na

herring *arenque* a·ren·ke

high *alto/a* ⓜ/ⓕ al·to/a

high school *instituto* ⓜ een·stee·too·to

hike *ir de excursión* eer de ek·skoor·syon

hiking *excursionismo* ⓜ ek·skoor·syo·nees·mo

hiking boots *botas* ⓕ pl *de montaña* bo·tas de mon·ta·nya

hiking route *camino* ⓜ *rural* ka·mee·no roo·ral

hill *colina* ⓕ ko·lee·na

Hindu *hindú* een·doo

hire *alquilar* al·kee·lar

his *su* soo

historical *histórico/a* ⓜ/ⓕ ees·to·ree·ko/a

hitchhike *hacer dedo* a·ser de·do

HIV positive *seropositivo/a* ⓜ/ⓕ se·ro·po·see·tee·vo/a

hockey *hockey* ⓜ kho·kee

holiday *día* ⓜ *festivo* dee·a fes·tee·vo

holidays *vacaciones* ⓕ pl va·ka·syo·nes

Holy Week *Semana* ⓕ *Santa* se·ma·na san·ta

home *casa* ⓕ ka·sa

homeless *sin techo* seen te·cho

homemaker *ama* ⓕ *de casa* a·ma de ka·sa

homosexual *homosexual* o·mo·sek·swal

Honduras *Honduras* ⓕ on·doo·ras

honey *miel* ⓕ myel

honeymoon *luna* ⓕ *de miel* loo·na de myel

horoscope *horóscopo* ⓜ o·ros·ko·po

horse *caballo* ⓜ ka·ba·lyo

horse riding *equitación* ⓕ e·kee·ta·syon

horseradish *rábano* ⓜ *picante* ra·ba·no pee·kan·te

hospital *hospital* ⓜ os·pee·tal

hospitality *hospitalidad* ⓕ os·pee·ta·lee·da

hot *caliente* ka·lyen·te

hot water *agua* ⓕ *caliente* a·gwa ka·lyen·te

hotel *hotel* ⓜ o·tel

house *casa* ⓕ ka·sa

how *como* ko·mo

how much *cuanto* kwan·to

hug *abrazo* ⓜ a·bra·so

huge *enorme* e·nor·me

human rights *derechos* ⓜ pl *humanos* de·re·chos oo·ma·nos

hummingbird *colibrí* ⓜ ko·lee·bree

(be) hungry *tener hambre* te·ner am·bre

hunting *caza* ⓕ ka·sa

(be in a) hurry *tener prisa* te·*ner* *pree*·sa

hurt *dañar* da·*nyar*

husband *esposo* ⓜ es·po·so

hut *cabaña* ⓕ ka·ba·nya

I

I *yo* yo

ice *hielo* ⓜ *ye*·lo

ice axe *piolet* ⓜ pyo·*let*

ice cream *helado* ⓜ e·*la*·do

ice-cream parlour *heladería* ⓕ
e·la·de·*ree*·a

ice hockey *hockey* ⓜ *sobre hielo*
kho·kee so·bre ye·lo

identification *identificación* ⓕ
ee·den·tee·fee·ka·*syon*

identification card (ID) *cédula* ⓜ *de
identidad* se·doo·la de ee·den·tee·*da*

idiot *idiota* ⓜ&ⓕ ee·*dyo*·ta

if *si* see

ill *enfermo/a* ⓜ/ⓕ en·*fer*·mo/a

illegal *ilegal* ee·le·*gal*

immigration *inmigración* ⓕ
een·mee·gra·*syon*

important *importante* eem·por·*tan*·te

impossible *imposible* eem·po·*see*·ble

included *incluido/a* ⓜ/ⓕ
een·kloo·*ee*·do/a

income tax *impuesto* ⓜ *sobre la renta*
eem·*pwes*·to so·bre la *ren*·ta

India *India* ⓕ *een*·dya

indicators (car) *direccionales* ⓜ pl
dee·rek·syo·*na*·les

indigestion *indigestion* ⓕ
een·dee·khes·*tyon*

industry *industria* ⓕ een·*doos*·trya

infection *infección* ⓕ een·fek·*syon*

inflammation *inflamación* ⓕ
een·fla·ma·*syon*

information *información* ⓕ
een·for·ma·*syon*

influenza *gripe* ⓕ *gree*·pe

ingredient *ingrediente* ⓜ
een·gre·*dyen*·te

inhaler *inhalador* ⓜ ee·na·la·*dor*

inject *inyectarse* een·yek·*tar*·se

injection *inyección* ⓕ een·yek·*syon*

injury *herida* ⓕ e·*ree*·da

innocent *inocente* ee·no·*sen*·te

inside *adentro* a·*den*·tro

instructor *instructor/instructora* ⓜ/ⓕ
een·strook·*tor*/een·strook·*to*·ra

instructor (skiing) *monitor/monitora*
ⓜ/ⓕ mo·nee·*tor*/mo·nee·*to*·ra

insurance *seguro* ⓜ se·*goo*·ro

interesting *interesante*
een·te·re·*san*·te

intermission *descanso* ⓜ des·*kan*·so

international *internacional*
een·ter·na·syo·*nal*

Internet *Internet* ⓜ een·ter·*net*

Internet cafe *cibercafé* ⓜ see·ber·ka·*fe*

interpreter *intérprete* ⓜ&ⓕ
een·*ter*·pre·te

interview *entrevista* ⓕ en·tre·*vees*·ta

invite *invitar* een·vee·*tar*

Ireland *Irlanda* ⓕ eer·*lan*·da

iron (clothes) *plancha* ⓕ *plan*·cha

island *isla* ⓕ *ees*·la

IT *informática* ⓕ een·for·*ma*·tee·ka

itch *picazón* ⓕ pee·ka·*son*

itemised *detallado/a* ⓜ/ⓕ
de·ta·*lya*·do/a

itinerary *itinerario* ⓜ ee·tee·ne·*ra*·ryo

IUD (contraceptive device) *DIU* ⓜ
de ee oo

J

jacket *chaqueta* ⓕ cha·*ke*·ta

jaguar *jaguar* ⓜ kha·*gwar*

jail *cárcel* ⓕ *kar*·sel

jam *mermelada* ⓕ mer·me·*la*·da

Japan *Japón* ⓜ kha·*pon*

jar *jarra* ⓕ kha·ra

jaw *mandíbula* ⓕ man·*dee*·boo·la

jealous *celoso/a* ⓜ/ⓕ se·*lo*·so/a

jeans *bluejeans* ⓜ pl *bloo*·jeens

jeep *yip* ⓜ yeep

jet lag *jet lag* ⓜ dyet lag

jewellery *joyería* ⓕ kho·ye·*ree*·a

Jewish *judío/a* ⓜ/ⓕ khoo·*dee*·o/a

job *trabajo* ⓜ tra·*ba*·kho
jockey *jockey* ⓜ *yo*·kee
jogging *footing* foo·*teen*
joke *broma* ⓕ *bro*·ma
journalist *periodista* ⓜ&ⓕ
pe·ryo·*dees*·ta
judge *juez* ⓜ&ⓕ khwes
juice *jugo* ⓜ *khoo*·go
jump *saltar* sal·*tar*
jumper (sweater) *chompa* ⓜ *chom*·pa
jumper leads *cables* ⓜ pl *de arranque*
ka·bles de a·*ran*·ke

K

ketchup *salsa* ⓕ *de tomate* *sal*·sa de
to·*ma*·te
key *llave* ⓕ *lya*·ve
keyboard *teclado* ⓜ te·*kla*·do
kick *patada* ⓕ pa·*ta*·da
kick *dar una patada* dar *oo*·na pa·*ta*·da
kill *matar* ma·*tar*
kilogram *kilo* ⓜ *kee*·lo
kilometre *kilómetro* ⓜ kee·*lo*·me·tro
kind *amable* a·*ma*·ble
kindergarten *jardín* ⓜ *de infancia* •
kinder ⓜ khar·*deen* de een·*fan*·sya •
keen·der
king *rey* ⓜ ray
kiss *beso* ⓜ *be*·so
kiss *besar* be·*sar*
kitchen *cocina* ⓕ ko·*see*·na
kitten *gatito/a* ⓜ/ⓕ ga·*tee*·to/a
kiwifruit *kiwi* ⓜ *kee*·wee
knapsack *mochila* ⓕ mo·*chee*·la
knee *rodilla* ⓕ ro·*dee*·lya
knife *cuchillo* ⓜ koo·*chee*·lyo
know (someone) *conocer* ko·no·*ser*
know (something) *saber* sa·*ber*
kosher *kosher* ko·*sher*

L

labourer *obrero/a* ⓜ/ⓕ o·*bre*·ro/a
lace *encaje* ⓜ en·*ka*·khe
lager *cerveza* ⓕ *rubia* ser·*ve*·sa *roo*·bya
lake *lago* ⓜ *la*·go

lamb *cordero* ⓜ kor·*de*·ro
land *tierra* ⓕ *tye*·ra
landlady *propietaria* ⓕ pro·pye·*ta*·rya
landlord *propietario* ⓜ pro·pye·*ta*·ryo
language *idioma* ⓜ ee·*dyo*·ma
laptop *computadora* ⓕ *portátil*
kom·poo·ta·*do*·ra por·*ta*·teel
lard *manteca* ⓕ *de cerdo* man·*te*·ka
de *ser*·do
large *grande* *gran*·de
laser pointer *puntero* ⓜ *láser*
poon·*te*·ro *la*·ser
late *tarde* *tar*·de
Latin America *Latinoamérica* ⓕ
la·tee·no·a·*me*·ree·ka
Latin American *latinoamericano/a*
ⓜ/ⓕ la·tee·no·a·me·ree·*ka*·no/a
laugh *reírse* re·*eer*·se
laundrette *lavandería* ⓕ la·van·de·*ree*·a
laundry *lavandería* ⓕ la·van·de·*ree*·a
law *ley* ⓕ lay
lawyer *abogado/a* ⓜ/ⓕ a·bo·*ga*·do/a
laxatives *laxantes* ⓜ pl lak·*san*·tes
lazy *perezoso/a* ⓜ/ⓕ pe·re·*so*·so/a
leader *jefe/a* ⓜ/ⓕ *khe*·fe/a
leaf *hoja* ⓕ *o*·kha
learn *aprender* a·pren·*der*
leather *cuero* ⓜ *kwe*·ro
leave *partir* par·*teer*
lecturer *profesor/profesora* ⓜ/ⓕ
pro·fe·*sor*/pro·fe·*so*·ra
leek *puerro* ⓜ *pwe*·ro
left (direction) *izquierda* ⓕ ees·*kyer*·da
left luggage office *consigna* ⓕ
kon·*seekh*·na
left-wing *izquierdista* ees·kyer·*dees*·ta
leg (body) *pierna* ⓕ *pyer*·na
legal *legal* le·*gal*
legislation *legislación* ⓕ
le·khees·la·*syon*
lemon *limón* ⓜ lee·*mon*
lemonade *limonada* ⓕ lee·mo·*na*·da
lens *objetivo* ⓜ ob·khe·*tee*·vo
Lent *Cuaresma* ⓕ kwa·*res*·ma
lentils *lentejas* ⓕ pl len·*te*·khas
lesbian *lesbiana* ⓕ les·*bya*·na
less *de menos* de *me*·nos

letter carta ① kar·ta
lettuce lechuga ① le·choo·ga
liar mentiroso/a ⓜ/① men·tee·ro·so/a
library biblioteca ① bee·blyo·te·ka
lice piojos ⓜ pl pyo·khos
license plate number matrícula ①
  ma·tree·koo·la
lie (not stand) tumbarse toom·bar·se
life vida ① vee·da
lifejacket chaleco ⓜ salvavidas
  cha·le·ko sal·va·vee·das
lift (elevator) ascensor ⓜ a·sen·sor
lift levantar le·van·tar
light luz ① loos
light (colour) claro/a ⓜ/① kla·ro/a
light (not heavy) ligero/a ⓜ/①
  lee·khe·ro/a
light bulb bombilla ① bom·bee·lya
light meter fotómetro ⓜ fo·to·me·tro
lighter encendedor ⓜ en·sen·de·dor
lights (on car) faros ⓜ pl fa·ros
like (affection) gustar(le) goos·tar(le)
lime lima ① lee·ma
line línea ① lee·ne·a
lip balm bálsamo ⓜ de labios
  bal·sa·mo de la·byos
lips labios ⓜ pl la·byos
lipstick lápiz ⓜ de labios la·pees de
  la·byos
liquor store bodega ① bo·de·ga
listen escuchar es·koo·char
live vivir vee·veer
liver hígado ⓜ ee·ga·do
lizard lagartija ① la·gar·tee·kha
local local lo·kal
lock (door) cerradura ① se·ra·doo·ra
lock cerrar se·rar
locked cerrado/a ⓜ/① con llave
  se·ra·do/a kon lya·ve
locker lócker ① lo·ker
lollies caramelos ⓜ pl ka·ra·me·los
long largo/a ⓜ/① lar·go/a
long-distance larga distancia lar·ga
  dees·tan·sya
look mirar mee·rar
look after cuidar de kwee·dar de
look for buscar boos·kar
lookout mirador ⓜ mee·ra·dor

loose change monedas ① pl sueltas
  mo·ne·das swel·tas
lose perder per·der
lost perdido/a ⓜ/① per·dee·do/a
lost property office oficina ① de
  objetos perdidos o·fee·see·na de
  ob·khe·tos per·dee·dos
loud ruidoso/a ⓜ/① rwee·do·so/a
love querer ke·rer
lover amante ⓜ&① a·man·te
low bajo/a ⓜ/① ba·kho/a
lubricant lubricante ⓜ loo·bree·kan·te
luck suerte ① swer·te
lucky afortunado/a ⓜ/①
  a·for·too·na·do/a
luggage equipaje ⓜ e·kee·pa·khe
luggage lockers consigna ①
  automática kon·seeg·na
  ow·to·ma·tee·ka
luggage tag etiqueta ① de equipaje
  e·tee·ke·ta de e·kee·pa·khe
lump bulto ⓜ bool·to
lunch almuerzo ⓜ al·mwer·so
lungs pulmones ⓜ pl pool·mo·nes
luxurious de lujo de loo·kho

M

macaw papagayo ⓜ pa·pa·ga·yo
machine máquina ① ma·kee·na
made of (cotton) hecho/a ⓜ/① de
  (algodón) e·cho/a de (al·go·don)
magazine revista ① re·vees·ta
magician mago/a ⓜ/① ma·go/a
mail correo ⓜ ko·re·o
mailbox buzón ⓜ boo·son
main principal preen·see·pal
make hacer a·ser
make-up maquillaje ⓜ ma·kee·lya·khe
malaria malaria ① ma·la·rya
mallet mazo ⓜ ma·so
mammogram mamograma ⓜ
  ma·mo·gra·ma
man hombre ⓜ om·bre
manager director/directora ⓜ/①
  dee·rek·tor/dee·rek·to·ra

mandarin *mandarina* ① man·da·*ree*·na

mango *mango* ⓜ *man*·go

manual *manual* ma·*nwal*

many *muchos/as* ⓜ/① pl *moo*·chos/as

map *mapa* ⓜ *ma*·pa

margarine *margarina* ① mar·ga·*ree*·na

marijuana *marihuana* ① ma·ree·*wa*·na

marital status *estado* ⓜ *civil* es·*ta*·do see·*veel*

market *mercado* ⓜ mer·*ka*·do

marmalade *mermelada* ① mer·me·*la*·da

marriage *matrimonio* ⓜ ma·tree·*mo*·nyo

married *casado/a* ⓜ/① ka·*sa*·do/a

marry *casarse* ka·*sar*·se

martial arts *artes* ⓜ pl *marciales* *ar*·tes mar·*sya*·les

mass (Catholic) *misa* ① *mee*·sa

massage *masaje* ⓜ ma·*sa*·khe

masseur/masseuse *masajista* ⓜ&① ma·sa·*khees*·ta

mat *esterilla* ① es·te·*ree*·lya

match (sport) *partido* ⓜ par·*tee*·do

matches *fósforos* ⓜ pl *fos*·fo·ros

matte (photos) *mate* *ma*·te

mattress *colchón* ⓜ kol·*chon*

maybe *quizás* kee·*sas*

mayonnaise *mayonesa* ① ma·yo·*ne*·sa

mayor *alcalde* ⓜ&① al·*kal*·de

measles *sarampión* ⓜ sa·ram·*pyon*

meat *carne* ① *kar*·ne

mechanic *mecánico/a* ⓜ/① me·*ka*·nee·ko/a

media *medios* ⓜ pl *de comunicación* *me*·dyos de ko·moo·nee·ka·*syon*

medicine *medicina* ① me·dee·*see*·na

meditation *meditación* ① me·dee·ta·*syon*

meet *encontrar* en·kon·*trar*

melon *melón* ⓜ me·*lon*

member *miembro* ⓜ&① *myem*·bro

menstruation *menstruación* ① mens·trwa·*syon*

menu *menú* ⓜ me·*noo*

message *mensaje* ⓜ men·*sa*·khe

metal *metal* ⓜ me·*tal*

metre (distance) *metro* ⓜ *me*·tro

metro *subterráneo* ⓜ soob·te·*ra*·ne·o

metro station *estación* ① *de subterráneo* es·ta·*syon* de soob·te·*ra*·ne·o

Mexico *México* ⓜ *me*·khee·ko

microwave oven *microondas* ⓜ mee·kro·*on*·das

midnight *medianoche* ① me·dya·*no*·che

migraine *migraña* ① mee·*gra*·nya

military *militares* ⓜ pl mee·lee·*ta*·res

military service *servicio* ⓜ *militar* ser·*vee*·syo mee·lee·*tar*

milk *leche* ① *le*·che

millimetre *milímetro* ⓜ mee·*lee*·me·tro

million *millón* ⓜ mee·*lyon*

mince (meat) *carne* ① *molida* *kar*·ne mo·*lee*·da

mind (look after) *cuidar* kwee·*dar*

mineral water *agua* ⓜ *mineral* *a*·gwa mee·ne·*ral*

mints *pastillas* ① pl *de menta* pas·*tee*·lyas de *men*·ta

minute *minuto* ⓜ mee·*noo*·to

mirror *espejo* ⓜ es·*pe*·kho

miscarriage *aborto* ⓜ *natural* a·*bor*·to na·too·*ral*

miss (feel absence of) *extrañar* ek·stra·*nyar*

mistake *error* ⓜ e·*ror*

mix *mezclar* mes·*klar*

mobile phone *teléfono* ⓜ *móvil/ celular* te·*le*·fo·no *mo*·veel/se·loo·*lar*

modem *módem* ⓜ *mo*·dem

moisturiser *crema* ① *hidratante* *kre*·ma ee·dra·*tan*·te

monastery *monasterio* ⓜ mo·nas·*te*·ryo

money *dinero* ⓜ dee·*ne*·ro

month *mes* ⓜ mes

monument *monumento* ⓜ mo·noo·*men*·to

moon *luna* ① *loo*-na
more *más* mas
morning *mañana* ① ma-*nya*-na
morning sickness *náuseas* ① pl *del
embarazo* now-se-as del em-ba-*ra*-so
mosque *mezquita* ① mes-*kee*-ta
mosquito *mosquito* ⑩ mos-*kee*-to
mosquito coil *espiral* ⑩ *repelente
contra mosquitos* es-pee-*ral
re-pe-len*-te kon-tra mos-*kee*-tos
mosquito net *mosquitera* ①
mos-kee-*te*-ra
mother *madre* ① *ma*-dre
mother-in-law *suegra* ① *swe*-gra
motorboat *motora* ① mo-*to*-ra
motorcycle *motocicleta* ①
mo-to-see-*kle*-ta
motorway *autopista* ① ow-to-*pees*-ta
mountain *montaña* ① mon-*ta*-nya
mountain bike *bicicleta* ① *de montaña*
bee-see-*kle*-ta de mon-*ta*-nya
mountain path *sendero* ⑩ sen-*de*-ro
mountain range *cordillera* ①
kor-dee-*lye*-ra
mountaineering *alpinismo* ⑩
al-pee-*nees*-mo
mouse *ratón* ⑩ ra-*ton*
mouth *boca* ① *bo*-ka
movie *película* ① pe-*lee*-koo-la
MP3 player *reproductor* ⑩ *de MP3*
re-pro-dook-*tor* de *e*-me pe tres
mud *lodo* ⑩ *lo*-do
muesli *muesli* ⑩ *mwes*-lee
mum *mamá* ① ma-*ma*
muscle *músculo* ⑩ *moos*-koo-lo
museum *museo* ⑩ moo-*se*-o
mushroom *champiñón* ⑩
cham-pee-*nyon*
music *música* ① *moo*-see-ka
musician *músico/a* ⑩/① *moo*-see-ko/a
Muslim *musulmán/musulmana* ⑩/①
moo-sool-*man*/moo-sool-*ma*-na
mussels *mejillones* ⑩ pl
me-khee-*lyo*-nes
mustard *mostaza* ① mos-*ta*-sa
mute *mudo/a* ⑩/① *moo*-do/a
my *mi* mee

N

nail clippers *cortauñas* ⑩ kor-ta-*oo*-nyas
name *nombre* ⑩ *nom*-bre
napkin *servilleta* ① ser-vee-*lye*-ta
nappy *pañal* ⑩ pa-*nyal*
nappy rash *irritación* ① *de pañal*
ee-ree-ta-*syon* de pa-*nyal*
national *nacional* na-syo-*nal*
national park *parque* ⑩ *nacional
par*-ke na-syo-*nal*
nationality *nacionalidad* ①
na-syo-na-lee-*da*
nature *naturaleza* ① na-too-ra-*le*-sa
naturopathy *naturopatia* ①
na-too-ro-*pa*-tya
nausea *náusea* ① *now*-se-a
near (to) *cerca (de)* ser-ka (de)
nearby *cerca* ser-ka
nearest *más cercano/a* ⑩/① mas
ser-*ka*-no/a
necessary *necesario/a* ⑩/①
ne-se-*sa*-ryo/a
neck *cuello* ⑩ *kwe*-lyo
need *necesitar* ne-se-see-*tar*
needle (sewing) *aguja* ① a-*goo*-kha
needle (syringe) *jeringuilla* ①
khe-reen-*gee*-lya
neither *tampoco* tam-*po*-ko
net *red* ⑩ re
Netherlands *Holanda* ① o-*lan*-da
never *nunca* *noon*-ka
new *nuevo/a* ⑩/① *nwe*-vo/a
New Year *Año Nuevo* ⑩ a-nyo *nwe*-vo
New Year's Day *dia de Año Nuevo* ⑩
dee-a de a-nyo *nwe*-vo
New Year's Eve *Nochevieja* ①
no-che-*vye*-kha
New Zealand *Nueva Zelanda* ①
nwe-va se-*lan*-da
news *noticias* ① pl no-*tee*-syas
newsagency *quiosco* ⑩ kee-os-ko
newspaper *periódico* ⑩ pe-ryo-*dee*-ko
next *próximo/a* ⑩/① *prok*-see-mo/a
next to *al lado de* al *la*-do de
Nicaragua *Nicaragua* ① nee-ka-*ra*-gwa
nice (object) *bueno/a* ⑩/① *bwe*-no/a

nice (person) *simpático/a* ⓜ/ⓕ
seem·*pa*·tee·ko/a
nickname *apodo* ⓜ a·*po*·do
night *noche* ⓕ *no*·che
night life *vida* ⓕ *nocturna* vee·da
nok·*toor*·na
no *no* no
noisy *ruidoso/a* ⓜ/ⓕ rwee·*do*·so/a
non-direct *indirecto/a* een·dee·*rek*·to/a
none *nada* na·da
non-fiction *literatura* ⓕ *no novelesca*
lee·te·ra·*too*·ra no no·ve·*les*·ka
non-smoking *no fumadores* no
foo·ma·*do*·res
noodles *fideos* ⓜ pl fee·*de*·os
noon *mediodía* ⓜ me·dyo·*dee*·a
north *norte* ⓜ *nor*·te
nose *nariz* ⓕ na·*rees*
notebook *cuaderno* ⓜ kwa·*der*·no
nothing *nada* na·da
novel *novela* ⓕ no·*ve*·la
now *ahora* a·o·ra
nuclear energy *energía* ⓕ *nuclear*
e·ner·*khee*·a noo·kle·*ar*
nuclear testing *pruebas* ⓕ pl
nucleares prwe·bas noo·kle·*a*·res
nuclear waste *desperdicios* ⓜ pl
nucleares des·per·*dee*·syos
noo·kle·*a*·res
number *número* ⓜ *noo*·me·ro
nun *monja* ⓕ *mon*·kha
nurse *enfermero/a* ⓜ/ⓕ en·fer·me·ro/a
nut *nuez* ⓕ nwes

O

oats *avena* ⓕ a·*ve*·na
ocean *océano* ⓜ o·se·a·no
off (spoiled) *pasado/a* ⓜ/ⓕ pa·*sa*·do/a
office *oficina* ⓕ o·fee·*see*·na
office worker *oficinista* ⓜ&ⓕ
o·fee·see·*nees*·ta
often *a menudo* a me·*noo*·do
oil *aceite* ⓜ a·*say*·te
old *viejo/a* ⓜ/ⓕ *vye*·kho/a
olive *aceituna* ⓕ a·say·*too*·na
olive oil *aceite* ⓜ *de oliva* a·*say*·te de
o·*lee*·va

Olympic Games *juegos* ⓜ pl *olímpicos* khwe·gos o·*leem*·pee·kos
on *en* en
once *una vez* oo·na ves
one-way ticket *boleto* ⓜ *sencillo*
bo·*le*·to sen·*see*·lyo
onion *cebolla* ⓕ se·*bo*·lya
only *sólo* so·lo
open *abierto/a* ⓜ/ⓕ a·*byer*·to/a
open *abrir* a·*breer*
opening hours *horas* ⓕ pl *de
apertura* o·ras de a·per·*too*·ra
opera *ópera* ⓕ o·pe·ra
opera house *teatro* ⓜ *de la ópera*
te·*a*·tro de la o·pe·ra
operation (medical) *operación* ⓕ
o·pe·ra·*syon*
operator *operador/operadora* ⓜ/ⓕ
o·pe·ra·*dor*/o·pe·ra·*do*·ra
opinion *opinión* ⓕ o·pee·*nyon*
opposite *frente a* *fren*·te a
or *o* o
orange (fruit) *naranja* ⓕ na·*ran*·kha
orange (colour) *naranjo/a* ⓜ/ⓕ
na·*ran*·kho/a
orange juice *jugo* ⓜ *de naranja*
khoo·go de na·*ran*·kha
orchestra *orquesta* ⓕ or·kes·ta
orchid *orquídea* ⓕ or·kee·de·a
order (command) *orden* ⓕ *or*·den
order (placement) *orden* ⓜ *or*·den
order *ordenar* or·de·*nar*
ordinary *corriente* ko·*ryen*·te
orgasm *orgasmo* ⓜ or·gas·mo
original *original* o·ree·khee·*nal*
other *otro/a* ⓜ/ⓕ o·tro/a
our *nuestro/a* ⓜ/ⓕ *nwes*·tro/a
outside *exterior* ⓜ ek·ste·*ryor*
ovarian cyst *quiste* ⓜ *ovárico*
kees·te o·va·ree·ko
oven *horno* ⓜ *or*·no
over (above) *sobre* so·bre
overcoat *abrigo* ⓜ a·*bree*·go
overdose *sobredosis* ⓕ so·bre·*do*·sees
owner *dueño/a* ⓜ/ⓕ *dwe*·nyo/a
oxygen *oxígeno* ⓜ ok·*see*·khe·no
oyster *ostra* ⓕ o·stra
ozone layer *capa* ⓕ *de ozono* ka·pa
de o·*so*·no

P

pacemaker marcapasos ⓜ mar·ka·pa·sos
pacifier chupete ⓜ choo·pe·te
package paquete ⓜ pa·ke·te
packet paquete ⓜ pa·ke·te
padlock candado ⓜ kan·da·do
page página ⓕ pa·khee·na
pain dolor ⓜ do·lor
painful doloroso/a ⓜ/ⓕ do·lo·ro·so/a
painkillers analgésicos ⓜ pl a·nal·khe·see·kos
paint pintar peen·tar
painter pintor/pintora ⓜ/ⓕ peen·tor/peen·to·ra
painting (art) pintura ⓕ peen·too·ra
painting (canvas) cuadro ⓜ kwa·dro
pair (couple) pareja ⓕ pa·re·kha
palace palacio ⓜ pa·la·syo
palm pilot palm pilot ⓜ palm pee·lot
pan olla ⓕ o·lya
panoramic panorámico/a ⓜ/ⓕ pa·no·ra·mee·ko/a
Panama Panamá ⓜ pa·na·ma
panther pantera ⓕ pan·te·ra
pants pantalones ⓜ pl pan·ta·lo·nes
panty liners salvaslips ⓜ pl sal·vas·leeps
pantyhose medias ⓕ pl me·dyas
pap smear citología ⓕ see·to·lo·khee·a
paper papel ⓜ pa·pel
paperwork trabajo ⓜ administrativo tra·ba·kho ad·mee·nees·tra·tee·vo
Paraguay Paraguay ⓜ pa·ra·gway
parcel paquete ⓜ pa·ke·te
parents padres ⓜ pl pa·dres
park parque ⓜ par·ke
park (car) estacionar es·ta·syo·nar
parliament parlamento ⓜ par·la·men·to
parrot loro ⓜ lo·ro
part parte ⓕ par·te
partner (relationship) pareja ⓜ&ⓕ pa·re·kha
part-time a tiempo parcial a tyem·po par·syal
party (celebration) fiesta ⓕ fyes·ta

party (politics) partido ⓜ par·tee·do
pass (mountain) paso ⓜ pa·so
pass (permit) pase ⓜ pa·se
passenger pasajero/a ⓜ/ⓕ pa·sa·khe·ro/a
passport pasaporte ⓜ pa·sa·por·te
passport number número ⓜ de pasaporte noo·me·ro de pa·sa·por·te
past pasado ⓜ pa·sa·do
pasta pasta ⓕ pas·ta
pate (food) paté ⓜ pa·te
path sendero ⓜ sen·de·ro
pay pagar pa·gar
payment pago ⓜ pa·go
pea guisante ⓕ gee·san·te
peace paz ⓕ pas
peach durazno ⓜ doo·ras·no
peak cumbre ⓕ koom·bre
peanut maní ⓜ ma·nee
pear pera ⓕ pe·ra
pedal pedal ⓜ pe·dal
pedestrian peatón ⓜ&ⓕ pe·a·ton
pegs (tent) estacas ⓕ pl es·ta·kas
pen (ballpoint) bolígrafo ⓜ bo·lee·gra·fo
pencil lápiz ⓜ la·pees
penis pene ⓜ pe·ne
penicillin penicilina ⓕ pe·nee·see·lee·na
penknife navaja ⓕ na·va·kha
pensioner pensionado/a ⓜ/ⓕ pen·syo·na·do/a
people gente ⓕ khen·te
pepper (spice) pimienta ⓕ pee·myen·ta
per (day) por (día) por (dee·a)
percent por ciento por syen·to
performance actuación ⓕ ak·twa·syon
perfume perfume ⓜ per·foo·me
period pain dolor ⓜ menstrual do·lor mens·trwal
permission permiso ⓜ per·mee·so
permit permiso ⓜ per·mee·so
permit permitir per·mee·teer
person persona ⓕ per·so·na
perspire sudar soo·dar
Peru Perú ⓜ pe·roo
petition petición ⓕ pe·tee·syon

petrol *gasolina* ⓕ ga·so·*lee*·na
pharmacy *farmacia* ⓕ far·*ma*·sya
pharmacist *farmacéutico/a* ⓜ/ⓕ far·ma·see·oo·tee·ko/a
phone book *guía* ⓕ *telefónica* gee·a te·le·fo·nee·ka
phone box *cabina* ⓕ *telefónica* ka·*bee*·na te·le·fo·nee·ka
phone card *tarjeta* ⓕ *de teléfono* tar·*khe*·ta de te·le·fo·no
photo *fotografía* ⓕ fo·to·gra·*fee*·a
photocopier *fotocopiadora* ⓕ fo·to·ko·pya·*do*·ra
photographer *fotógrafo/a* ⓜ/ⓕ fo·*to*·gra·fo/a
photography *fotografía* ⓕ fo·to·gra·*fee*·a
phrasebook *libro* ⓜ *de frases* *lee*·bro de *fra*·ses
pick (up) *levantar* le·van·*tar*
pickaxe *piqueta* ⓕ pee·*ke*·ta
pickles *pepinillos* ⓜ pl pe·pee·*nee*·lyos
picnic *picnic* ⓜ peek·*neek*
pie *empanada* ⓕ em·pa·*na*·da
piece *pedazo* ⓜ pe·*da*·so
pig *cerdo* ⓜ *ser*·do
pill *pastilla* ⓕ pas·*tee*·lya
the Pill *la píldora* ⓕ la *peel*·do·ra
pillow *almohada* ⓕ al·mo·*a*·da
pillowcase *funda* ⓕ *de almohada* *foon*·da de al·mo·*a*·da
pineapple *ananá(s)* ⓜ a·na·*na(s)*
pink *rosa* *ro*·sa
pistachio *pistacho* pees·*ta*·cho
place *lugar* loo·*gar*
place of birth *lugar* ⓜ *de nacimiento* loo·*gar* de na·see·*myen*·to
plane *avión* ⓜ a·*vyon*
planet *planeta* ⓜ pla·*ne*·ta
plant *planta* ⓕ *plan*·ta
plant *sembrar* sem·*brar*
plastic *plástico* ⓜ *plas*·tee·ko
plate *plato* ⓜ *pla*·to
plateau *meseta* ⓕ me·*se*·ta
platform *plataforma* ⓕ pla·ta·*for*·ma
play *obra* ⓕ o·*bra*
play (a game) *jugar* khoo·*gar*

play (the guitar) *tocar (la guitarra)* to·*kar* (la gee·*ta*·ra)
play (tennis) *jugar (al tenis)* khoo·*gar* (al *te*·nees)
plug (bath) *tapón* ⓜ ta·*pon*
plug (electricity) *enchufe* ⓜ en·*choo*·fe
plum *ciruela* ⓕ see·*rwe*·la
pocket *bolsillo* ⓜ bol·*see*·lyo
poetry *poesía* ⓕ po·e·*see*·a
point *punto* ⓜ *poon*·to
point *apuntar* a·poon·*tar*
poisonous *venenoso/a* ⓜ/ⓕ ve·ne·*no*·so/a
police *policía* ⓕ po·lee·*see*·a
police station *comisaría* ⓕ ko·mee·sa·*ree*·a
policy *política* ⓕ po·*lee*·tee·ka
policy (insurance) *póliza* ⓕ po·*lee*·sa
politician *político/a* ⓜ/ⓕ po·*lee*·tee·ko/a
politics *política* ⓕ po·*lee*·tee·ka
pollen *polen* ⓜ *po*·len
polls *sondeos* ⓜ pl son·*de*·os
pollution *contaminación* ⓕ kon·ta·mee·na·*syon*
pony *potro* ⓜ *po*·tro
pool (game) *billar* ⓜ bee·*lyar*
pool (swimming) *piscina* ⓕ pee·*see*·na
poor *pobre* *po*·bre
popular *popular* po·poo·*lar*
pork *cerdo* ⓜ *ser*·do
port *puerto* ⓜ *pwer*·to
port (wine) *oporto* ⓜ o·*por*·to
portable CD player *reproductor* ⓜ *de compacts portátil* re·pro·dook·*tor* de *kom*·paks por·*ta*·teel
possible *posible* po·*see*·ble
post code *código* ⓜ *postal* *ko*·dee·go pos·*tal*
post office *correos* ⓜ pl ko·*re*·os
postage *franqueo* ⓕ fran·*ke*·o
postcard *postal* ⓕ pos·*tal*
pot (ceramic) *cacharro* ⓜ ka·*cha*·ro
pot (kitchen) *olla* ⓕ *o*·lya
pot (dope) *chocolate* ⓜ cho·ko·*la*·te
potato *papa* ⓕ *pa*·pa
pottery *alfarería* ⓕ al·fa·re·*ree*·a
pound (money) *libra* ⓕ *lee*·bra

poverty *pobreza* ⓕ po·*bre*·sa
power *poder* ⓜ po·*der*
prawn *langostino* ⓜ lan·gos·*tee*·no
prayer *oración* ⓕ o·ra·*syon*
prefer *preferir* pre·fe·*reer*
pregnancy test kit *prueba* ⓕ *del embarazo* prwe·ba del em·ba·*ra*·so
pregnant *embarazada* em·ba·ra·*sa*·da
premenstrual tension *tensión* ⓕ *premenstrual* ten·*syon* pre·mens·*trwal*
prepare *preparar* pre·pa·*rar*
present (gift) *regalo* ⓜ re·*ga*·lo
presentation *presentación* ⓕ pre·sen·ta·*syon*
president *presidente/a* ⓜ/ⓕ pre·see·*den*·te/a
pressure *presión* ⓕ pre·*syon*
pretty *bonito/a* ⓜ/ⓕ bo·*nee*·to/a
prevent *prevenir* pre·ve·*neer*
price *precio* ⓜ *pre*·syo
priest *sacerdote* ⓜ sa·ser·*do*·te
prime minister (man) *primer ministro* ⓜ pree·*mer* mee·*nees*·tro
prime minister (woman) *primera ministra* ⓕ pree·*me*·ra mee·*nees*·tra
prison *cárcel* ⓕ *kar*·sel
prisoner *prisionero/a* ⓜ/ⓕ pree·syo·ne·*ro*/a
private *privado/a* ⓜ/ⓕ pree·*va*·do/a
produce *producir* pro·doo·*seer*
profit *beneficio* ⓜ be·ne·*fee*·syo
programme *programa* ⓜ pro·*gra*·ma
projector *proyector* ⓜ pro·yek·*tor*
promise *promesa* ⓕ pro·*me*·sa
proposal *propuesta* ⓕ pro·*pwes*·ta
protect *proteger* pro·te·*kher*
protected *protegido/a* ⓜ/ⓕ pro·te·*khee*·do/a
protest *protesta* ⓕ pro·*tes*·ta
protest *protestar* pro·tes·*tar*
provisions *provisiones* ⓕ pl pro·vee·*syo*·nes
prune *ciruela* ⓕ pasa see·*rwe*·la *pa*·sa
pub *pub* ⓜ poob
public telephone *teléfono* ⓜ *público* te·*le*·fo·no *poo*·blee·ko

public toilet *baños* ⓜ pl *ba*·nyos
Puerto Rico *Puerto* ⓜ *Rico* pwer·to *ree*·ko
pull *jalar* kha·*lar*
pump *bomba* ⓕ *bom*·ba
pumpkin *calabaza* ⓕ ka·la·*ba*·sa
puncture *pinchar* peen·*char*
punish *castigar* kas·tee·*gar*
puppy *cachorro* ⓜ ka·*cho*·ro
pure *puro/a* ⓜ/ⓕ *poo*·ro/a
purple *morado/a* ⓜ/ⓕ mo·*ra*·do/a
push *empujar* em·poo·*khar*
put *poner* po·*ner*

Q

qualifications *cualificaciones* ⓕ pl kwa·lee·fee·ka·*syo*·nes
quality *calidad* ⓕ ka·lee·*da*
quarantine *cuarentena* ⓕ kwa·ren·*te*·na
quarrel *pelea* ⓕ pe·*le*·a
quarter *cuarto* ⓜ *kwar*·to
queen *reina* ⓕ *ray*·na
question *pregunta* ⓕ pre·*goon*·ta
queue *cola* ⓕ *ko*·la
quick *rápido/a* ⓜ/ⓕ *ra*·pee·do/a
quiet *tranquilo/a* ⓜ/ⓕ tran·*kee*·lo/a

R

rabbit *conejo* ⓜ ko·*ne*·kho
race (people) *raza* ⓕ *ra*·sa
race (sport) *carrera* ⓕ ka·*re*·ra
racetrack (sport) *pista* ⓕ *pees*·ta
racing bike *bicicleta* ⓕ *de carreras* bee·see·*kle*·ta de ka·*re*·ras
racquet *raqueta* ⓕ ra·*ke*·ta
radiator *radiador* ⓜ ra·dya·*dor*
radish *rábano* ⓜ *ra*·ba·no
railway *ferrocarril* ⓜ fe·ro·ka·*reel*
railway station *estación* ⓕ *de tren* es·ta·*syon* de tren
rain *lluvia* ⓕ *lyoo*·vya
raincoat *impermeable* ⓜ eem·per·me·*a*·ble
raisin *pasa* ⓕ *de uva* *pa*·sa de *oo*·va

rape *violar* vyo·lar
rare *raro/a* ⓜ/ⓕ ra·ro/a
rash *irritación* ⓕ ee·ree·ta·syon
raspberry *frambuesa* ⓕ fram·bwe·sa
rat *rata* ⓕ ra·ta
raw *crudo/a* ⓜ/ⓕ kroo·do/a
razor *afeitadora* ⓕ a·fay·ta·do·ra
razor blade *hoja* ⓕ *de afeitar* o·kha
   de a·fay·tar
read *leer* le·er
ready *listo/a* ⓜ/ⓕ lees·to/a
real estate agent *agente* ⓜ
   inmobiliario a·khen·te
   een·mo·bee·lya·ryo
realistic *realista* re·a·lees·ta
reason *razón* ⓕ ra·son
receipt *recibo* ⓜ re·see·bo
receive *recibir* re·see·beer
recently *recientemente*
   re·syen·te·men·te
recognise *reconocer* re·ko·no·ser
recommend *recomendar*
   re·ko·men·dar
recording *grabación* ⓕ gra·ba·syon
recyclable *reciclable* re·see·kla·ble
recycle *reciclar* re·see·klar
red *rojo/a* ⓜ/ⓕ ro·kho/a
referee *árbitro* ⓜ ar·bee·tro
references (work) *referencias* ⓕ pl
   re·fe·ren·syas
refrigerator *refrigeradora* ⓕ
   re·free·khe·ra·do·ra
refugee *refugiado/a* ⓜ/ⓕ
   re·foo·khya·do/a
refund *reembolso* ⓜ re·em·bol·so
refuse *negar(se)* ne·gar(·se)
registered mail *correo* ⓜ *certificado*
   ko·re·o ser·tee·fee·ka·do
relationship *relación* ⓕ re·la·syon
relax *relajarse* re·la·khar·se
relic *reliquia* ⓕ re·lee·kya
religion *religión* ⓕ re·lee·khyon
religious *religioso/a* ⓜ/ⓕ
   re·lee·khyo·so/a
remote *remoto/a* ⓜ/ⓕ re·mo·to/a
remote control *mando* ⓜ *a distancia*
   man·do a dees·tan·sya

rent *alquiler* ⓜ al·kee·ler
rent *alquilar* al·kee·lar
repair *reparar* re·pa·rar
republic *república* ⓕ re·poo·blee·ka
reservation *reserva* ⓕ re·ser·va
reserve *hacer una reserva* a·ser oo·na
   re·ser·va
rest *descansar* des·kan·sar
restaurant *restaurante* ⓜ res·tow·ran·te
resume *currículum* ⓜ koo·ree·koo·loom
retired *jubilado/a* ⓜ/ⓕ
   khoo·bee·la·do/a
return *volver* vol·ver
return ticket *boleto* ⓜ *de ida y vuelta*
   (bo·le·to) de ee·da ee vwel·ta
reverse charge call *llamada* ⓕ *a
   cobro revertido* lya·ma·da a ko·bro
   re·ver·tee·do
review *crítica* ⓕ kree·tee·ka
rhythm *ritmo* ⓜ reet·mo
rice *arroz* ⓜ a·ros
rich *rico/a* ⓜ/ⓕ ree·ko/a
ride *paseo* ⓜ pa·se·o
ride *montar* mon·tar
right (correct) *correcto/a* ⓜ/ⓕ
   ko·rek·to/a
right (direction) *derecha* de·re·cha
right-wing *derechista* de·re·chees·ta
ring (on finger) *anillo* ⓜ a·nee·lyo
ring (by phone) *llamar por teléfono*
   lya·mar por te·le·fo·no
rip-off *estafa* ⓕ es·ta·fa
risk *riesgo* ⓜ ryes·go
river *río* ⓜ ree·o
road *calle* ⓕ ka·lye
rob *robar* ro·bar
rock (stone) *roca* ⓕ ro·ka
rock (music) *rock* ⓜ rok
rock climbing *escalada* ⓕ es·ka·la·da
rock group *grupo* ⓜ *de rock* groo·po
   de rok
roll (bread) *bollo* ⓜ bo·lyo
romance novel *novela* ⓕ *rosa* no·ve·la
   ro·sa
romantic *romántico/a* ⓜ/ⓕ
   ro·man·tee·ko/a
roof *techo* ⓜ te·cho

room *habitación* ① a·bee·ta·*syon*
room number *numero* ⑩ *de habitación*
noo·me·ro de a·bee·ta·*syon*
rope *cuerda* ① kwer·da
round *redondo/a* ⑩/① re·don·do/a
roundabout *glorieta* ① glo·*rye*·ta
route *ruta* ① roo·ta
rowing *remo* ⑩ re·mo
rubbish *basura* ① ba·soo·ra
rug *alfombra* ① al·*fom*·bra
rugby *rugby* ⑩ roog·bee
ruins *ruinas* ① pl rwee·nas
rules *reglas* ① pl re·glas
rum *ron* ⑩ ron
running (sport) *footing* ⑩ foo·teen

S

Sabbath *sábado* ⑩ sa·ba·do
sad *triste* trees·te
saddle *sillín* ⑩ see·*lyeen*
safe *caja* ① *fuerte* ka·kha fwer·te
safe *seguro/a* ⑩/① se·goo·ro/a
safe sex *sexo* ⑩ *seguro* sek·so
se·goo·ro
sail *vela* ① ve·la
sailing boat *barco* ⑩ *de vela* bar·ko
de ve·la
saint *santo/a* ⑩/① san·to/a
salad *ensalada* ① en·sa·la·da
salami *salami* ⑩ sa·la·mee
salary *salario* ⑩ sa·la·ryo
sales tax IVA ⑩ ee·va
salmon *salmón* ⑩ sal·mon
salt *sal* ① sal
same *igual* ee·gwal
sand *arena* ① a·re·na
sandals *sandalias* ① pl san·da·lyas
sandwich *sandwich* ⑩ san·weech
sanitary napkins *compresas* ① pl
kom·pre·sas
saucepan *olla* ① o·lya
sauna *sauna* ① sow·na
sausage *salchicha* ① sal·chee·cha
say *decir* de·seer
scale (climb) *trepar* tre·par
scarf *bufanda* ① boo·fan·da
school *escuela* ① es·kwe·la

science *ciencia* ① syen·sya
science fiction *ciencia* ① *ficción*
syen·sya feek·syon
scientist *científico/a* ⑩/①
syen·tee·fee·ko/a
scissors *tijeras* ① pl tee·khe·ras
score *marcar* mar·kar
scoreboard *marcador* ⑩ mar·ka·dor
Scotland *Escocia* ① es·ko·sya
screen *pantalla* ① pan·ta·lya
sea *mar* ⑩ mar
seasickness *mareo* ⑩ ma·re·o
seaside *orilla* ① *del mar* o·ree·lya
del mar
season *estación* ① es·ta·syon
seat *asiento* ⑩ a·syen·to
seatbelt *cinturón* ⑩ *de seguridad*
seen·too·ron de se·goo·ree·da
second *segundo* ⑩ se·goon·do
second *segundo/a* ⑩/① se·goon·do/a
second-hand *de segunda mano* de
se·goon·da ma·no
secretary *secretario/a* ⑩/①
se·kre·ta·ryo/a
see *ver* ver
selfish *egoista* ⑩&① e·go·ees·ta
self-service *autoservicio* ⑩
ow·to·ser·vee·syo
sell *vender* ven·der
send *enviar* en·vyar
sensible *juicioso/a* ⑩/① khwee·syo·so/a
sensual *sensual* sen·swal
separate *separado/a* ⑩/① se·pa·ra·do/a
separate *separar* se·pa·rar
series *serie* ① se·rye
serious *serio/a* ⑩/① se·ryo/a
service charge *servicio* ⑩ ser·vee·syo
service station *gasolinera* ①
ga·so·lee·ne·ra
several *varios/as* ⑩/① va·ryos/as
sew *coser* ko·ser
sex *sexo* ⑩ sek·so
sexism *sexismo* ⑩ sek·sees·mo
sexy *sexy* sek·see
shade *sombra* ① som·bra
shadow *sombra* ① som·bra

shampoo *champú* ⓜ cham·poo
shape *forma* ⓕ for·ma
share (with) *compartir* kom·par·teer
shave *afeitarse* a·fay·tar·se
shaving cream *espuma* ⓕ *de afeitar* es·poo·ma de a·fay·tar
she *ella* e·lya
sheep *oveja* ⓕ o·ve·kha
sheet (bed) *sábana* ⓕ sa·ba·na
ship *barco* ⓜ bar·ko
shirt *camisa* ⓕ ka·mee·sa
shoe shop *zapatería* ⓕ sa·pa·te·ree·a
shoes *zapatos* ⓜ pl sa·pa·tos
shoot *disparar* dees·pa·rar
shop *tienda* ⓕ tyen·da
(go) shopping *ir de compras* eer de kom·pras
shopping centre *centro* ⓜ *comercial* sen·tro ko·mer·syal
short (height) *bajo/a* ⓜ/ⓕ ba·kho/a
short (length) *corto/a* ⓜ/ⓕ kor·to/a
shortage *escasez* ⓕ es·ka·ses
shorts *pantalones* ⓜ *cortos* pan·ta·lo·nes kor·tos
short stories *cuentos* ⓜ pl kwen·tos
shoulders *hombros* ⓜ pl om·bros
shout *gritar* gree·tar
show *espectáculo* ⓜ es·pek·ta·koo·lo
show *mostrar* mos·trar
shower *ducha* ⓕ doo·cha
shrine *capilla* ⓕ ka·pee·lya
shut *cerrado/a* ⓜ/ⓕ se·ra·do/a
shy *tímido/a* ⓜ/ⓕ tee·mee·do/a
sick *enfermo/a* ⓜ/ⓕ en·fer·mo/a
side *lado* ⓜ la·do
sign *señal* ⓕ se·nyal
signature *firma* ⓕ feer·ma
silk *seda* ⓕ se·da
silver *plata* ⓕ pla·ta
SIM card *tarjeta* ⓕ *SIM* tar·khe·ta seem
similar *similar* see·mee·lar
simple *sencillo/a* ⓜ/ⓕ sen·see·lyo/a
since (time) *desde* des·de
sing *cantar* kan·tar
Singapore *Singapur* ⓜ seen·ga·poor
singer *cantante* ⓜ&ⓕ kan·tan·te
single (unmarried) *soltero/a* ⓜ/ⓕ sol·te·ro/a

single room *habitación* ⓕ *individual* a·bee·ta·syon een·dee·vee·dwal
singlet *camiseta* ⓕ ka·mee·se·ta
sister *hermana* ⓕ er·ma·na
sit *sentarse* sen·tar·se
size (clothes) *talla* ⓕ ta·lya
size (general) *tamaño* ta·ma·nyo
skateboarding *monopatinaje* ⓜ mo·no·pa·tee·na·khe
ski *esquiar* es·kyar
skiing *esquí* ⓜ es·kee
ski lift *telesquí* ⓜ te·le·skee
skis *esquís* ⓜ pl es·kees
skimmed milk *leche* ⓕ *desnatada* le·che des·na·ta·da
skin *piel* ⓕ pyel
skirt *falda* ⓕ fal·da
sky *cielo* ⓜ sye·lo
sleep *dormir* dor·meer
sleeping bag *saco* ⓜ *de dormir* sa·ko de dor·meer
sleeping car *coche* ⓜ *cama* ko·che ka·ma
sleeping pills *pastillas* ⓕ pl *para dormir* pas·tee·lyas pa·ra dor·meer
(be) sleepy *tener sueño* te·ner swe·nyo
slide (film) *diapositiva* ⓕ dya·po·see·tee·va
slow *lento/a* ⓜ/ⓕ len·to/a
slowly *despacio* des·pa·syo
small *pequeño/a* ⓜ/ⓕ pe·ke·nyo/a
smell *olor* ⓜ o·lor
smile *sonreír* son·re·eer
smoke *fumar* foo·mar
SMS *SMS* e·se·e·me e·se
snack *tentempié* ⓜ ten·tem·pye
snail *caracol* ⓜ ka·ra·kol
snake *serpiente* ⓕ ser·pyen·te
snorkelling *buceo* ⓜ boo·se·o
snow *nieve* ⓕ nye·ve
snowboarding *surf* ⓜ *sobre la nieve* soorf so·bre la nye·ve
soap *jabón* ⓜ kha·bon
soap opera *telenovela* ⓕ te·le·no·ve·la
soccer *fútbol* ⓜ foot·bol
social welfare *asistencia* ⓕ *social* a·sees·ten·sya so·syal

socialist socialista so·sya·lees·ta
socks calcetines ⓜ pl kal·se·tee·nes
soft drink gaseosa ⓕ ga·se·o·sa
soldier soldado ⓜ sol·da·do
some algún al·goon
someone alguien al·gyen
something algo al·go
sometimes de vez en cuando de ves en kwan·do
son hijo ⓜ ee·kho
song canción ⓕ kan·syon
soon pronto pron·to
sore dolorido/a ⓜ/ⓕ do·lo·ree·do/a
soup sopa ⓕ so·pa
sour cream crema ⓕ agria kre·ma a·grya
south sur ⓜ soor
South America Sudamérica ⓕ soo·da·me·ree·ka
South American sudamericano/a ⓜ/ⓕ soo·da·me·ree·ka·no/a
souvenir recuerdo ⓜ re·kwer·do
souvenir shop tienda ⓕ de recuerdos tyen·da de re·kwer·dos
soy milk leche ⓕ de soya le·che de so·ya
soy sauce salsa ⓕ de soya sal·sa de so·ya
space espacio ⓜ es·pa·syo
spade pala ⓕ pa·la
Spain España ⓕ es·pa·nya
speak hablar a·blar
special especial es·pe·syal
specialist especialista ⓜ&ⓕ es·pe·sya·lees·ta
speed velocidad ⓕ ve·lo·see·da
speed limit límite ⓜ de velocidad lee·mee·te de ve·lo·see·da
speedometer velocímetro ⓜ ve·lo·see·me·tro
spermicide espermicida ⓕ es·per·mee·see·da
spider araña ⓕ a·ra·nya
spinach espinacas ⓕ pl es·pee·na·kas
spoon cuchara ⓕ koo·cha·ra
sport deportes ⓜ pl de·por·tes

sports store tienda ⓕ deportiva tyen·da de·por·tee·va
sportsperson deportista ⓜ&ⓕ de·por·tees·ta
sprain torcedura ⓕ tor·se·doo·ra
spring (mechanical) muelle ⓜ mwe·lye
spring (season) primavera ⓕ pree·ma·ve·ra
square (shape) cuadrado ⓜ kwa·dra·do
square (town) plaza ⓕ pla·sa
stadium estadio ⓜ es·ta·dyo
stage escenario ⓜ e·se·na·ryo
stairway escalera ⓕ es·ka·le·ra
stamp sello ⓜ se·lyo
standby ticket boleto ⓜ de lista de espera bo·le·to de lees·ta de es·pe·ra
stars estrellas ⓕ pl es·tre·lyas
start comenzar ko·men·sar
station estación ⓕ es·ta·syon
statue estatua ⓕ es·ta·twa
stay (at a hotel) alojarse a·lo·khar·se
stay (remain) quedarse ke·dar·se
STD (sexually transmitted disease) enfermedad ⓕ de transmisión sexual en·fer·me·da de trans·mee·syon sek·swal
steak (beef) bistec ⓜ bees·tek
steal robar ro·bar
steep escarpado/a ⓜ/ⓕ es·kar·pa·do/a
step paso ⓜ pa·so
stereo equipo ⓜ estereofónico e·kee·po es·te·re·o·fo·nee·ko
stingy tacaño/a ⓜ/ⓕ ta·ka·nyo/a
stockings medias ⓕ pl me·dyas
stomach estómago ⓜ es·to·ma·go
stomachache dolor ⓜ de estómago do·lor de es·to·ma·go
stone piedra ⓕ pye·dra
stoned (drugged) volado/a ⓜ/ⓕ vo·la·do/a
stop parada ⓕ pa·ra·da
stop parar pa·rar
storm tormenta ⓕ tor·men·ta
story cuento ⓜ kwen·to
stove estufa ⓕ es·too·fa
straight recto/a ⓜ/ⓕ rek·to/a

strange *extraño/a* ⓜ/ⓕ ek·*stra*·nyo/a
stranger *extraño/a* ⓜ/ⓕ ek·*stra*·nyo/a
strawberry *frutilla* ⓕ froo·*tee*·lya
stream *arroyo* ⓜ a·*ro*·yo
street *calle* ⓕ *ka*·lye
street market *feria* ⓕ *fe*·rya
string *cuerda* ⓕ *kwer*·da
strong *fuerte* *fwer*·te
stubborn *testarudo/a* ⓜ/ⓕ tes·ta·*roo*·do/a
student *estudiante* ⓜ&ⓕ es·too·*dyan*·te
studio *estudio* ⓜ es·*too*·dyo
stupid *estúpido/a* ⓜ/ⓕ es·*too*·pee·do/a
style *estilo* ⓜ es·*tee*·lo
subtitles *subtítulos* ⓜ pl soob·*tee*·too·los
suburb *barrio* ⓜ *ba*·ryo
subway *subterráneo* soob·te·*ra*·ne·o
sugar *azúcar* ⓜ a·*soo*·kar
sugar cane *caña* ⓕ *de azúcar ka*·nya de a·*soo*·kar
suit *traje* ⓜ *tra*·khe
suitcase *maleta* ⓕ ma·*le*·ta
summer *verano* ⓜ ve·*ra*·no
sun *sol* ⓜ sol
sunblock *crema* ⓕ *solar kre*·ma so·*lar*
sunburn *quemadura* ⓕ *de sol* ke·ma·*doo*·ra de sol
sunglasses *anteojos* ⓕ pl *de sol* an·te·o·khos de sol
sunny *soleado/a* ⓜ/ⓕ so·le·*a*·do/a
sunrise *amanecer* ⓜ a·ma·ne·*ser*
sunset *puesta* ⓕ *del sol pwes*·ta del sol
sunstroke *insolación* ⓕ een·so·la·*syon*
supermarket *supermercado* ⓜ soo·per·mer·*ka*·do
superstition *superstición* ⓕ soo·per·stee·*syon*
supporters *hinchas* ⓜ&ⓕ pl *een*·chas
surf *hacer surf* a·ser soorf
surface mail *por vía terrestre* por *vee*·a te·*res*·tre
surf *hacer surfing* ⓜ a·ser *soorf*·een
surfboard *tabla* ⓕ *de surf ta*·bla de soorf
surname *apellido* ⓜ a·pe·*lyee*·do
surprise *sorpresa* ⓕ sor·*pre*·sa
sweater (jumper) *jersey* ⓜ kher·say

sweet *dulce dool*·se
swim *nadar* na·*dar*
swimming pool *piscina* ⓕ pee·*see*·na
swimsuit *traje* ⓜ *de baño tra*·khe de *ba*·nyo
synagogue *sinagoga* ⓕ see·na·*go*·ga
synthetic *sintético/a* ⓜ/ⓕ seen·*te*·tee·ko/a
syringe *jeringa* ⓕ khe·*reen*·ga

T

table *mesa* ⓕ *me*·sa
table tennis *ping pong* ⓜ peen pon
tablecloth *mantel* ⓜ man·*tel*
tail *rabo* ⓜ *ra*·bo
tailor *sastre* ⓜ *sas*·tre
take *tomar* to·*mar*
talk *hablar* a·*blar*
tall *alto/a* ⓜ/ⓕ *al*·to/a
tampons *tampones* ⓜ pl tam·*po*·nes
tanning lotion *bronceador* ⓜ bron·se·a·*dor*
tap (faucet) *grifo* ⓜ *gree*·fo
tapir *danta* ⓕ *dan*·ta
tasty *sabroso/a* ⓜ/ⓕ sa·*bro*·so/a
tax *impuesto* ⓜ eem·*pwes*·to
taxi *taxi* ⓜ *tak*·see
taxi stand *parada* ⓕ *de taxis* pa·*ra*·da de *tak*·sees
tea *té* ⓜ te
teacher *profesor/profesora* ⓜ/ⓕ pro·fe·*sor*/pro·fe·*so*·ra
team *equipo* ⓜ e·*kee*·po
teaspoon *cucharita* ⓕ koo·cha·*ree*·ta
teeth *dientes* ⓜ pl *dyen*·tes
telegram *telegrama* ⓜ te·le·*gra*·ma
telephone *teléfono* ⓜ te·*le*·fo·no
telephone *llamar (por teléfono)* lya·*mar* (por te·*le*·fo·no)
telephone centre *central* ⓕ *telefónica* sen·*tral* te·le·fo·*nee*·ka
telephoto lens *teleobjetivo* ⓜ te·le·ob·khe·*tee*·vo
television *televisión* ⓕ te·le·vee·*syon*
tell *decir* de·*seer*
temperature (fever) *fiebre* ⓕ *fye*·bre

temperature (weather) *temperatura* ①
tem·pe·ra·*too*·ra

temple *templo* ⓜ *tem*·plo

tennis *tenis* ⓜ *te*·nees

tennis court *cancha* ① *de tenis*
kan·cha de te·nees

tent *carpa* ① *kar*·pa

tent pegs *estacas* ① *de carpa* es·*ta*·kas
de *kar*·pa

terrible *terrible* te·*ree*·ble

test *prueba* ① *prwe*·ba

testimonial literature *literatura* ①
testimonial lee·te·ra·*too*·ra
tes·tee·mo·*nyal*

thank *dar gracias* dar *gra*·syas

the Pill *píldora* ① *peel*·do·ra

theatre *teatro* ⓜ te·*a*·tro

their *su* soo

they *ellos/ellas* ⓜ/① pl e·lyos/e·lyas

thief *ladrón/ladrona* ⓜ/①
la·*dron*/la·*dro*·na

thin *delgado/a* ⓜ/① del·*ga*·do/a

think *pensar* pen·*sar*

third *tercio* ⓜ *ter*·syo

thirst *sed* ① se

(be) thirsty *tener sed* te·*ner* se

this *éste/a* ⓜ/① *es*·te/a

throat *garganta* ① gar·*gan*·ta

thrush (medical) *aftas* ⓜ pl *af*·tas

ticket *boleto* ⓜ bo·*le*·to

ticket collector *revisor/revisora* ⓜ/①
re·vee·*sor*/re·vee·*so*·ra

ticket machine *máquina* ① *de boletos*
ma·kee·na de bo·*le*·tos

ticket office (theatre, cinema)
taquilla ① ta·*kee*·lya

ticket office (general) *boletería* ①
bo·le·te·*ree*·a

tide *marea* ① ma·*re*·a

tight *apretado/a* ⓜ/① a·pre·*ta*·do/a

time (hour) *hora* ① *o*·ra

time (period) *tiempo* ⓜ *tyem*·po

time difference *diferencia* ① *de horas*
dee·fe·*ren*·sya de *o*·ras

timetable *horario* ⓜ o·*ra*·ryo

tin (can) *lata* ① *la*·ta

tin opener *abrelatas* ⓜ a·bre·*la*·tas

tiny *pequeñito/a* ⓜ/① pe·ke·*nyee*·to/a

tip (gratuity) *propina* ① pro·*pee*·na

tired *cansado/a* ⓜ/① kan·*sa*·do/a

tissues *pañuelos* ⓜ pl *de papel*
pa·*nywe*·los de pa·*pel*

toast *tostada* ① tos·*ta*·da

toaster *tostadora* ① tos·ta·*do*·ra

tobacco *tabaco* ⓜ ta·*ba*·ko

tobacconist *estanquero* ⓜ es·tan·*ke*·ro

tobogganing *ir en tobogán* eer en
to·bo·*gan*

today *hoy* oy

toe *dedo* ⓜ *del pie* *de*·do del pye

tofu *tofú* ⓜ to·*foo*

together *juntos/as* ⓜ/① pl
khoon·tos/as

toilet *baño* ⓜ • *servicio* ⓜ
ba·nyo • ser·*vee*·syo

toilet paper *papel* ⓜ *higiénico* pa·*pel*
ee·*khye*·nee·ko

tomato *tomate* ⓜ to·*ma*·te

tomato sauce *salsa* ① *de tomate*
sal·sa de to·*ma*·te

tomorrow *mañana* ① ma·*nya*·na

tonight *esta noche* *es*·ta *no*·che

too (expensive) *demasiado (caro/a)*
ⓜ/① de·ma·*sya*·do (*ka*·ro/a)

tooth (back) *muela* ① *mwe*·la

toothache *dolor* ⓜ *de muelas* do·*lor*
de *mwe*·las

toothbrush *cepillo* ⓜ *de dientes*
se·*pee*·lyo de *dyen*·tes

toothpaste *pasta* ① *dentífrica* *pas*·ta
den·*tee*·free·ka

toothpick *palillo* ⓜ pa·*lee*·lyo

torch (flashlight) *linterna* ①
leen·*ter*·na

touch *tocar* to·*kar*

tour *excursión* ① ek·skoor·*syon*

tourist *turista* ⓜ&① too·*rees*·ta

tourist office *oficina* ① *de turismo*
o·fee·*see*·na de too·*rees*·mo

towards *hacia* *a*·sya

towel *toalla* ① to·*a*·lya

tower *torre* ① *to*·re

toxic waste *residuos* ⓜ pl *tóxicos*
re·*see*·dwos *tok*·see·kos

toy shop *juguetería* ① khoo·ge·te·*ree*·a
track (path) *camino* ⓜ ka·*mee*·no
track (sports) *pista* ① *pees*·ta
trade *comercio* ⓜ ko·*mer*·syo
traffic *tráfico* ⓜ *tra*·fee·ko
traffic lights *semáforos* ⓜ pl se·*ma*·fo·ros
trail *camino* ⓜ ka·*mee*·no
train *tren* ⓜ tren
train station *estación* ① *de tren* es·ta·*syon* de tren
tram *tranvía* ⓜ tran·*vee*·a
transit lounge *sala* ① *de tránsito* *sa*·la de *tran*·see·to
translate *traducir* tra·doo·*seer*
transport *transporte* ⓜ trans·*por*·te
travel *viajar* vya·*khar*
travel agency *agencia* ① *de viajes* a·*khen*·sya de *vya*·khes
travel books *libros* ⓜ pl *de viajes* *lee*·bros de *vya*·khes
travel sickness *mareo* ⓜ ma·*re*·o
travellers cheque *cheque* ⓜ *de viajero* *che*·ke de vya·*khe*·ro
tree *árbol* ⓜ *ar*·bol
trip *viaje* ⓜ *vya*·khe
trousers *pantalones* ⓜ pl pan·ta·*lo*·nes
truck *camión* ⓜ ka·*myon*
trust *confianza* ① kon·*fyan*·sa
trust *confiar* kon·*fyar*
try (attempt) *probar* pro·*bar*
T-shirt *camiseta* ① ka·mee·*se*·ta
tube (tyre) *cámara* ① *de aire* *ka*·ma·ra de *ai*·re
tuna *atún* ⓜ a·*toon*
tune *melodía* ① me·lo·*dee*·a
turkey *pavo* ⓜ *pa*·vo
turn *doblar* do·*blar*
TV *tele* ① *te*·le
tweezers *pinzas* ① pl *peen*·sas
twice *dos veces* dos *ve*·ses
twin beds *dos camas* ① pl dos *ka*·mas
twins *gemelos/as* ⓜ/① pl khe·*me*·los/as
type *tipo* ⓜ *tee*·po
typical *típico/a* ⓜ/① *tee*·pee·ko/a
tyre *llanta* ① *lyan*·ta

ultrasound *ecografía* ① e·ko·gra·*fee*·a
umbrella *paraguas* ① pa·ra·gwas
umpire *árbitro/a* ⓜ/① *ar*·bee·tro/a
uncle *tío* ⓜ *tee*·o
uncomfortable *incómodo/a* ⓜ/① een·*ko*·mo·do/a
underpants (men) *calzoncillos* ⓜ pl kal·son·*see*·lyos
underpants (women) *bragas* ① pl *bra*·gas
understand *entender* en·ten·*der*
underwater camera *cámara* ① *submarina* *ka*·ma·ra soob·ma·*ree*·na
underwear *ropa* ① *interior* *ro*·pa een·te·*ryor*
unemployed *desempleado/a* ⓜ/① des·em·*ple*·a·do/a
unfair *injusto/a* ⓜ/① een·*khoos*·to/a
uniform *uniforme* ⓜ oo·nee·*for*·me
universe *universo* ⓜ oo·nee·*ver*·so
university *universidad* ① oo·nee·ver·see·*da*
unleaded *sin plomo* seen *plo*·mo
unsafe *inseguro/a* ⓜ/① een·se·*goo*·ro/a
until *hasta* *as*·ta
unusual *extraño/a* ⓜ/① ek·*stra*·nyo/a
up *arriba* a·*ree*·ba
uphill *cuesta arriba* kwes·ta a·*ree*·ba
urgent *urgente* oor·*khen*·te
Uruguay *Uruguay* ⓜ oo·roo·*gway*
USA *Los Estados* ⓜ pl *Unidos* los es·*ta*·dos oo·*nee*·dos
useful *útil* oo·*teel*

vacant *vacante* va·*kan*·te
vacation *vacaciones* ① pl va·ka·*syo*·nes
vaccination *vacuna* ① va·*koo*·na
vagina *vagina* ① va·*khee*·na
vaginal discharge *flujo* ⓜ *vaginal* *floo*·kho va·khee·*nal*
validate *validar* va·lee·*dar*
valley *valle* ⓜ *va*·lye
valuable *valioso/a* ⓜ/① va·*lyo*·so/a

value *valor* ⓜ va·lor
van *caravana* ⓕ ka·ra·va·na
veal *ternera* ⓕ ter·ne·ra
vegan *vegetariano/a estricto/a* ⓜ/ⓕ ve·khe·ta·rya·no/a es·treek·to/a
vegetable *verdura* ⓕ ver·doo·ra
vegetable garden *huerta* ⓕ wer·ta
vegetarian *vegetariano/a* ⓜ/ⓕ ve·khe·ta·rya·no/a
vein *vena* ⓕ ve·na
venereal disease *enfermedad* ⓕ *venérea* en·fer·me·da ve·ne·re·a
Venezuela *Venezuela* ⓕ ve·ne·swe·la
venue *local* ⓜ lo·kal
very *muy* mooy
video *vídeo* ⓜ vee·de·o
video tape *cinta* ⓕ *de vídeo* seen·ta de vee·de·o
view *vista* ⓕ vees·ta
village *pueblo* ⓜ pwe·blo
vinegar *vinagre* ⓜ vee·na·gre
vineyard *viñedo* ⓜ vee·nye·do
virus *virus* ⓜ vee·roos
visa *visado* ⓜ vee·sa·do
visit *visitar* vee·see·tar
vitamins *vitaminas* ⓕ pl vee·ta·mee·nas
voice *voz* ⓕ vos
volleyball *vóleibol* ⓜ vo·lay·bol
vote *votar* vo·tar
vulture *buitre* ⓜ bwee·tre

W

wage *sueldo* ⓜ swel·do
wait *esperar* es·pe·rar
waiter *camarero/a* ⓜ/ⓕ ka·ma·re·ro/a
waiting room *sala* ⓕ *de espera* sa·la de es·pe·ra
wake up *despertarse* des·per·tar·se
walk *caminar* ka·mee·nar
wall (inside) *pared* ⓕ pa·re
wallet *cartera* ⓕ kar·te·ra
want *querer* ke·rer
WAP *WAP* ⓜ gwap
WAP-enabled *capacidad* ⓕ *de WAP* ka·pa·see·da de gwap
war *guerra* ⓕ ge·ra

wardrobe *vestuario* ⓜ ves·twa·ryo
warm *templado/a* ⓜ/ⓕ tem·pla·do/a
warn *advertir* ad·ver·teer
wash (oneself) *lavarse* la·var·se
wash (something) *lavar* la·var
wash cloth (flannel) *toallita* ⓕ to·a·lyee·ta
washing machine *lavadora* ⓕ la·va·do·ra
watch *reloj* ⓜ *de pulsera* re·lokh de pool·se·ra
watch *mirar* mee·rar
water *agua* ⓕ a·gwa
  boiled water *agua* ⓕ *hervida* a·gwa er·vee·da
  still water *agua* ⓕ *sin gas* a·gwa seen gas
  tap water *agua* ⓕ *del grifo* a·gwa del gree·fo
water bottle *cantimplora* ⓕ kan·teem·plo·ra
waterfall *cascada* ⓕ kas·ka·da
watermelon *sandía* ⓕ san·dee·a
waterproof *impermeable* eem·per·me·a·ble
waterskiing *esquí* ⓜ *acuático* es·kee a·kwa·tee·ko
water skis *esquís* ⓜ pl *acuáticos* es·kees a·kwa·tee·kos
wave *ola* ⓕ o·la
way *camino* ⓜ ka·mee·no
we *nosotros/as* ⓜ/ⓕ no·so·tros/as
weak *débil* de·beel
wealthy *rico/a* ⓜ/ⓕ ree·ko/a
wear *llevar* lye·var
weather *tiempo* ⓜ tyem·po
wedding *boda* ⓕ bo·da
wedding cake *tarta* ⓕ *nupcial* tar·ta noop·syal
wedding present *regalo* ⓜ *de bodas* re·ga·lo de bo·das
week *semana* ⓕ se·ma·na
weekend *fin* ⓜ *de semana* feen de se·ma·na
weight *peso* ⓜ pe·so
welcome *dar la bienvenida* dar la byen·ve·nee·da
welfare *bienestar* ⓜ byen·es·tar

well *bien* byen
well (water) *pozo* ⓜ po·so
west *oeste* ⓜ o·es·te
wet *mojado/a* ⓜ/ⓕ mo·kha·do/a
what *que* ke
wheel *rueda* ⓕ rwe·da
wheelchair *silla* ⓕ *de ruedas* see·lya de rwe·das
when *cuando* kwan·do
where *donde* don·de
white *blanco/a* ⓜ/ⓕ blan·ko/a
whiteboard *pizarra* ⓕ *blanca* pee·sa·ra blan·ka
who *quien* kyen
why *por qué* por ke
wide *ancho/a* ⓜ/ⓕ an·cho/a
widow *viuda* ⓕ vyoo·da
widower *viudo* ⓜ vyoo·do
wife *esposa* ⓕ es·po·sa
win *ganar* ga·nar
wind *viento* ⓜ vyen·to
window *ventana* ⓕ ven·ta·na
window-shopping *mirar escaparates* mee·rar es·ka·pa·ra·tes
windscreen *parabrisas* ⓜ pa·ra·bree·sas
windsurfing *hacer windsurfing* a·ser gween·soorf·een
wine *vino* ⓜ vee·no
  red wine *vino* ⓜ *tinto* vee·no teen·to
  sparkling wine *vino* ⓜ *espumoso* vee·no es·poo·mo·so
  white wine *vino* ⓜ *blanco* vee·no blan·ko
winery *bodega* ⓕ bo·de·ga
wings *alas* ⓕ pl a·las
winner *ganador/ganadora* ⓜ/ⓕ ga·na·dor/ga·na·do·ra
winter *invierno* ⓜ een·vyer·no
wire *alambre* ⓜ a·lam·bre
wish *desear* de·se·ar
with *con* kon
within (an hour) *dentro de (una hora)* den·tro de (oo·na o·ra)
without *sin* seen
woman *mujer* ⓕ moo·kher
wonderful *maravilloso/a* ⓜ/ⓕ ma·ra·vee·lyo·so/a
wood *madera* ⓕ ma·de·ra

wool *lana* ⓕ la·na
word *palabra* pa·la·bra
work (occupation) *trabajo* ⓜ tra·ba·kho
work (of art) *obra* ⓕ o·bra
work *trabajar* tra·ba·khar
work experience *experiencia* ⓕ *laboral* ek·spe·ryen·sya la·bo·ral
work permit *permiso* ⓜ *de trabajo* per·mee·so de tra·ba·kho
workout *entreno* ⓜ en·tre·no
workshop *taller* ⓜ ta·lyer
world *mundo* ⓜ moon·do
World Cup *La Copa* ⓕ *Mundial* la ko·pa moon·dyal
worried *preocupado/a* ⓜ/ⓕ pre·o·koo·pa·do/a
worship (pray) *rezar* re·sar
wrist *muñeca* ⓕ moo·nye·ka
write *escribir* es·kree·beer
writer *escritor/escritora* ⓜ/ⓕ es·kree·tor/es·kree·to·ra
wrong *equivocado/a* ⓜ/ⓕ e·kee·vo·ka·do/a

Y

(this) year *(este) año (es·te)* a·nyo

yellow *amarillo/a* ⓜ/ⓕ a·ma·ree·lyo/a
yellow fever *fiebre* ⓕ *amarilla* fye·bre a·ma·ree·lya
yes *sí* see
(not) yet *todavía (no)* to·da·vee·a (no)
yesterday *ayer* a·yer
yoga *yoga* ⓜ yo·ga
yogurt *yogur* ⓜ yo·goor
you sg inf *tú* too
you sg pol *usted* oos·te
you pl inf&pol *ustedes* oos·te·des
young *joven* kho·ven
youth hostel *albergue* ⓜ *juvenil* al·ber·ge khoo·ve·neel

Z

zodiac *zodíaco* ⓜ so·dee·a·ko
zoo *zoológico* ⓜ so·o·lo·khee·ko
zoom lens *zoom* ⓜ soom

A

Nouns in the dictionary have their gender indicated by ⓜ or ⓕ. If it's a plural noun, you'll also see pl. When a word that could be either a noun or a verb has no gender indicated, it's a verb.

A

a bordo a *bor*·do *aboard*
a larga distancia a *lar*·ga dees·*tan*·sya *long-distance*
a menudo a me·*noo*·do *often*
a tiempo a *tyem*·po *on time*
a través a tra·*ves across*
abajo a·*ba*·kho *below*
abarrotado/a ⓜ/ⓕ a·ba·ro·*ta*·do/a *crowded*
abeja ⓕ a·*be*·kha *bee*
abierto/a ⓜ/ⓕ a·*byer*·to/a *open*
abogado/a ⓜ/ⓕ a·bo·*ga*·do/a *lawyer*
aborto ⓜ a·*bor*·to *abortion*
— **natural** na·too·*ral miscarriage*
abrazo ⓜ a·*bra*·so *hug*
abrebotellas ⓜ a·bre·bo·*te*·lyas *bottle opener*
abrelatas ⓜ a·bre·*la*·tas *can opener* • *tin opener*
abrigo ⓜ a·*bree*·go *overcoat*
abrir a·*breer open*
abuela ⓕ a·*bwe*·la *grandmother*
abuelo ⓜ a·*bwe*·lo *grandfather*
aburrido/a ⓜ/ⓕ a·boo·*ree*·do/a *boring*
acabar a·ka·*bar end*
acampar a·*kam*·par *camp*
acantilado ⓜ a·kan·tee·*la*·do *cliff*
accidente ⓜ ak·see·*den*·te *accident*
aceite ⓜ a·*say*·te *oil*
— **de oliva** de o·*lee*·va *olive oil*
aceituna ⓕ a·say·*too*·na *olive*
aceptar a·sep·*tar accept*

acera ⓕ a·*se*·ra *footpath*
acondicionador ⓜ a·kon·dee·syo·na·*dor conditioner*
aconsejar a·kon·se·*khar advise*
acoso ⓜ a·*ko*·so *harassment*
activista ⓜ&ⓕ ak·tee·*vees*·ta *activist*
actuación ⓕ ak·twa·*syon gig* • *performance*
acupuntura ⓕ a·koo·poon·*too*·ra *acupuncture*
adaptador ⓜ a·dap·ta·*dor adaptor*
addicto/a ⓜ/ⓕ a·*deek*·to/a *addicted*
adentro a·*den*·tro *inside*
adivinar a·dee·vee·*nar guess*
administración ⓕ ad·mee·nees·tra·*syon administration*
admitir ad·mee·*teer admit* • *accept* • *acknowledge*
aduana ⓕ a·*dwa*·na *customs*
adulto/a ⓜ/ⓕ a·*dool*·to/a *adult*
advertir ad·ver·*teer warn*
aeróbic ⓜ a·e·*ro*·beek *aerobics*
aerolínea ⓕ a·e·ro·*lee*·ne·a *airline*
aeropuerto ⓜ a·e·ro·*pwer*·to *airport*
afeitadora ⓕ a·fay·ta·*do*·ra *razor*
afeitarse a·fay·*tar*·se *shave*
afortunado/a ⓜ/ⓕ a·for·too·*na*·do/a *lucky*
África ⓕ *a*·free·ka *Africa*
agencia ⓕ a·*khen*·sya **de viajes** de *vya*·khes *travel agency*
agenda ⓕ a·*khen*·da *diary*
agente ⓜ **inmobiliario** a·*khen*·te een·mo·bee·*lya*·ryo *real estate agent*
agresivo/a ⓜ/ⓕ a·gre·*see*·vo/a *aggressive*

agricultor(a) ⓜ/ⓕ a·gree·kool·tor/ a·gree·kool·to·ra *farmer*

agricultura ⓕ a·gree·kool·too·ra *agriculture*

agua ⓕ a·gwa *water*
— **caliente** ka·lyen·te *hot water*
— **del grifo** del gree·fo *tap water*
— **hervida** er·vee·da *boiled water*
— **mineral** mee·ne·ral *mineral water*
— **sin gas** seen gas *still water*

aguja ⓕ a·goo·kha *needle (sewing)*

ahora a·o·ra *now*

aire ⓜ ai·re *air*
— **acondicionado** a·kon·dee·syo·na·do *air-conditioning*

ajedrez ⓜ a·khe·dres *chess*

ají ⓜ a·khee *chilli*

ajo ⓜ a·kho *garlic*

al fondo de al fon·do de *at the bottom*

al lado de al la·do de *next to*

alambre ⓜ a·lam·bre *wire*

alas ⓜ pl a·las *wings*

albergue ⓜ **juvenil** al·ber·ge khoo·ve·neel *youth hostel*

alcalde ⓜ&ⓕ al·kal·de *mayor*

alcohol ⓜ al·kol *alcohol*

Alemania a·le·ma·nya *Germany*

alergia ⓕ a·ler·khya *allergy*

alfarería ⓕ al·fa·re·ree·a *pottery*

alfombra ⓕ al·fom·bra *rug*

algo al·go *something*

algodón ⓜ al·go·don *cotton*

alguien al·gyen *someone*

algún al·goon *some*

alguno/a ⓜ/ⓕ sg al·goo·no/a *any (singular)*

algunos/as ⓜ/ⓕ pl al·goo·nos/as *any (plural)*

almacén ⓜ al·ma·sen *general store*

almendra ⓕ al·men·dra *almond*

almohada ⓕ al·mo·a·da *pillow*

almuerzo ⓜ al·mwer·so *lunch*

alojamiento ⓜ a·lo·kha·myen·to *accommodation*

alojarse a·lo·khar·se *stay (at a hotel)*

alpinismo ⓜ al·pee·nees·mo *mountaineering*

alquilar al·kee·lar *hire • rent*
— **un carro** oon ka·ro *hire a car*

alquiler ⓜ al·kee·ler *hire • rental*

altar ⓜ al·tar *altar*

alto/a ⓜ/ⓕ al·to/a *high • tall*

altura ⓕ al·too·ra *altitude*

alucinar a·loo·see·nar *hallucinate*

ama ⓕ **de casa** a·ma de ka·sa *homemaker*

amable a·ma·ble *kind*

amanecer ⓜ a·ma·ne·ser *sunrise*

amante ⓜ&ⓕ a·man·te *lover*

amarillo/a ⓜ/ⓕ a·ma·ree·lyo/a *yellow*

amateur ⓜ&ⓕ a·ma·toor *amateur*

ambulancia ⓕ am·boo·lan·sya *ambulance*

América ⓕ a·me·ree·ka *America*

amigo/a ⓜ/ⓕ a·mee·go/a *friend*

ampolla ⓕ am·po·lya *blister*

analgésicos ⓜ pl a·nal·khe·see·kos *painkillers*

análisis ⓜ **de sangre** a·na·lee·sees de san·gre *blood test*

ananas ⓜ a·na·nas *pineapple*

anaranjado/a ⓜ/ⓕ a·na·ran·kha·do/a *orange (colour)*

anarquista ⓜ&ⓕ a·nar·kees·ta *anarchist*

ancho/a ⓜ/ⓕ an·cho/a *wide*

andar an·dar *walk*
— **en bicicleta** en bee·see·kle·ta *cycle*

anillo ⓜ a·nee·lyo *ring (on finger)*

animal ⓜ a·nee·mal *animal*

año a·nyo *year*

Año Nuevo ⓜ a·nyo nwe·vo *New Year*

anteayer an·te·a·yer *day before yesterday*

anteojos ⓜ pl an·te·o·khos *glasses • goggles*
— **de sol** de sol *sunglasses*

antes an·tes *before*

antibióticos ⓜ pl an·tee·byo·tee·kos *antibiotics*

anticonceptivo ⓜ an·tee·kon·sep·tee·vo *contraceptive*

antigüedad ⓕ an·tee·gwe·da *antique*

antiguo/a ⓜ/ⓕ an·*tee*·gwo/a *ancient*

antihistamínicos ⓜ pl an·tee·ees·ta·*mee*·nee·kos *antihistamines*

antinuclear an·tee·noo·kle·*ar* *antinuclear*

antiséptico ⓜ an·tee·*sep*·tee·ko *antiseptic*

anuncio ⓜ a·*noon*·syo *advertisement*

apellido ⓜ a·pe·*lyee*·do *family name • surname*

apéndice ⓜ a·*pen*·dee·se *appendix*

apodo ⓜ a·*po*·do *nickname*

aprender a·pren·*der* *learn*

apretado/a ⓜ/ⓕ a·pre·*ta*·do/a *tight*

apuesta ⓕ a·*pwes*·ta *bet*

apuntar a·poon·*tar* *point*

aquí a·*kee* *here*

araña ⓕ a·*ra*·nya *spider*

árbitro ⓜ ar·bee·tro *referee*

árbol ⓜ ar·bol *tree*

arena ⓕ a·*re*·na *sand*

arenque a·*ren*·ke *herring*

aretes ⓜ pl a·*re*·tes *earrings*

Argentina ⓕ ar·khen·*tee*·na *Argentina*

armadillo ⓜ ar·ma·*dee*·lyo *armadillo*

armario ⓜ ar·*ma*·ryo *cupboard*

arqueológico/a ⓜ/ⓕ ar·ke·o·*lo*·khee·ko/a *archaeological*

arquitecto/a ⓜ/ⓕ ar·kee·*tek*·to/a *architect*

arquitectura ⓕ ar·kee·*tek*·too·ra *architecture*

arrendar a·ren·*dar* *hire • rent*

arriba a·*ree*·ba *above • up*

arroyo ⓜ a·*ro*·yo *stream*

arroz ⓜ a·*ros* *rice*

arte ⓜ ar·te *art*

artes ⓜ pl **marciales** ar·tes *mar*·sya·les *martial arts*

artesanía ⓕ ar·te·sa·*nee*·a *craft • handicraft*

artista ⓜ&ⓕ ar·*tees*·ta *artist*

— **callejero/a** ⓜ/ⓕ ka·lye·*khe*·ro/a *busker*

arveja ⓕ ar·*ve*·kha *pea*

ascensor ⓜ a·sen·*sor* *elevator • lift*

Asia a·sya *Asia*

asiento ⓜ a·*syen*·to *seat*

— **de seguridad para bebés** de se·goo·ree·*da* para be·*bes* *child's car seat*

asistencia ⓕ **social** a·sees·*ten*·sya so·*syal* *social welfare*

asma ⓜ as·ma *asthma*

aspirina ⓕ as·pee·*ree*·na *aspirin*

atascado/a ⓜ/ⓕ a·tas·*ka*·do/a *blocked*

atletismo ⓜ at·le·*tees*·mo *athletics*

atmósfera ⓕ at·*mos*·fe·ra *atmosphere*

atún ⓜ a·*toon* *tuna*

audífono ⓜ ow·*dee*·fo·no *hearing aid*

Australia ⓕ ows·*tra*·lya *Australia*

auto ⓜ ow·to *car*

autobús ⓜ ow·to·*boos* *bus (city)*

automatico/a ⓜ/ⓕ ow·to·*ma*·tee·ko/a *automatic*

autopista ⓕ ow·to·*pees*·ta *motorway*

autoservicio ⓜ ow·to·ser·*vee*·syo *self-service*

avena ⓕ a·*ve*·na *oats*

avenida ⓕ a·ve·*nee*·da *avenue*

avergonzado/a ⓜ/ⓕ a·ver·gon·*sa*·do/a *embarrassed*

averiado/a ⓜ/ⓕ a·ve·*rya*·do/a *broken down (machine)*

avión ⓜ a·*vyon* *plane*

ayer a·*yer* *yesterday*

ayudar a·yoo·*dar* *help*

azúcar ⓜ a·*soo*·kar *sugar*

azul a·*sool* *blue*

B

babysitter ⓜ&ⓕ be·bee·*see*·ter *babysitter*

baila ⓕ *bai*·la *dance*

bailar bai·*lar* *dance*

bajo/a ⓜ/ⓕ *ba*·kho/a *low • short (height)*

balcón ⓜ bal·*kon* *balcony*

balde ⓜ *bal*·de *bucket*

ballet ⓜ ba·*le* *ballet*

bálsamo ⓜ **de labios** *bal*·sa·mo de *la*·byos *lip balm*

banco ⓜ ban·ko *bank (money)*

bandera ⓕ ban·*de*·ra *flag*

baño ⓜ ba·nye·ra *bath • bathroom • toilet*

baños ⓜ pl *ba*·nyos *toilets*

bar ⓜ bar *bar*

barato/a ⓜ/ⓕ ba·ra·to/a *cheap*

barbero ⓜ bar·be·ro *barber*

barco ⓜ bar·ko *boat • ship*
— **de vela** de ve·la *sailing boat*

barrio ⓜ ba·ryo *suburb*

basquetbol ⓜ bas·ket·bol *basketball*

basura ⓕ ba·soo·ra *rubbish*

batería ⓕ ba·te·ree·a *battery (car) • drums*

bautizo ⓜ bow·tee·so *baptism*

bebé ⓜ&ⓕ be·be *baby*

béisbol ⓜ bays·bol *baseball*

Belice ⓕ be·lee·se *Belize*

bello/a ⓜ/ⓕ be·lyo/a *beautiful*

beneficio ⓜ be·ne·fee·syo *profit*

berenjena ⓕ be·ren·khe·na *aubergine • eggplant*

besar be·sar *kiss*

beso ⓜ be·so *kiss*

biblia ⓕ bee·blya *bible*

biblioteca ⓕ bee·blyo·te·ka *library*

bicho ⓜ bee·cho *bug*

bici ⓕ bee·see *bike*

bicicleta ⓕ bee·see·kle·ta *bicycle*
— **de carreras** de ka·re·ras *racing bike*
— **de montaña** de mon·ta·nya *mountain bike*

bien byen *well*

bienestar ⓜ byen·es·tar *welfare*

billar ⓜ bee·lyar *pool (game)*

billetes ⓜ pl **de banco** bee·lye·tes de ban·ko *banknotes*

biodegradable byo·de·gra·da·ble *biodegradable*

biografía ⓕ byo·gra·fya *biography*

birome ⓕ bee·ro·me *ballpoint pen (Arg)*

bistec ⓜ bees·tek *steak (beef)*

blanco y negro blan·ko ee ne·gro *B&W (film)*

blanco/a ⓜ/ⓕ blan·ko/a *white*

bluejeans ⓜ pl bloo·jeens *jeans*

boca ⓕ bo·ka *mouth*

boda ⓕ bo·da *wedding*

bodega ⓕ bo·de·ga *liquor store • winery*

bol ⓜ bol *bowl*

bolas ⓕ pl **de algodón** bo·las de al·go·don *cotton balls*

boletería ⓕ bo·le·te·ree·a *ticket office*

boleto ⓜ bo·le·to *ticket*
— **de ida y vuelta** de ee·da ee vwel·ta *return ticket*
— **de lista de espera** de lees·ta de es·pe·ra *standby ticket*
— **sencillo** sen·see·lyo *one-way ticket*

bolígrafo ⓜ bo·lee·gra·fo *pen (ballpoint)*

Bolivia ⓕ bo·lee·vya *Bolivia*

bollos ⓜ pl bo·lyos *bread rolls*

bolsa ⓕ **de compras** bol·sa de kom·pras *shopping bag*

bolsillo ⓜ bol·see·lyo *pocket*

bolso ⓜ bol·so *bag (general) • handbag*

bomba ⓕ bom·ba *pump • bomb*

bombillo ⓜ bom·bee·lyo *light bulb*

bondadoso/a ⓜ/ⓕ bon·da·do·so/a *caring*

bonito/a ⓜ/ⓕ bo·nee·to/a *pretty*

bosque ⓜ bos·ke *forest*

botas ⓕ pl bo·tas *boots*
— **de montaña** de mon·ta·nya *hiking boots*

botella ⓕ bo·te·lya *bottle*

botón ⓜ bo·ton *button*

boxeo ⓜ bok·se·o *boxing*

bragas ⓕ pl bra·gas *underpants (women)*

Braille ⓜ bray·e·le *Braille*

Brasil ⓜ bra·seel *Brazil*

brazo ⓜ bra·so *arm*

briliante bree·lyan·te *brilliant • glossy*

broma ⓕ bro·ma *joke*

bronceador ⓜ bron·se·a·dor *tanning lotion*

bronquitis ⓜ bron·kee·tees *bronchitis*

brújula ⓕ broo·khoo·la *compass*

brumoso/a ⓜ/ⓕ broo·mo·so/a *foggy*

buceo ⓜ boo·se·o *snorkelling*

budista ⓜ&ⓕ boo·dees·ta *Buddhist*

bueno/a ⓜ/ⓕ *bwe*·no/a *good • nice*
bufanda ⓕ boo·*fan*·da *scarf*
buffet ⓜ boo·fe *buffet (meal)*
bulto ⓜ *bool*·to *lump*
burro ⓜ *boo*·ro *donkey*
buscar boos·*kar* *look for*
buzón ⓜ boo·*son* *mailbox*

C

caballo ⓜ ka·*ba*·lyo *horse*
cabaña ⓕ ka·*ba*·nya *hut*
cabeza ⓕ ka·*be*·sa *head*
cabina ⓕ **telefónica** ka·*bee*·na
te·le·fo·*nee*·ka *phone box*
cable ⓜ *ka*·ble *cable*
cables ⓜ pl **de arranque** *ka*·bles de
a·*ran*·ke *jumper leads*
cabra ⓕ *ka*·bra *goat*
cacao ⓜ ka·*kow* *cocoa*
cacharro ⓜ ka·*cha*·ro *pot (ceramic)*
cachorro ⓜ ka·*cho*·ro *puppy*
cacto ⓜ *kak*·to *cactus*
cada *ka*·da *each*
cadena ⓕ ka·*de*·na *chain*
— **de bici** de *bee*·see *bike chain*
café ⓜ ka·fe *cafe • coffee*
cafetería ⓕ ka·fe·te·*ree*·a *cafe*
caída ⓕ ka·*ee*·da *fall (tumble)*
caja ⓕ *ka*·kha *box*
— **fuerte** *fwer*·te *safe*
— **registradora** re·khees·tra·*do*·ra
cash register
cajero automático ka·*khe*·ro
ow·to·*ma*·tee·ko *automatic teller
machine*
cajero/a ⓜ/ⓕ ka·*khe*·ro/a *cashier*
cajón con llave ka·*khon* kon *lya*·ve
locker
calabacín ⓜ ka·la·ba·*seen* *courgette*
calabaza ⓕ ka·la·*ba*·sa *pumpkin*
calcetines ⓜ pl kal·se·*tee*·nes *socks*
calculadora ⓕ kal·koo·la·*do*·ra *calculator*
calefacción ⓕ ka·le·fak·*syon* *heating*
— **central** sen·*tral* *central heating*
calendario ⓜ ka·len·*da*·ryo *calendar*

calidad ⓕ ka·lee·*da* *quality*
caliente ka·*lyen*·te *hot*
calle ⓕ *ka*·lye *road*
calor ⓜ ka·*lor* *heat*
calzoncillos ⓜ pl kal·son·*see*·lyos
underpants (men)
cama ⓕ *ka*·ma *bed*
— **de matrimonio** de
ma·tree·mo·nyo *double bed*
cámara ⓕ **(fotográfica)** *ka*·ma·ra
(fo·to·*gra*·fee·ka) *camera*
— **de aire** de *ai*·re *tube (tyre)*
— **descartable** des·kar·*ta*·ble
disposable camera
— **digital** de·khee·*tal* *digital camera*
— **submarina** soob·ma·*ree*·na
underwater camera
camarero/a ⓜ/ⓕ ka·ma·*re*·ro/a *waiter*
cambiar kam·*byar* *change • exchange*
cambio ⓜ *kam*·byo *change (coins) •
exchange*
— **de dinero** de dee·*ne*·ro *currency
exchange*
caminar ka·mee·*nar* *walk*
camino ⓜ ka·*mee*·no *track • trail • way*
— **de bici** de *bee*·see *bike path*
— **rural** roo·*ral* *hiking route*
camión ⓜ ka·*myon* *truck*
camisa ⓕ ka·*mee*·sa *shirt*
camiseta ⓕ ka·mee·*se*·ta *singlet •
T-shirt*
cámping ⓜ *kam*·peen *campsite*
campo ⓜ *kam*·po *countryside*
caña ⓕ **de azúcar** *ka*·nya de a·*soo*·kar
sugar cane
Canadá ka·na·*da* *Canada*
canasta ⓕ ka·*nas*·ta *basket*
cancelar kan·se·*lar* *cancel*
cáncer ⓜ *kan*·ser *cancer*
cancha de golf *kan*·cha de golf
golf course
cancha de tenis *kan*·cha de *te*·nees
tennis court
canción ⓕ kan·*syon* *song*
candado ⓜ kan·*da*·do *padlock*
candidiasis ⓜ kan·dee·*dya*·sees
thrush (medical)

cansado/a ⓜ/ⓕ kan·*sa*·do/a *tired*
cantalupo ⓜ kan·ta·*loo*·po *cantaloupe*
cantante ⓜ&ⓕ kan·*tan*·te *singer*
cantar kan·*tar* *sing*
cantidad ⓕ kan·tee·*da amount*
cantimplora ⓕ kan·teem·*plo*·ra *water bottle*
capa ⓕ **de ozono** *ka*·pa de o·*so*·no *ozone layer*
capacidad ⓕ **de SMS** ka·pa·see·*da* de *e*·se em·e *e·se SMS capability*
capacidad ⓕ **de WAP** ka·pa·see·*da* de gwap *WAP-enabled*
capilla ⓕ ka·*pee*·lya *shrine*
capote ⓜ ka·*po*·te *cloak*
cara ⓕ *ka*·ra *face*
caracol ⓜ ka·ra·*kol snail*
caramelos ⓜ pl ka·ra·*me*·los *lollies*
caravana ⓕ ka·ra·*va*·na *caravan • van*
cárcel ⓕ *kar*·sel *jail • prison*
caries ⓕ *ka*·ryes *cavity (tooth)*
carne ⓕ *kar*·ne *meat*
— **de vaca** de *va*·ka *beef*
— **molida** mo·*lee*·da *mince*
carnet ⓜ *kar*·net *drivers licence*
carnicería ⓕ kar·nee·se·*ree*·a *butcher's shop*
caro/a ⓜ/ⓕ *ka*·ro/a *expensive*
carpa ⓕ *kar*·pa *tent*
carpintero ⓜ kar·peen·*te*·ro *carpenter*
carrera ⓕ ka·*re*·ra *race (sport)*
carro ⓜ *ka*·ro *car*
carta ⓕ *kar*·ta *letter*
cartas ⓕ pl *kar*·tas *cards*
cartera ⓕ kar·*te*·ra *wallet*
cartón ⓜ kar·*ton carton*
cartucho ⓜ **de gas** kar·*too*·cho de gas *gas cartridge*
casa ⓕ *ka*·sa *house • home*
casado/a ⓜ/ⓕ ka·*sa*·do/a *married*
casarse ka·*sar*·se *marry*
cascada ⓕ kas·*ka*·da *waterfall*
casco ⓜ *kas*·ko *helmet*
casete ⓕ ka·*set cassette*
casi *ka*·see *almost*
casino ⓜ ka·*see*·no *casino*

castaña ⓕ **de cajú** kas·*ta*·nya de ka·*khoo cashew*
castigar kas·tee·*gar punish*
castillo ⓜ kas·*tee*·lyo *castle*
catedral ⓕ ka·te·*dral cathedral*
católico/a ⓜ/ⓕ ka·to·*lee*·ko/a *Catholic*
caza ⓕ *ka*·sa *hunting*
cebolla ⓕ se·*bo*·lya *onion*
cédula ⓜ **de identidad** *se*·doo·la de ee·den·tee·*da identification card (ID)*
celebración ⓕ se·le·bra·*syon celebration*
celoso/a ⓜ/ⓕ se·*lo*·so/a *jealous*
cementerio ⓜ se·men·*te*·ryo *cemetery*
cena ⓕ *se*·na *dinner*
cenicero ⓜ se·nee·*se*·ro *ashtray*
centavo ⓜ sen·*ta*·vo *cent*
centímetro ⓜ sen·*tee*·me·tro *centimetre*
central ⓕ **telefónica** sen·*tral* te·le·*fo*·nee·ka *telephone centre*
centro ⓜ *sen*·tro *centre*
— **comercial** ko·mer·*syal shopping centre*
— **de la ciudad** de la syoo·*da city centre*
Centroamérica ⓕ sen·tro·a·*me*·ree·ka *Central America*
centroamericano/a ⓜ/ⓕ sen·tro·a·me·ree·*ka*·no/a *Central American*
cepillo ⓜ **de dientes** se·*pee*·lyo de *dyen*·tes *toothbrush*
cerámica ⓕ se·*ra*·mee·ka *ceramic*
cerca ⓕ *ser*·ka *fence*
cerca *ser*·ka *near • nearby*
cerdo ⓜ *ser*·do *pig • pork*
cereales ⓜ pl se·re·*a*·les *cereal*
cerrado/a ⓜ/ⓕ se·*ra*·do/a *closed • shut • locked*
— **con llave** kon *lya*·ve *locked*
cerradura ⓕ se·ra·*doo*·ra *lock (door)*
cerrar se·*rar close • lock • shut*
certificado ⓜ ser·tee·fee·*ka*·do *certificate*
cerveza ⓕ ser·*ve*·sa *beer*
— **rubia** *roo*·bya *lager*

chaleco ⓜ **salvavidas** cha·le·ko sal·va·vee·das *life jacket*
champiñón ⓜ cham·pee·nyon *mushroom*
champú ⓜ cham·poo *shampoo*
chancho ⓜ chan·cho *pig • pork*
chaqueta ① cha·ke·ta *jacket*
cheque ⓜ che·ke *cheque*
— **de viajero** de vya·khe·ro *travellers cheque*
chica ① chee·ka *girl*
chicle ⓜ chee·kle *chewing gum*
chico ⓜ chee·ko *boy*
Chile ⓜ chee·le *Chile*
chocolate ⓜ cho·ko·la·te *chocolate • pot (dope)*
choque ⓜ cho·ke *crash (accident)*
chupete ⓜ choo·pe·te *dummy • pacifier*
cibercafé ⓜ see·ber·ka·fe *Internet cafe*
ciclismo ⓜ see·klees·mo *cycling*
ciclista ⓜ&① see·klees·ta *cyclist*
ciego/a ⓜ/① sye·go/a *blind*
cielo ⓜ sye·lo *sky*
ciencia ① syen·sya *science*
— **ficción** feek·syon *science fiction*
científico/a ⓜ/① syen·tee·fee·ko/a *scientist*
cigarillo ⓜ see·ga·ree·lyo *cigarette*
cigarro ⓜ see·ga·ro *cigar*
cine ⓜ see·ne *cinema*
cinta ① **de vídeo** seen·ta de vee·de·o *video tape*
cinturón ⓜ **de seguridad** seen·too·ron de se·goo·ree·da *seatbelt*
circo ⓜ seer·ko *circus*
ciruela ① see·rwe·la *plum*
— **pasa** pa·sa *prune*
cistitis ① sees·tee·tees *cystitis*
cita ① see·ta *appointment • date*
citología ① see·to·lo·khee·a *pap smear*
ciudad ① syoo·da *city*
ciudadanía ① syoo·da·da·nee·a *citizenship*
claro/a ⓜ/① kla·ro/a *light (colour)*

clase ① kla·se *class*
— **preferente** pre·fe·ren·te *business class*
— **turística** too·rees·tee·ka *economy class*
clásico/a ⓜ/① kla·see·ko/a *classical*
cliente/a ⓜ/① klyen·te/a *client*
cobrar (un cheque) ko·brar (oon che·ke) *cash (a cheque)*
coca ① ko·ka *coke (drug) • coca plant*
cocaína ① ko·ka·ee·na *cocaine*
coche ⓜ **cama** ko·che ka·ma *sleeping car*
cocina ① ko·see·na *kitchen • cuisine*
cocinar ko·see·nar *cook*
cocinero/a ⓜ/① ko·see·ne·ro/a *chef • cook*
coco ⓜ ko·ko *coconut*
cocodrilo ⓜ ko·ko·dree·lo *crocodile*
codeína ① ko·de·ee·na *codeine*
código ⓜ **postal** ko·dee·go pos·tal *post code*
coima ① koy·ma *bribe*
coimear koy·me·ar *bribe*
cola ① ko·la *queue*
colchón ⓜ kol·chon *mattress*
colega ⓜ&① ko·le·ga *colleague*
cólera ① ko·le·ra *cholera*
coles ⓜ pl **de Bruselas** ko·les de broo·se·las *Brussels sprouts*
colibrí ⓜ ko·lee·bree *hummingbird*
coliflor ko·lee·flor *cauliflower*
colina ① ko·lee·na *hill*
Colombia ① ko·lom·bya *Colombia*
color ⓜ ko·lor *colour*
comedia ① ko·me·dya *comedy*
comenzar ko·men·sar *begin • start*
comer ko·mer *eat*
comerciante ⓜ&① ko·mer·syan·te *business person*
comercio ⓜ ko·mer·syo *trade*
cómics ⓜ pl ko·meeks *comics*
comida ① ko·mee·da *food*
— **de bebé** de be·be *baby food*
comisaría ① ko·mee·sa·ree·a *police station*
como ko·mo *how*

cómodo/a ⓜ/ⓕ *ko*-mo-do/a *comfortable*

cómpact ⓜ *kom*-pakt *CD*

compañero/a ⓜ/ⓕ kom-pa-*nye*-ro/a *companion*

compañía ⓕ kom-pa-*nyee*-a *company*

compartir kom-par-*teer* *share (with)*

comprar kom-*prar* *buy*

compresas ⓕ pl kom-*pre*-sas *sanitary napkins*

compromiso ⓜ kom-pro-*mee*-so *engagement (marriage)*

computadora ⓕ kom-poo-ta-*do*-ra *computer*
  — **portátil** por-*ta*-teel *laptop*

comunión ⓕ ko-moo-*nyon* *communion*

comunista ⓜ&ⓕ ko-moo-*nees*-ta *communist*

con kon *with*
  — **filtro** *feel*-tro *filtered*

coñac ko-*nyak* *brandy*

concierto ⓜ kon-*syer*-to *concert*

condición ⓕ **cardíaca** kon-dee-*syon* kar-*dee*-a-ka *heart condition*

condon ⓜ kon-*don* *condom*

cóndor ⓜ *kon*-dor *condor*

conducir kon-doo-*seer* *drive*

conejo ⓜ ko-*ne*-kho *rabbit*

conexión ⓕ ko-nek-*syon* *connection*

confesión ⓕ kon-fe-*syon* *confession*

confianza ⓕ kon-*fyan*-sa *trust*

confiar kon-*fyar* *trust*

confirmar kon-feer-*mar* *confirm*

congelación ⓕ kon-khe-la-*syon* *frostbite*

conocer ko-no-*ser* *know (a person)*

conocido/a ⓜ/ⓕ ko-no-*see*-do/a *famous*

consejo ⓜ kon-*se*-kho *advice*

conservador(a) ⓜ/ⓕ kon-ser-va-*dor*/ kon-ser-va-*do*-ra *conservative*

consigna ⓕ kon-*see*-nya *left luggage office*
  — **automática** ow-to-*ma*-tee-ka *luggage lockers*

construir kon-stroo-*eer* *build*

consulado ⓜ kon-soo-*la*-do *consulate*

contaminación ⓕ kon-ta-mee-na-*syon* *pollution*

contar kon-*tar* *count*

contemporáneo/a ⓜ/ⓕ kon-tem-po-*ra*-ne-o/a *contemporary*

contestador ⓜ **automático** kon-tes-ta-*dor* ow-to-*ma*-tee-ko *answering machine*

contrato ⓜ kon-*tra*-to *contract*

control ⓜ kon-*trol* *checkpoint*

convento ⓜ kon-*ven*-to *convent*

copa ⓕ *ko*-pa *drink*

Copa ⓕ **Mundial** *ko*-pa moon-*dyal* *World Cup*

copos ⓜ pl **de maíz** *ko*-pos de ma-*ees* *cornflakes*

corazón ⓜ ko-ra-*son* *heart*

cordero ⓜ kor-*de*-ro *lamb*

cordillera ⓕ kor-dee-*lye*-ra *mountain range*

corpiño ⓜ kor-*pee*-nyo *bra (Arg)*

correcto/a ⓜ/ⓕ ko-*rek*-to/a *right (correct)*

correo ⓜ ko-*re*-o *mail*
  — **aereo** a-*e*-re-o *airmail*
  — **certificado** ser-tee-fee-*ka*-do *registered mail*
  — **urgente** oor-*khen*-te *express mail*

correos ⓜ pl ko-*re*-os *post office*

corrida ⓕ ko-*ree*-da *bullfight*

corriente ⓕ ko-*ryen*-te *current*

corriente ko-*ryen*-te *ordinary*

corrupto/a ⓜ/ⓕ ko-*roop*-to/a *corrupt*

cortar kor-*tar* *cut*

cortauñas ⓜ kor-ta-oo-*nyas* *nail clippers*

corte ⓜ **de pelo** *kor*-te de *pe*-lo *haircut*

corto/a ⓜ/ⓕ *kor*-to/a *short (length)*

cosecha ⓕ ko-*se*-cha *crop • harvest*

coser ko-*ser* *sew*

costa ⓕ *kos*-ta *coast*

Costa Rica ⓕ *kos*-ta *ree*-ka *Costa Rica*

costar kos-*tar* *cost*

crecer kre-*ser* *grow*

crema ⓕ *kre*-ma *cream*
  — **agria** *a*-grya *sour cream*
  — **hidratante** ee-dra-*tan*-te *moisturiser*
  — **solar** so-*lar* *sunblock*

críquet ⓜ *kree*·ket *cricket (sport)*
cristiano/a ⓜ/ⓕ krees·*tya*·no/a *Christian*
crítica ⓕ *kree*·tee·ka *review*
crudo/a ⓜ/ⓕ *kroo*·do/a *raw*
cuaderno ⓜ kwa·*der*·no *notebook*
cuadrado ⓜ kwa·*dra*·do *square (place)*
cuadro ⓜ *kwa*·dro *painting (canvas)*
cualificaciones ⓕ pl kwa·lee·fee·ka·*syo*·nes *qualifications*
cuando *kwan*·do *when*
cuanto *kwan*·to *how much*
cuarentena ⓕ kwa·ren·*te*·na *quarantine*
Cuaresma ⓕ kwa·*res*·ma *Lent*
cuarto ⓜ *kwar*·to *quarter*
Cuba ⓕ *koo*·ba *Cuba*
cubiertos ⓜ pl koo·*byer*·tos *cutlery*
cucaracha ⓕ koo·ka·*ra*·cha *cockroach*
cuchara ⓕ koo·*cha*·ra *spoon*
cucharita ⓕ koo·cha·*ree*·ta *teaspoon*
cuchillo ⓜ koo·*chee*·lyo *knife*
cuenta ⓕ *kwen*·ta *bill · check*
   — bancaria ban·*ka*·rya *bank account*
cuento ⓜ *kwen*·to *story · short story*
cuerda ⓕ *kwer*·da *rope · string*
   — para tender la ropa *pa*·ra ten·*der* la *ro*·pa *clothes line*
cuero ⓜ *kwe*·ro *leather*
cuerpo ⓜ *kwer*·po *body*
cuervo ⓜ *kwer*·vo *vulture*
cuesta abajo *kwes*·ta a·*ba*·kho *downhill*
cuesta arriba *kwes*·ta a·*ree*·ba *uphill*
cueva ⓕ *kwe*·va *cave*
cuidar kwee·*dar* *care for · mind (an object)*
culo ⓜ *koo*·lo *bum (ass)*
culpa ⓕ *kool*·pa *(someone's) fault*
culpable kool·*pa*·ble *guilty*
cumbre ⓕ *koom*·bre *peak*
cumpleaños ⓜ koom·ple·*a*·nyos *birthday*
cupón ⓜ koo·*pon* *coupon*
curitas ⓕ pl koo·*ree*·tas *Band-Aids*
currículum ⓜ koo·*ree*·koo·loom *resume*
curry ⓜ *koo*·ree *curry*
   — en polvo en *pol*·vo *curry powder*
cuy ⓜ kooy *guinea pig*

D

damasco da·*mas*·ko *apricot*
dañar da·*nyar* *hurt*
danta ⓕ *dan*·ta *tapir*
dar dar *give*
   — gracias *gra*·syas *thank*
   — la bienvenida la byen·ve·*nee*·da *welcome*
   — una patada *oo*·na pa·*ta*·da *kick*
de de *from*
   — cercanías ser·ka·*nee*·as *local*
   — (cuatro) estrellas (*kwa*·tro) es·*tre*·lyas *(four-)star*
   — derecha de·*re*·cha *right-wing*
   — izquierda ees·*kyer*·da *left-wing*
   — lujo *loo*·kho *luxurious*
   — menos *me*·nos *less*
   — segunda mano se·*goon*·da *ma*·no *second-hand*
   — vez en cuando ves en *kwan*·do *sometimes*
débil *de*·beel *weak*
decidir de·see·*deer* *decide*
decir de·*seer* *say · tell*
dedo ⓜ *de*·do *finger*
   — del pie del pye *toe*
defectuoso/a ⓜ/ⓕ de·fek·*two*·so/a *faulty*
deforestación ⓕ de·fo·res·ta·*syon* *deforestation*
dejar entrar de·*khar* en·*trar* *admit (allow to enter)*
delgado/a ⓜ/ⓕ del·*ga*·do/a *thin*
demasiado (caro/a) ⓜ/ⓕ de·ma·*sya*·do (*ka*·ro/a) *too (expensive)*
democracia ⓕ de·mo·kra·*see*·a *democracy*
demora ⓕ de·*mo*·ra *delay*
dentista ⓜ&ⓕ den·*tees*·ta *dentist*
dentro de (una hora) *den*·tro de (*oo*·na *o*·ra) *within (an hour)*
deportes ⓜ pl de·*por*·tes *sport*
deportista ⓜ&ⓕ de·por·*tees*·ta *sportsperson*
depósito ⓜ de·*po*·see·to *deposit (bank)*
derecha de·*re*·cha *right (direction)*
derechista de·re·*chees*·ta *right-wing*

derechos ⓜ pl de·*re*·chos *rights*
— **civiles** see·*vee*·les *civil rights*
— **de animales** de a·nee·*ma*·les *animal rights*
— **humanos** oo·*ma*·nos *human rights*
desayuno ⓜ de·sa·*yoo*·no *breakfast*
descansar des·kan·*sar rest*
descanso ⓜ des·*kan*·so *intermission*
descendiente ⓜ de·sen·*dyen*·te *descendant*
descomponerse des·kom·po·*ner*·se *break down*
descubrir des·koo·*breer discover*
descuento ⓜ des·*kwen*·to *discount*
desde *des*·de *since (time)*
desear de·se·*ar wish*
desempleado/a ⓜ/ⓕ des·em·*ple*·a·do/a *unemployed*
desierto ⓜ de·*syer*·to *desert*
desodorante ⓜ de·so·do·*ran*·te *deodorant*
despacio des·*pa*·syo *slowly*
desperdicios ⓜ pl des·per·*dee*·syos noo·kle·*a*·res *nuclear waste*
despertador ⓜ des·per·ta·*dor alarm clock*
despertarse des·per·*tar*·se *wake up*
después de des·*pwes de after*
destino ⓜ des·*tee*·no *destination*
detallado/a ⓜ/ⓕ de·ta·*lya*·do/a *itemised*
detalle ⓜ de·*ta*·lye *detail*
detener de·te·*ner arrest*
detrás de de·*tras de behind*
día ⓜ *dee*·a *day*
— **de Año Nuevo** de a·nyo *nwe*·vo *New Year's Day*
— **festivo** fes·*tee*·vo *holiday*
diabetes ⓕ dya·*be*·tes *diabetes*
diafragma ⓜ dya·*frag*·ma *diaphragm*
diapositiva ⓕ dya·po·see·*tee*·va *(film)*
diariamente dya·rya·*men*·te *daily*
diarrea ⓕ dya·*re*·a *diarrhoea*
dibujar dee·boo·*khar draw*
diccionario ⓜ deek·syo·*na*·ryo *dictionary*

dientes ⓜ pl *dyen*·tes *teeth*
diferencia ⓕ **de horas** dee·fe·*ren*·sya de o·ras *time difference*
diferente dee·fe·*ren*·te *different*
difícil dee·*fee*·seel *difficult*
dinero ⓜ dee·*ne*·ro *money*
— **en efectivo** en e·fek·*tee*·vo *cash*
dios dyos *god (general)*
dirección ⓕ dee·rek·*syon address*
direccionales ⓜ pl dee·rek·syo·*na*·les *indicators (car)*
directo/a ⓜ/ⓕ dee·*rek*·to/a *direct*
director(a) ⓜ/ⓕ dee·rek·*tor*/ dee·rek·*to*·ra *director*
disco ⓜ *dees*·ko *disk*
discoteca ⓕ dees·ko·*te*·ka *disco*
discriminación ⓕ dees·kree·mee·na·*syon discrimination*
discutir dees·koo·*teer argue*
diseño ⓜ dee·*se*·nyo *design*
disentería ⓕ dees·en·te·*ree*·a *dysentry*
disparar dees·pa·*rar shoot*
DIU ⓜ de·ee·*oo IUD (contraceptive device)*
diversión ⓕ dee·ver·*syon fun*
divertirse dee·ver·*teer*·se *enjoy (oneself)*
doblar do·*blar turn*
doble *do*·ble *double*
docena ⓕ do·*se*·na *dozen*
dólar ⓜ *do*·lar *dollar*
dolor ⓜ do·*lor pain*
— **de cabeza** de ka·*be*·sa *headache*
— **de estómago** de es·*to*·ma·go *stomachache*
— **de muelas** de *mwe*·las *toothache*
— **menstrual** mens·*trwal period pain*
dolorido/a ⓜ/ⓕ do·lo·*ree*·do/a *sore*
doloroso/a ⓜ/ⓕ do·lo·ro·*so*/a *painful*
donde *don*·de *where*
dormir dor·*meer sleep*
dos ⓜ/ⓕ dos *two*
— **camas** ⓕ pl *ka*·mas *twin beds*
— **copias** ⓕ pl *ko*·pyas *double copies (photos)*
— **veces** *ve*·ses *twice*

drama ⓜ *dra*·ma *drama*
droga ① *dro*·ga *drug (illegal)*
drogadicción ① dro·ga·deek·*syon* *drug addiction*
drogas ① pl *dro*·gas *drugs (illegal)*
ducha ① *doo*·cha *shower*
dueño/a ⓜ/① *dwe*·nyo/a *owner*
dulce ① *dool*·se *sweet • candy*
durante doo·*ran*·te *during*
durazno ⓜ doo·*ras*·no *peach*
duro/a ⓜ/① *doo*·ro/a *hard (not soft)*

E

ecografía ① e·ko·gra·*fee*·a *ultrasound*
Ecuador ⓜ e·kwa·*dor* *Ecuador*
eczema ① *ek*·se·ma *eczema*
edad ① e·*da* *age*
edificio ⓜ e·dee·*fee*·syo *building*
educación ① e·doo·ka·*syon* *education*
egoísta ⓜ&① e·go·*ees*·ta *selfish*
ejemplo ⓜ e·*khem*·plo *example*
ejército ⓜ e·*kher*·see·to *army*
él ⓜ el *he*
El Salvador ⓜ el sal·va·*dor* *El Salvador*
elecciones ① pl e·lek·*syo*·nes *elections*
electricidad ① e·lek·tree·see·*da* *electricity*
electricista ⓜ&① e·lek·tree·*sees*·ta *electrician*
ella ① *e*·lya *she*
ellos/ellas ⓜ/① pl *e*·lyos/*e*·lyas *they*
embajada ① em·ba·*kha*·da *embassy*
embajador(a) ⓜ/① em·ba·kha·*dor*/ em·ba·kha·*do*·ra *ambassador*
embarazada em·ba·ra·*sa*·da *pregnant*
embarcarse em·bar·*kar*·se *board (plane, ship)*
emborrachado/a ⓜ/① em·bo·ra·*cha*·do/a *drunk*
embrague ⓜ em·*bra*·ge *clutch*
emergencia ① e·mer·*khen*·sya *emergency*
emocional e·mo·syo·*nal* *emotional*
empanada ① em·pa·*na*·da *pie*

empleado/a ⓜ/① em·ple·*a*·do/a *employee*
empujar em·poo·*khar* *push*
en en *on • in*
— **el extranjero** el ek·stran·*khe*·ro *abroad*
encaje ⓜ en·*ka*·khe *lace*
encantador(a) ⓜ/① en·kan·ta·*dor*/ en·kan·ta·*do*·ra *charming*
encendedor ⓜ en·sen·de·*dor* *lighter*
enchufe ⓜ en·*choo*·fe *plug (electricity)*
encía ① en·*see*·a *gum (mouth)*
encontrar en·kon·*trar* *find • meet*
energía ① *nuclear* e·ner·*khee*·a noo·kle·*ar* *nuclear energy*
enfadado/a ⓜ/① en·fa·*da*·do/a *angry*
enfermedad ① en·fer·mee·*da* *disease*
— **de transmisión sexual** de trans·mee·*syon* sek·*swal* *STD (sexually transmitted disease)*
— **venérea** ve·ne·re·a *venereal disease*
enfermero/a ⓜ/① en·fer·*me*·ro/a *nurse*
enfermo/a ⓜ/① en·*fer*·mo/a *sick*
enorme e·*nor*·me *huge*
ensalada ① en·sa·*la*·da *salad*
entender en·ten·*der* *understand*
entrar en·*trar* *enter*
entre *en*·tre *among • between*
entregar en·tre·*gar* *deliver*
entrenador(a) ⓜ/① en·tre·na·*dor*/ en·tren·na·*do*·ra *coach*
entreno en·*tre*·no *workout*
entrevista ① en·tre·*vees*·ta *interview*
enviar en·*vyar* *send*
epilepsia ① e·pee·*lep*·sya *epilepsy*
equipaje ⓜ e·kee·*pa*·khe *luggage*
equipo ⓜ e·*kee*·po *equipment • team*
— **de inmersión** de een·mer·*syon* *diving equipment*
— **estereofónico** es·te·re·o·fo·nee·ko *stereo*
equitación ① e·kee·ta·*syon* *horse riding*
equivocado/a ⓜ/① e·kee·vo·*ka*·do/a *wrong*
error ⓜ e·*ror* *mistake*
escalada ① es·ka·*la*·da *rock climbing*

escalera ① es·ka·*le*·ra *stairway*
— **electrica** e·*lek*·tree·ka *escalator*
escape ⓜ es·*ka*·pe *exhaust (car)*
escarcha ① es·*kar*·cha *frost*
escarpado/a ⓜ/① es·kar·*pa*·do/a *steep*
escasez ① es·ka·*ses* *shortage*
escenario ⓜ e·se·*na*·ryo *stage*
Escocia es·*ko*·sya *Scotland*
escoger es·ko·*kher* *choose*
escribir es·kree·*beer* *write*
escritor(a) ⓜ/① es·kree·*tor*/
es·kree·*to*·ra *writer*
escuchar es·koo·*char* *listen*
escuela ① es·*kwe*·la *school*
esgrima ① es·*gree*·ma *fencing (sport)*
espacio ⓜ es·*pa*·syo *space*
espalda ① es·*pal*·da *back (body)*
España es·*pa*·nya *Spain*
especial es·pe·*syal* *special*
especialista ⓜ&① es·pe·sya·*lees*·ta
specialist
especies ① pl **en peligro de
extinción** es·*pe*·syes en pe·*lee*·gro
de ek·steen·*syon* *endangered species*
espectáculo ⓜ es·pek·*ta*·koo·lo *show*
espejo ⓜ es·*pe*·kho *mirror*
esperar es·pe·*rar* *wait*
espermicida ① es·per·mee·*see*·da
spermicide
espinacas ① pl es·pee·*na*·kas *spinach*
espiral ⓜ **repelente contra
mosquitos** es·pee·*ral* re·pe·*len*·te
kon·tra mos·*kee*·tos *mosquito coil*
esposa ① es·*po*·sa *wife*
esposo ⓜ es·*po*·so *husband*
espuma ① **de afeitar** es·*poo*·ma de
a·fay·*tar* *shaving cream*
esquí ⓜ es·*kee* *skiing*
— **acuático** a·*kwa*·tee·ko
waterskiing
esquiar es·*kyar* *ski*
esquina ① es·*kee*·na *corner*
esquís ⓜ pl es·*kees* *skis*
— **acuáticos** a·*kwa*·tee·kos *water skis*
esta noche *es*·ta *no*·che *tonight*
estacas ① pl es·*ta*·kas *pegs (tent)*

estación ① es·ta·*syon* *station* • *season*
— **de tren** de tren *railway station*
— **de autobuses** de ow·to·*boo*·ses
bus station (city)
— **de ómnibuses** de om·nee·*boo*·ses
bus station (inter-city)
— **de subterráneo** de
soob·te·*ra*·ne·o *metro station*
estacionamiento ⓜ
es·ta·syo·na·*myen*·to *car park*
estacionar es·ta·syo·*nar* *park (car)*
estadio ⓜ es·*ta*·dyo *stadium*
estado ⓜ **civil** es·*ta*·do see·*veel*
marital status
estafa ① es·*ta*·fa *rip-off*
estanquero ⓜ es·tan·*ke*·ro *tobacconist*
estar es·*tar* *be*
— **aburrido/a** ⓜ/① a·boo·*ree*·do/a
be bored
— **de acuerdo** de a·*kwer*·do *agree*
estatua ① es·*ta*·twa *statue*
este ⓜ *es*·te *east*
éste/a ⓜ/① *es*·te/a *this*
esterilla ① es·te·*ree*·lya *mat*
esteticista ⓜ&① es·te·tee·*sees*·ta
beautician
estilo ⓜ es·*tee*·lo *style*
estómago ⓜ es·*to*·ma·go *stomach*
estrellas ① pl es·*tre*·lyas *stars*
estreñimiento ⓜ es·tre·nyee·*myen*·to
constipation
estudiante ⓜ&① es·too·*dyan*·te
student
estudio ⓜ es·*too*·dyo *studio*
estufa ① es·*too*·fa *heater* • *stove*
estúpido/a ⓜ/① es·*too*·pee·do/a
stupid
etiqueta ① **de equipaje** e·tee·*ke*·ta
de e·kee·*pa*·khe *luggage tag*
euro ⓜ e·*oo*·ro *euro*
Europa ① e·oo·*ro*·pa *Europe*
eutanasia ① e·oo·ta·*na*·sya *euthanasia*
excelente ek·se·*len*·te *excellent*
exceso ⓜ **de equipage** ek·*se*·so de
e·kee·*pa*·khe *excess baggage*
excursión ① ek·skoor·*syon* *tour*

excursionismo ⓜ
ek·skoor·syo·*nees*·mo *hiking*

experiencia ① ek·spe·*ryen*·sya
experience
— **laboral** la·bo·*ral* *work experience*

explotación ① ek·splo·ta·*syon*
exploitation

exposición ① ek·spo·see·*syon*
exhibition

expreso/a ⓜ/① ek·*spre*·so/a *express*

exterior ⓜ ek·ste·*ryor* *outside*

extrañar ek·stra·*nyar*
miss (feel absence of)

extranjero/a ⓜ/① ek·stran·*khe*·ro/a
foreigner

extranjero/a ⓜ/① ek·stran·*khe*·ro/a
foreign

extraño/a ⓜ/① ek·*stra*·nyo/a *stranger*

extraño/a ⓜ/① ek·*stra*·nyo/a
strange • unusual

F

fábrica ① *fa*·bree·ka *factory*

fácil *fa*·seel *easy*

facturación ① fak·too·ra·*syon* *check-in (airport)*
— **de equipaje** de e·kee·*pa*·khe
check-in (luggage)

falda ① *fal*·da *skirt*

familia ① fa·*mee*·lya *family*

fantástico/a ⓜ/① fan·*tas*·tee·ko/a
fantasy • great

farmacia ① far·*ma*·sya *chemist • pharmacy*

faros ⓜ pl *fa*·ros *headlights*

fastidiado/a ⓜ/① fas·tee·*dya*·do/a
annoyed

fecha ① *fe*·cha *date (day)*
— **de nacimiento** de na·see·*myen*·to
date of birth

feliz fe·*lees* *happy*

feria ① *fe*·rya *street market*

ferretería ① fe·re·te·*ree*·a *hardware store*

festival ⓜ fes·tee·*val* *festival*

ficción ① feek·*syon* *fiction*

fideos ⓜ pl fee·*de*·os *noodles*

fiebre ① *fye*·bre *fever*
— **amarilla** a·ma·*ree*·lya *yellow fever*
— **del dengue** del *den*·ge *dengue fever*
— **del heno** del *e*·no *hay fever*
— **glandular** glan·doo·*lar* *glandular fever*

fiesta ① *fyes*·ta *party (celebration)*

film ⓜ feelm *film (cinema)*

fin ⓜ feen *end*
— **de semana** de se·*ma*·na *weekend*

firma ① *feer*·ma *signature*

flamenco ⓜ fla·*men*·ko *flamingo • flamenco (dance)*

flash flash *flash (camera)*

flor ① flor *flower*

florista ⓜ&① flo·*rees*·ta *florist*

flujo ⓜ **vaginal** *floo*·kho va·khee·*nal*
vaginal discharge

foco ⓜ *fo*·ko *lightbulb*

footing foo·*teen* *jogging*

forma ① *for*·ma *shape*

fósforos ⓜ pl *fos*·fo·ros *matches*

fotocopiadora ① fo·to·ko·pee·a·*do*·ra
photocopier

fotografía ① fo·to·gra·*fee*·a *photo • photography*

fotógrafo/a ⓜ/① fo·to·*gra*·fo/a
photographer

fotómetro ⓜ fo·to·*me*·tro *light meter*

frágil *fra*·kheel *fragile*

frambuesa ① fram·*bwe*·sa *raspberry*

Francia ① *fran*·sya *France*

franqueo ⓜ fran·*ke*·o *postage*

frazada ① fra·*sa*·da *blanket*

freír fre·*eer* *fry*

freno ⓜ pl *fre*·no *brake*

frente a *fren*·te a *opposite*

frigorífico ⓜ free·go·*ree*·fee·ko *fridge*

frijoles ⓜ pl free·*kho*·les *beans*

frío/a ⓜ/① *free*·o/a *cold*

frontera ① fron·*te*·ra *border (frontier)*

fruta ① *froo*·ta *fruit*

frutilla ① froo·*tee*·lya *strawberry*

fuego ⓜ *fwe*·go *fire*

fuerte *fwer*·te *strong*

fumar foo·*mar* *smoke*

funda ① de almohada *foon·*da de al·mo·*a·*da *pillowcase*
funeral ⓜ foo·ne·*ral funeral*
fútbol ⓜ *foot·*bol *football · soccer*
futuro ① foo·*too·*ro *future*

G

galleta ① ga·*lye·*ta *biscuit · cookie*
ganador(a) ⓜ/① ga·na·*dor/*ga·na·*do·*ra *winner*
ganar ga·*nar earn · win*
garage ⓜ ga·*ra·*khe *garage (car shelter)*
garbanzos ⓜ pl gar·*ban·*sos *chickpeas*
garganta ① gar·*gan·*ta *throat*
gas ⓜ gas *gas (for cooking)*
gasolina ① ga·so·*lee·*na *gas · petrol*
gasolinera ① ga·so·lee·*ne·*ra *service station*
gastroenteritis ①
gas·tro·en·te·re·*tees gastroenteritis*
gatito/a ⓜ/① ga·*tee·*to/a *kitten*
gato/a ⓜ/① ga·to/a *cat*
gay gay *gay*
gemelos/as ⓜ/① pl khe·*me·*los/as *twins*
general khe·ne·*ral general*
gente ① *khen·*te *people*
gimnasia ① kheem·*na·*sya *gymnastics*
ginecólogo/a ⓜ/①
khe·ne·*ko·*lo·go/a *gynaecologist*
glorieta ① glo·*rye·*ta *roundabout*
gobierno ⓜ go·*byer·*no *government*
goma ① go·ma *gum (chewing)*
gordo/a ⓜ/① gor·do/a *fat*
gotas ① pl para los ojos go·tas pa·ra los o·khos *eye drops*
grabación ① gra·ba·*syon recording*
gracioso/a ⓜ/① gra·*syo·*so/a *funny*
gramos ⓜ pl gra·mos *grams*
grande gran·de *big*
grandes almacenes ⓜ pl gran·des al·ma·se·nes *department store*
granizo ⓜ gra·*nee·*so *hail*
granja ① gran·kha *farm*

gratis gra·tees *free (gratis)*
grifo ⓜ gree·fo *tap · faucet*
gripe ① gree·pe *influenza*
gris grees *grey*
gritar gree·*tar shout*
grupo ⓜ groo·po *group · band (music)*
— **de rock** de rok *rock group*
— **sanguíneo** san·*gwee·*ne·o *blood group*
guantes ⓜ pl gwan·tes *gloves*
guardarropa ⓜ gwar·da·*ro·*pa *cloakroom*
guardería ① gwar·de·*ree·*a *childminding service · creche*
Guatemala ① gwa·te·*ma·*la *Guatemala*
guerra ① ge·ra *war*
guía ① gee·a *guidebook*
— **audio** ow·dyo *audio guide*
— **de espectaculos** de es·pek·*ta·*koo·los *entertainment guide*
— **telefónica** te·le·fo·nee·ka *phone book*
guía ⓜ&① gee·a *guide (person)*
guitarra ① gee·*ta·*ra *guitar*
gustar(le) goos·*tar(*le) *like*

H

habitación a·bee·ta·*syon room · bedroom*
— **doble** do·ble *double room*
— **individual** een·dee·vee·*dwal single room*
hablar a·blar *speak · talk*
hacer a·ser do · *make*
— **dedo** de·do *hitchhike*
— **surf** soorf *surf*
— **windsurf** gween·soorf *windsurfing*
hachís ⓜ a·chees *hash*
hacia a·sya *towards*
— **abajo** a·ba·kho *down*
halal a·lal *halal*
hamaca ① a·*ma·*ka *hammock*
harina ① a·*ree·*na *flour*
hasta as·ta *until*

hecho/a ⓜ/ⓕ *e*·cho/a *made*
— **a mano** a *ma*·no *handmade*
— **de (algodón)** de (al·go·*don*) *made of (cotton)*
heladería ⓕ e·la·de·*ree*·a *ice-cream parlour*
helado ⓜ e·*la*·do *ice cream*
helar e·*lar* *freeze*
hepatitis ⓕ e·pa·*tee*·tees *hepatitis*
herborista ⓜ&ⓕ er·bo·*rees*·ta *herbalist*
herida ⓕ e·*ree*·da *injury*
hermana ⓕ er·*ma*·na *sister*
hermano ⓜ er·*ma*·no *brother*
hermoso/a ⓜ/ⓕ er·*mo*·so/a *handsome*
heroína ⓕ e·ro·*ee*·na *heroin*
hielo ⓜ *ye*·lo *ice*
hierba ⓕ *yer*·ba *grass*
hierbas ⓕ pl *yer*·bas *herbs*
hígado ⓜ *ee*·ga·do *liver*
higo ⓜ *ee*·go *fig*
hija ⓕ *ee*·kha *daughter*
hijo ⓜ *ee*·kho *son*
hilo ⓜ *ee*·lo *thread*
— **dental** den·*tal* *dental floss*
hinchas ⓜ&ⓕ pl *een*·chas *fans (supporters)*
hindú een·*doo* *Hindu*
historial ⓜ **profesional** ees·to·*ryal* pro·fe·syo·*nal* *CV*
histórico/a ⓜ/ⓕ ees·*to*·ree·ko/a *historical*
hockey ⓜ *kho*·kee *hockey*
— **sobre hielo** *so*·bre *ye*·lo *ice hockey*
hoja ⓕ *o*·kha *leaf*
— **de afeitar** de a·fay·*tar* *razor blade*
Holanda ⓕ o·*lan*·da *Netherlands*
hombre ⓜ *om*·bre *man*
hombros ⓜ pl *om*·bros *shoulders*
homosexual o·mo·sek·*swal* *homosexual*
Honduras ⓕ on·*doo*·ras *Honduras*
hora ⓕ *o*·ra *time*
horario ⓜ o·*ra*·ryo *timetable*
horas ⓕ pl **de abrir** *o*·ras de a·*breer* *opening hours*
hormiga ⓕ or·*mee*·ga *ant*

horno ⓜ *or*·no *oven*
horóscopo ⓜ o·*ros*·ko·po *horoscope*
hospital ⓜ os·pee·*tal* *hospital*
hostelería ⓕ os·te·le·*ree*·a *hospitality*
hotel ⓜ o·*tel* *hotel*
hoy oy *today*
huerta ⓕ *wer*·ta *vegetable garden*
hueso ⓜ *we*·so *bone*
huevo ⓜ *we*·vo *egg*

I

identificación ⓕ ee·den·tee·fee·ka·*syon* *identification*
idioma ⓜ ee·*dyo*·ma *language*
idiota ⓜ&ⓕ ee·*dyo*·ta *idiot*
iglesia ⓕ ee·*gle*·sya *church*
igual ee·*gwal* *same*
igualdad ⓕ ee·gwal·*da* *equality*
ilegal ee·le·*gal* *illegal*
impermeable ⓜ eem·per·me·*a*·ble *raincoat*
impermeable eem·per·me·*a*·ble *waterproof*
importante eem·por·*tan*·te *important*
imposible eem·po·*see*·ble *impossible*
impuesto ⓜ eem·*pwes*·to *tax*
— **sobre la renta** *so*·bre la *ren*·ta *income tax*
incluido/a ⓜ/ⓕ een·kloo·*ee*·do/a *included*
incómodo/a ⓜ/ⓕ een·*ko*·mo·do/a *uncomfortable*
India *een*·dya *India*
indigestion ⓕ een·dee·khes·*tyon* *indigestion*
industria ⓕ een·*doos*·trya *industry*
infección ⓕ een·fek·*syon* *infection*
inflamación ⓕ een·fla·ma·*syon* *inflammation*
información ⓕ een·for·ma·*syon* *information*
informática ⓕ een·for·*ma*·tee·ka *IT*
informativo ⓜ een·for·ma·*tee*·vo *current affairs*
ingeniería ⓕ een·khe·nye·*ree*·a *engineering*

ingeniero/a ⓜ/ⓕ een·khe·*nye*·ro/a
engineer
Inglaterra een·gla·*te*·ra *England*
inglés ⓜ een·*gles* *English (language)*
inglés(a) ⓜ/ⓕ een·*gles*/een·*gle*·sa
English
ingrediente ⓜ een·gre·*dyen*·te
ingredient
inhalador ⓜ een·a·la·*dor* *inhaler*
injusto/a ⓜ/ⓕ een·*khoos*·to/a *unfair*
inmigración ⓕ een·mee·gra·*syon*
immigration
inocente ee·no·*sen*·te *innocent*
inseguro/a ⓜ/ⓕ een·se·*goo*·ro/a
unsafe
insolación ⓕ een·so·la·*syon* *sunstroke*
instituto ⓜ een·stee·*too*·to *high
school*
instructor(a) ⓜ/ⓕ een·strook·*tor*/
een·strook·*to*·ra *instructor*
interesante een·te·re·*san*·te
interesting
internacional een·ter·na·syo·*nal*
international
Internet ⓜ&ⓕ een·ter·*net* *Internet*
intérprete ⓜ&ⓕ een·*ter*·pre·te
interpreter
intoxicación ⓕ **alimenticia**
een·tok·see·ka·*syon*
a·lee·men·*tee*·sya *food poisoning*
inundación ⓕ ee·noon·da·*syon* *flood*
invierno ⓜ een·*vyer*·no *winter*
invitar een·vee·*tar* *invite*
inyección ⓕ een·yek·*syon* *injection*
inyectarse een·yek·*tar*·se *inject*
ir eer *go*
  — **de compras** de *kom*·pras *shop*
  — **de excursión** de ek·skoor·*syon*
hike
  — **en tobogán** en to·bo·*gan*
tobogganing
Irlanda ⓕ eer·*lan*·da *Ireland*
irritación ⓕ ee·rree·ta·*syon*
irritation · rash
  — **de pañal** de pa·*nyal* *nappy rash*
isla ⓕ *ees*·la *island*
itinerario ⓜ ee·tee·ne·*ra*·ryo *itinerary*
IVA ⓜ *ee*·va *sales tax*
izquierda ⓕ ees·*kyer*·da *left (direction)*

jabón ⓜ kha·*bon* *soap*
jaguar ⓜ kha·*gwar* *jaguar*
jalar kha·*lar* *pull*
jamón ⓜ kha·*mon* *ham*
Japón ⓜ kha·*pon* *Japan*
jarabe ⓜ kha·*ra*·be *cough medicine*
jardín ⓜ khar·*deen* *garden*
  — **botánico** bo·*ta*·nee·ko *botanic
garden*
  — **de infantes** de een·*fan*·tes
kindergarten
jardinería ⓕ khar·dee·ne·*ree*·a
gardening
jarra ⓕ *kha*·ra *jar*
jefe/a ⓜ/ⓕ *khe*·fe/a *boss · leader ·
manager*
jengibre ⓜ khen·*khee*·bre *ginger*
jeringa ⓕ khe·*reen*·ga *syringe*
jersey ⓜ kher·*say* *sweater · jumper*
jet lag ⓜ dyet lag *jet lag*
jockey ⓜ kho·*kay* *jockey*
joven kho·ven *young*
joyería ⓕ kho·ye·*ree*·a *jewellery*
jubilado/a ⓜ/ⓕ khoo·bee·*la*·do/a
retired
judío/a ⓜ/ⓕ khoo·*dee*·o/a *Jewish*
juego ⓜ *khwe*·go *game (play)*
  — **de computadora** de
kom·poo·ta·*do*·ra *computer game*
juegos ⓜ pl **olímpicos** *khwe*·gos
o·*leem*·pee·kos *Olympic Games*
juez ⓜ&ⓕ *khwes* *judge*
jugar khoo·*gar* *play (a game)*
  — **al tenis** al te·nees *play tennis*
jugo ⓜ *khoo*·go *juice*
  — **de naranja** de na·*ran*·kha *orange
juice*
juguetería ⓕ khoo·ge·te·*ree*·a *toy shop*
juicioso/a ⓜ/ⓕ khwee·*syo*·so/a *sensible*
juntos/as ⓜ/ⓕ pl *khoon*·tos/as *together*

K

kilo ⓜ *kee*·lo *kilogram*
kilómetro ⓜ kee·*lo*·me·tro *kilometre*
kiwi *kee*·wee *kiwifruit*
kosher ko·sher *kosher*

L

La Copa ① **Mundial** la *ko*·pa moon·*dyal the World Cup*

la píldora ① la *peel*·do·ra *the Pill*

labios ⓜ pl *la*·byos *lips*

lado ⓜ *la*·do *side*

ladrón(a) ⓜ/① la·dron/la·*dro*·na *thief*

lagartija ① la·gar·*tee*·kha *lizard*

lago ⓜ *la*·go *lake*

lana ① *la*·na *wool*

langostino ⓜ lan·gos·*tee*·no *prawn*

lápiz ⓜ *la*·pees *pencil*
— **de labios** de *la*·byos *lipstick*

largo/a ⓜ/① *lar*·go/a *long*

lata ① *la*·ta *can · tin*

Latinoamérica ①
la·tee·no·a·*me*·ree·ka *Latin America*

latinoamericano/a ⓜ/①
la·tee·no·a·me·ree·*ka*·no/a *Latin American*

lavadora ① la·va·*do*·ra *washing machine*

lavandería ① la·van·de·*ree*·a *laundrette · laundry*

lavar la·*var wash (something)*

lavarse la·*var*·se *wash (oneself)*

laxantes ⓜ pl lak·*san*·tes *laxatives*

leche ① *le*·che *milk*
— **de soya** de *so*·ya *soy milk*
— **semi** *se*·mee *skimmed milk*

lechuga ① le·*choo*·ga *lettuce*

leer le·*er read*

legal le·*gal legal*

legislación ① le·khees·la·*syon legislation*

lejos *le*·khos *far*

leña ① *le*·nya *firewood*

lenteja ① pl len·*te*·kha *lentil*

lentes ⓜ pl *len*·tes *lenses*
— **de contacto** de kon·*tak*·to *contact lenses*

lento/a ⓜ/① *len*·to/a *slow*

lesbiana ① les·*bya*·na *lesbian*

levantar le·van·*tar lift*

levantarse le·van·*tar*·se *get up*

ley ① lay *law*

libra ① *lee*·bra *pound (money)*

libre *lee*·bre *free (not bound)*

librería ① lee·bre·*ree*·a *bookshop*

libro ⓜ *lee*·bro *book*
— **de frases** de *fra*·ses *phrasebook*

libros ⓜ pl **de viajes** *lee*·bros de *vya*·khes *travel books*

ligar lee·*gar chat up*

ligero/a ⓜ/① lee·*khe*·ro/a *light (not heavy)*

lila *lee*·la *purple*

lima ① *lee*·ma *lime*

limite ⓜ *lee*·mee·te *limit*
— **de equipaje** de e·kee·*pa*·khe *baggage allowance*
— **de velocidad** de ve·lo·see·*da speed limit*

limón ⓜ lee·*mon lemon*

limonada ① lee·mo·*na*·da *lemonade*

limpio/a ⓜ/① *leem*·pyo/a *clean*

línea ① *lee*·ne·a *line*

linterna ① leen·*ter*·na *flashlight · torch*

listo/a ⓜ/① *lees*·to/a *ready*

literatura ① lee·te·ra·*too*·ra *literature*
— **de ficción** de feek·*syon fiction (literature)*
— **no novelesca** no no·ve·*les*·ka *non-fiction (literature)*

llamada ① lya·*ma*·da *phone call*
— **a cobro revertido** a *ko*·bro re·ver·*tee*·do *collect call*

llamar lya·*mar call*
— **por telefono** por te·*le*·fo·no *ring (by phone)*

llano/a ⓜ/① *lya*·no/a *flat*

llanta ① *lyan*·ta *tyre*

llave ① *lya*·ve *key*

llegadas ① pl lye·*ga*·das *arrivals*

llegar lye·*gar arrive*

lleno/a ⓜ/① *lye*·no/a *full · booked out*

llevar lye·*var carry · wear*

lluvia ① *lyoo*·vya *rain*

local ⓜ lo·*kal venue*

loción ① lo·*syon lotion*
 — para después del afeitado
 pa·ra des·*pwes* del a·fay·*ta*·do
 aftershave
loco/a ⓜ/① *lo*·ko/a *crazy*
lodo ⓜ *lo*·do *mud*
loro ⓜ *lo*·ro *parrot*
Los Estados ⓜ pl **Unidos** los es·*ta*·dos
 oo·*nee*·dos *the USA*
los/las dos ⓜ/① pl los/las dos *both*
lubricante ⓜ loo·bree·*kan*·te
 lubricant
lucha ① *loo*·cha *fight*
lugar ⓜ loo·*gar place*
 — de nacimiento de
 na·see·*myen*·to *place of birth*
luna ① *loo*·na *moon*
 — llena *lye*·na *full moon*
 — de miel de myel *honeymoon*
luz ① loos *light*

M

madera ① ma·*de*·ra *wood*
madre ① *ma*·dre *mother*
madrugada ① ma·droo·*ga*·da *dawn*
mago/a ⓜ/① *ma*·go/a *magician*
maíz ⓜ ma·*ees corn*
malaria ① ma·*la*·rya *malaria*
maleta ① ma·*le*·ta *suitcase*
maletín ⓜ ma·le·*teen briefcase*
 — de primeros auxilios
 de pree·*me*·ros ow·*see*·lyos
 first-aid kit
malla ① *ma*·lya *bathing suit*
malo/a ⓜ/① *ma*·lo/a *bad*
mamá ① ma·*ma mum*
mamograma ⓜ ma·mo·*gra*·ma
 mammogram
mañana ① ma·*nya*·na *tomorrow •*
 morning
mandarina ① man·da·*ree*·na
 mandarin
mandíbula ① man·*dee*·boo·la *jaw*
mando ⓜ **a distancia** man·do a
 dees·*tan*·sya *remote control*

mango ⓜ *man*·go *mango*
maní ⓜ ma·*nee groundnut • peanut*
manifestación ① ma·nee·fes·ta·*syon*
 demonstration (protest)
manillar ⓜ ma·nee·*lyar handlebar*
mano ① *ma*·no *hand*
manteca ① **de cerdo** man·*te*·ka de
 ser·do *lard*
mantel ⓜ man·*tel tablecloth*
mantequilla ① man·te·*kee*·lya *butter*
manual ma·*nwal manual*
manzana ① man·*sa*·na *apple*
mapa ⓜ *ma*·pa *map*
maquillaje ⓜ ma·kee·*lya*·khe *make-up*
máquina ① *ma*·kee·na *machine*
 — de boletos de bo·*le*·tos *ticket*
 machine
mar ⓜ mar *sea*
maravilloso/a ⓜ/① ma·ra·vee·*lyo*·so/a
 wonderful
marcador ⓜ mar·ka·*dor scoreboard*
marcapasos ⓜ mar·ka·*pa*·sos
 pacemaker
marcar mar·*kar score*
marchas ① pl *mar*·chas *gears*
marcos ⓜ pl *mar*·kos *borders*
 (photography)
marea ① ma·*re*·a *tide*
mareado/a ⓜ/① ma·re·*a*·do/a *dizzy*
mareo ⓜ ma·*re*·o *seasickness • travel*
 sickness
margarina ① mar·ga·*ree*·na *margarine*
marihuana ① ma·ree·*wa*·na *marijuana*
mariposa ① ma·ree·*po*·sa *butterfly*
marrón ma·*ron brown*
martillo ⓜ mar·*tee*·lyo *hammer*
más mas *more • most*
más cercano/a ⓜ/① mas ser·*ka*·no
 nearest
masaje ⓜ ma·*sa*·khe *massage*
masajista ⓜ&① ma·sa·*khees*·ta
 masseur/masseuse
matar ma·*tar kill*
mate ⓜ *ma*·te *type of tea popular in*
 South America
mate *ma*·te *matte (photos)*

matrícula ⓕ ma·*tree*·koo·la *car registration* · *license plate number*

matrimonio ⓜ ma·tree·*mo*·nyo *marriage*

mayonesa ⓕ ma·yo·*ne*·sa *mayonnaise*

mazo ⓜ *ma*·so *mallet*

mecánico/a ⓜ/ⓕ me·*ka*·nee·ko/a *mechanic*

mechero ⓜ me·*che*·ro *cigarette lighter*

medianoche ⓕ me·dya·*no*·che *midnight*

medias ⓕ pl *me*·dyas *pantyhose* · *stockings*

medicina ⓕ me·dee·*see*·na *drug (medicinal)* · *medicine*

medico/a ⓜ/ⓕ me·dee·ko/a *doctor*

medio ⓜ **ambiente** *me*·dyo am·*byen*·te *environment*

medio/a ⓜ/ⓕ *me*·dyo/a *half*

mediodía ⓜ me·dyo·*dee*·a *noon*

medios ⓜ pl *me*·dyos *resources*
— **de comunicación** de ko·moo·nee·ka·*syon* *media*
— **de transporte** de trans·*por*·te *transport*

meditación ⓕ me·dee·ta·*syon* *meditation*

mejillones ⓜ pl me·khee·*lyo*·nes *mussels*

mejor me·*khor* *best* · *better*

melodía ⓕ me·lo·*dee*·a *tune*

melón ⓜ me·*lon* *melon*

mendigo/a ⓜ/ⓕ men·*dee*·go/a *beggar*

mensaje ⓜ men·*sa*·khe *message*

menstruación ⓕ mens·trwa·*syon* *menstruation*

mentiroso/a ⓜ/ⓕ men·tee·ro·so/a *liar*

menú ⓜ me·*noo* *menu*

a menudo a me·*noo*·do *often*

mercado ⓜ mer·*ka*·do *market*
— **de artesanía** de ar·te·sa·*nee*·a *craft market*

mermelada ⓕ mer·me·*la*·da *jam* · *marmalade*

mes ⓜ mes *month*

mesa ⓕ *me*·sa *table*

meseta ⓕ me·*se*·ta *plateau*

metal ⓜ me·*tal* *metal*

metro ⓜ me·tro *metre (distance)*

México ⓜ *me*·khee·ko *Mexico*

mezclar mes·*klar* *mix*

mezquita ⓕ mes·*kee*·ta *mosque*

microondas ⓕ mee·kro·*on*·das *microwave oven*

miel ⓕ myel *honey*

miembro ⓜ&ⓕ *myem*·bro *member*

migraña ⓕ mee·*gra*·nya *migraine*

milímetro ⓜ mee·*lee*·me·tro *millimetre*

militares ⓜ pl mee·lee·*ta*·res *military*

millón ⓜ mee·*lyon* *million*

minusválido/a ⓜ/ⓕ mee·noos·*va*·lee·do/a *disabled*

minuto ⓜ mee·*noo*·to *minute*

mirador ⓜ mee·ra·*dor* *lookout*

mirar mee·*rar* *look* · *watch*
— **las vidrieras** las vee·*drye*·ras *window-shopping*

misa ⓕ *mee*·sa *mass (Catholic)*

mochila ⓕ mo·*chee*·la *backpack*

módem ⓜ *mo*·dem *modem*

mojado/a ⓜ/ⓕ mo·*kha*·do/a *wet*

monasterio ⓜ mo·nas·*te*·ryo *monastery*

monedas ⓕ pl mo·*ne*·das *coins*
— **sueltas** *swel*·tas *loose change*

monitor(a) ⓜ/ⓕ mo·nee·*tor*/ mo·nee·*to*·ra *(skiing) instructor*

monja ⓕ *mon*·kha *nun*

monopatinaje ⓜ mo·no·pa·tee·*na*·khe *skateboarding*

montaña ⓕ mon·*ta*·nya *mountain*

montar mon·*tar* *ride*

monumento ⓜ mo·noo·*men*·to *monument*

mordedura ⓕ mor·de·*doo*·ra *bite (dog)*

moretón ⓜ mo·re·*ton* *bruise*

morir mo·*reer* *die*

mosca ⓕ *mos*·ka *fly*

mosquitera ⓕ mos·kee·*te*·ra *mosquito net*

mosquito ⓜ mos·*kee*·to *mosquito*
mostaza ⓕ mos·*ta*·sa *mustard*
mostrador ⓜ mos·tra·*dor* *counter (shop)*
mostrar mos·*trar* *show*
motocicleta ⓕ mo·to·see·*kle*·ta
　motorcycle
motor ⓜ mo·*tor* *engine*
motora ⓕ mo·*to*·ra *motorboat*
muchos/as ⓜ/ⓕ pl *moo*·chos/as
　many
mudo/a ⓜ/ⓕ *moo*·do/a *mute*
muebles ⓜ pl *mwe*·bles *furniture*
muela ⓕ *mwe*·la *tooth (back)*
muelle ⓜ *mwe*·lye *spring*
muerto/a ⓜ/ⓕ *mwer*·to/a *dead*
muesli ⓜ *mwes*·lee *muesli*
mujer ⓕ moo·*kher* *woman*
multa ⓕ *mool*·ta *fine (payment)*
mundo ⓜ *moon*·do *world*
muñeca ⓕ moo·*nye*·ka *doll • wrist*
músculo ⓜ *moos*·koo·lo *muscle*
museo ⓜ moo·*se*·o *museum*
　— **de arte** de *ar*·te *art gallery*
música ⓕ *moo*·see·ka *music*
músico/a ⓜ/ⓕ *moo*·see·ko/a
　musician
musulmán(a) ⓜ/ⓕ moo·sool·*man*/
　moo·sool·*ma*·na *Muslim*
muy mooy *very*

N

nacional na·syo·*nal* *national*
nacionalidad ⓕ na·syo·na·lee·*da*
　nationality
nada *na*·da *none • nothing*
nadar na·*dar* *swim*
naranja ⓕ na·*ran*·kha *orange (fruit)*
nariz ⓕ na·*rees* *nose*
naturaleza ⓕ na·too·ra·*le*·sa *nature*
naturopatia ⓕ na·too·ro·*pa*·tya
　naturopathy
náusea ⓕ *now*·se·a *nausea*
náuseas ⓕ pl **del embarazo**
　now·se·as del em·ba·*ra*·so
　morning sickness
navaja ⓕ na·*va*·kha *penknife*

Navidad ⓕ na·vee·*da* *Christmas*
necesario/a ⓜ/ⓕ ne·se·*sa*·ryo/a
　necessary
necesitar ne·se·see·*tar* *need*
negar(se) ne·*gar*·(se) *refuse*
negocio ⓜ ne·*go*·syo *business*
　— **de artículos básicos** de
　ar·*tee*·koo·los ba·*see*·kos
　convenience store
negro/a ⓜ/ⓕ *ne*·gro/a *black*
Nicaragua ⓕ nee·ka·*ra*·gwa
　Nicaragua
nieto/a ⓜ/ⓕ *nye*·to/a *grandchild*
nieve ⓕ *nye*·ve *snow*
niño/a ⓜ/ⓕ *nee*·nyo/a *child*
no no *no*
　— **fumadores** foo·ma·*do*·res
　non-smoking
　— **incluido/a** ⓜ/ⓕ
　een·kloo·*ee*·do/a *excluded*
noche ⓕ *no*·che *evening • night*
Nochebuena ⓕ no·che·*bwe*·na
　Christmas Eve
Nochevieja ⓕ no·che·*vye*·kha
　New Year's Eve
nombre ⓜ *nom*·bre *name*
norte ⓜ *nor*·te *north*
nosotros/as ⓜ/ⓕ no·so·tros/as *we*
noticias ⓕ pl no·*tee*·syas *news*
novela ⓕ no·*ve*·la *novel*
　— **negra** *ne*·gra *detective novel*
　— **rosa** *ro*·sa *romance novel*
novia ⓕ *no*·vya *girlfriend*
novio ⓜ *no*·vyo *boyfriend*
nube ⓕ *noo*·be *cloud*
nublado/a ⓜ/ⓕ noo·*bla*·do/a
　cloudy
nuestro/a ⓜ/ⓕ *nwes*·tro/a *our*
Nueva Zelandia ⓕ *nwe*·va se·*lan*·dya
　New Zealand
nuevo/a ⓜ/ⓕ *nwe*·vo/a *new*
nuez ⓕ nwes *nut*
número ⓜ *noo*·me·ro *number*
　— **de habitación** de ha·bee·ta·*syon*
　room number
　— **de pasaporte** de pa·sa·*por*·te
　passport number
nunca *noon*·ka *never*

O

o o *or*

objetivo ⓜ ob·khe·*tee*·vo *lens*

obra ⓕ *o*·bra *play (theatre)* • *work (of art)*

obrero/a ⓜ/ⓕ o·*bre*·ro/a *factory worker* • *labourer*

océano ⓜ o·*se*·a·no *ocean*

ocupado/a ⓜ/ⓕ o·koo·*pa*·do/a *busy*

oeste ⓜ o·*es*·te *west*

oficina ⓕ o·fee·*see*·na *office*

  — de objetos perdidos de ob·*khe*·tos per·*dee*·dos *lost property office*

  — de turismo de too·*rees*·mo *tourist office*

oficinista ⓜ&ⓕ o·fee·see·*nees*·ta *office worker*

oír o·*eer* *hear*

ojo ⓜ *o*·kho *eye*

ola ⓕ *o*·la *saucepan* • *wave*

olor ⓜ o·*lor* *smell*

olvidar ol·vee·*dar* *forget*

ómnibus ⓜ *om*·nee·boos *bus (intercity)*

ópera ⓕ *o*·pe·ra *opera*

operación ⓕ o·pe·ra·*syon* *operation (medical)*

operador(a) ⓜ/ⓕ o·pe·ra·*dor*/o·pe·ra·*do*·ra *operator*

opinión ⓕ o·pee·*nyon* *opinion*

oporto ⓜ o·*por*·to *port (wine)*

oportunidad ⓕ o·por·too·nee·*da* *chance*

oración ⓕ o·ra·*syon* *prayer*

orden ⓜ *or*·den *order (placement)*

orden ⓜ *or*·den *order (command)*

ordenar or·de·*nar* *order (give command)*

oreja ⓕ o·*re*·kha *ear*

orgasmo ⓜ or·*gas*·mo *orgasm*

original o·ree·khee·*nal* *original*

orilla ⓕ o·*ree*·lya *seaside*

  — del mar o·*ree*·lya del mar *seaside*

oro ⓜ *o*·ro *gold*

orquesta ⓕ or·*kes*·ta *orchestra*

orquídea ⓕ or·*kee*·de·a *orchid*

oscuro/a ⓜ/ⓕ os·*koo*·ro/a *dark*

ostra ⓕ *os*·tra *oyster*

otoño ⓜ o·*to*·nyo *autumn*

otra vez *o*·tra ves *again*

otro/a ⓜ/ⓕ *o*·tro/a *other*

oveja ⓕ o·*ve*·kha *sheep*

oxígeno ⓜ ok·*see*·khe·no *oxygen*

P

padre ⓜ *pa*·dre *father*

padres ⓜ pl *pa*·dres *parents*

pagar pa·*gar* *pay*

página ⓕ *pa*·khee·na *page*

pago ⓜ *pa*·go *payment*

país ⓜ pa·*ees* *country (nation)*

pájaro ⓜ *pa*·kha·ro *bird*

pala ⓕ *pa*·la *spade*

palabra ⓕ pa·*la*·bra *word*

palacio ⓜ pa·*la*·syo *palace*

palillo ⓜ pa·*lee*·lyo *toothpick*

paloma ⓕ pa·*lo*·ma *dove*

palm ⓜ palm *palm pilot*

palma ⓕ **de coco** *pal*·ma de *ko*·ko *coconut palm*

palta ⓕ *pal*·ta *avocado*

pan ⓜ pan *bread*

  — blanco *blan*·ko *white bread*

  — de centeno de sen·*te*·no *rye bread*

  — de masa fermentada de *ma*·sa fer·men·*ta*·da *sourdough bread*

  — integral een·te·*gral* *wholemeal bread*

panadería ⓕ pa·na·de·*ree*·a *bakery*

pañal ⓜ pa·*nyal* *nappy* • *diaper*

Panamá ⓕ pa·na·*ma* *Panama*

panorámico/a ⓜ/ⓕ pa·no·ra·*mee*·ko/a *panoramic*

pantalla ⓕ pan·*ta*·lya *screen*

pantalones ⓜ pl pan·ta·*lo*·nes *pants* • *trousers*

  — cortos *kor*·tos *shorts*

pantera ⓕ pan·*te*·ra *panther*

pañuelo ⓜ pa·*nywe*·lo *handkerchief*

  — de papel de pa·*pel* *tissue*

papa ⓕ *pa*·pa *potato*

papá ⓜ pa·*pa* *dad*

papagayo ⓜ pa·pa·*ga*·yo *macaw*

papel ⓜ pa·*pel* paper
— **higiénico** ee·*khye*·nee·ko *toilet paper*
papeles ⓜ pl **del auto** pa·*pe*·les del *ow*·to *car owner's title*
paquete ⓜ pa·*ke*·te *package · packet · parcel*
para siempre pa·ra *syem*·pre *forever*
parabrisas ⓜ pa·ra·*bree*·sas *windscreen*
parada ⓕ pa·*ra*·da *stop*
— **de autobús** de ow·to·*boos* *bus stop (city)*
— **de ómnibus** de *om*·nee·boos *bus stop (intercity)*
— **de subteráneo** de soob·te·*ra*·ne·o *metro stop*
— **de taxis** de *tak*·sees *taxi stand*
paraguas ⓜ pa·*ra*·gwas *umbrella*
Paraguay ⓜ pa·ra·*gway* *Paraguay*
para pa·ra *for*
parar pa·*rar* *stop*
pared ⓕ pa·*re*·wall (inside)
pareja ⓕ pa·*re*·kha *partner · pair (couple)*
parlamento ⓜ par·*la*·men·to *parliament*
parque ⓜ *par*·ke *park*
— **nacional** na·syo·*nal* *national park*
parte ⓕ *par*·te *part*
partida ⓕ **de nacimiento** par·*tee*·da de na·see·*myen*·to *birth certificate*
partido ⓜ par·*tee*·do *match (sport) · party (politics)*
partir par·*teer* *leave*
pasa ⓕ **de uva** pa·sa de *oo*·va *raisin*
pasado ⓜ pa·*sa*·do *past*
— **mañana** ma·*nya*·na *day after tomorrow*
pasado/a ⓜ/ⓕ pa·*sa*·do/a *off (spoiled)*
pasajero/a ⓜ/ⓕ pa·sa·*khe*·ro/a *passenger*
pasaporte ⓜ pa·sa·*por*·te *passport*
Pascua ⓕ *pas*·kwa *Easter*
pase ⓜ pa·se *pass (permit)*
paseo ⓜ pa·*se*·o *ride · street*

pasillo ⓜ pa·*see*·lyo *aisle (plane, train)*
paso ⓜ pa·so *step · pass (mountain)*
pasta ⓕ *pas*·ta *pasta*
— **dentífrica** den·*tee*·free·ka *toothpaste*
pastelería ⓕ pas·te·le·*ree*·a *cake shop*
pastillas ⓕ pl pas·*tee*·lyas *pills*
— **antipalúdicas** an·tee·pa·*loo*·dee·kas *antimalarial tablets*
— **de menta** de *men*·ta *mints*
— **para dormir** pa·ra dor·*meer* *sleeping pills*
paté ⓜ pa·*te* *pate (food)*
pato ⓜ pa·to *duck*
patrón/patrona ⓜ/ⓕ pa·*tron*/pa·*tro*·na *employer*
pavo ⓜ *pa*·vo *turkey*
paz ⓕ pas *peace*
peatón ⓜ&ⓕ pe·a·*ton* *pedestrian*
pecho ⓜ *pe*·cho *chest*
pedal ⓜ pe·*dal* *pedal*
pedazo ⓜ pe·*da*·so *piece*
pedir pe·*deer* *ask (for something) · borrow*
peine ⓜ *pay*·ne *comb*
pelea ⓕ pe·*le*·a *quarrel*
película ⓕ pe·*lee*·koo·la *film (for camera) · movie*
peligroso/a ⓜ/ⓕ pe·lee·*gro*·so/a *dangerous*
pelo ⓜ *pe*·lo *hair*
pelota ⓕ pe·*lo*·ta *ball*
— **de golf** de golf *golf ball*
peluquero/a ⓜ/ⓕ pe·loo·*ke*·ro/a *hairdresser*
pene ⓜ *pe*·ne *penis*
penicilina ⓕ pe·nee·see·*lee*·na *penicillin*
pensar pen·*sar* *think*
pensión ⓕ pen·*syon* *boarding house*
pensionado/a ⓜ/ⓕ pen·syo·*na*·do/a *pensioner*
pepinillos ⓜ pl pe·pee·*nee*·lyos *pickles*
pepino ⓜ pe·*pee*·no *cucumber*
pequeñito/a ⓜ/ⓕ pe·ke·*nee*·to/a *tiny*
pequeño/a ⓜ/ⓕ pe·*ke*·nyo/a *small*

pera ⓕ *pe·ra pear*
perder per·*der lose*
perdido/a ⓜ/ⓕ per·*dee·do/a lost*
perdonar per·do·*nar forgive*
perezoso/a ⓜ/ⓕ pe·re·*so·so/a lazy*
perfume ⓜ per·*foo·me perfume*
periódico ⓜ pe·ryo·*dee·ko newspaper*
periodista ⓟ&ⓕ pe·ryo·*dees·ta journalist*
permiso ⓜ per·*mee·so permission • permit*
— de trabajo de tra·*ba·kho work permit*
permitir per·mee·*teer allow*
pero *pe·ro but*
perro/a ⓜ/ⓕ *pe·ro/a dog*
— guía *gee·a guide dog*
persona ⓕ per·*so·na person*
Perú ⓜ pe·*roo Peru*
pesado/a ⓜ/ⓕ pe·*sa·do/a heavy*
pesca ⓕ *pes·ka fishing*
pescadería ⓕ pes·ka·de·*ree·a fish shop*
pescado ⓜ pes·*ka·do fish (as food)*
peso ⓜ *pe·so weight*
petición ⓕ pe·tee·*syon petition*
pez ⓜ *pes fish*
picadura ⓕ pee·ka·*doo·ra bite (insect)*
picazón ⓜ pee·ka·*son itch*
picnic ⓜ *peek·neek picnic*
pie ⓜ *pye foot*
piedra ⓕ *pye·dra stone*
piel ⓕ *pyel skin*
pierna ⓕ *pyer·na leg (body)*
pila ⓕ *pee·la battery (small)*
píldora ⓕ *peel·do·ra pill • the Pill*
pimienta ⓕ pee·*myen·ta pepper*
pimiento ⓜ pee·*myen·to capsicum • bell pepper*
pinchar peen·*char puncture*
ping pong ⓜ *peen pon table tennis*
pintar peen·*tar paint*
pintor(a) ⓜ/ⓕ peen·*tor/peen·to·ra painter*
pintura ⓕ peen·*too·ra painting (art)*
pinzas ⓕ pl *peen·sas tweezers*
piojos ⓜ pl *pyo·khos lice*
piolet ⓜ pyo·*let ice axe*

piqueta ⓕ pee·*ke·ta pickaxe*
piscina ⓕ pee·*see·na swimming pool*
piso ⓜ *pee·so floor (storey)*
pista ⓕ *pees·ta sports track • tennis court*
pistacho ⓜ pees·*ta·cho pistachio*
pizarra ⓕ blanca pee·*sa·ra blan·ka whiteboard*
plancha ⓕ *plan·cha iron (clothes)*
planeta ⓜ pla·*ne·ta planet*
planta ⓕ *plan·ta plant*
plástico ⓜ *plas·tee·ko plastic*
plata ⓕ *pla·ta silver*
plataforma ⓕ pla·ta·*for·ma platform*
plátano ⓜ *pla·ta·no banana*
plato ⓜ *pla·to plate*
playa ⓕ *pla·ya beach*
plaza ⓕ *pla·sa square*
— de toros de *to·ros bullring*
pobre *po·bre poor*
pobreza ⓕ po·*bre·sa poverty*
pocos/as ⓜ/ⓕ pl *po·kos/as few*
poder ⓜ po·*der power*
poder po·*der can (be able)*
poesía ⓕ po·e·*see·a poetry*
polen ⓜ *po·len pollen*
policía ⓕ po·lee·*see·a police*
política ⓕ po·lee·*tee·ka policy • politics*
político/a ⓜ/ⓕ po·lee·*tee·ko/a politician*
póliza ⓕ *po·lee·sa policy (insurance)*
pollo ⓜ *po·lyo chicken*
pomelo ⓜ po·*me·lo grapefruit*
poner po·*ner put*
popular po·poo·*lar popular*
por por *for*
por (dia) por *(dee·a) per (day)*
por ciento por *syen·to percent*
por qué por *ke why*
por vía aérea por *vee·a a·e·re·a by airmail*
por vía terrestre por *vee·a te·res·tre surface mail*
porque por·*ke because*
posible po·*see·ble possible*
potable po·*ta·ble drinkable*
potro ⓜ *po·tro pony*
pozo ⓜ *po·so well (water)*

latin american spanish-english

precio ⓜ *pre·syo* price
— **de entrada** de en·tra·da admission price
— **del cubierto** del koo·byer·to cover charge (restaurant)
preferir pre·fe·reer prefer
pregunta ⓕ pre·goon·ta question
preguntar pre·goon·tar ask (a question)
preocupado/a ⓜ/ⓕ pre·o·koo·pa·do/a worried
preocuparse por pre·o·koo·par·se por care (about something)
preparar pre·pa·rar prepare
presentación ⓕ pre·sen·ta·syon presentation
presidente/a ⓜ/ⓕ pre·see·den·te/a president
presión ⓕ pre·syon pressure
— **arterial** ar·te·ryal blood pressure
presupuesto ⓜ pre·soo·pwes·to budget
prevenir pre·ve·neer prevent
primavera ⓕ pree·ma·ve·ra spring (season)
primer ministro/a ⓜ/ⓕ pree·mer mee·nees·tro/a prime minister
primera clase ⓕ pree·me·ra kla·se first class
primero/a ⓜ/ⓕ pree·me·ro/a first
primo/a ⓜ/ⓕ pree·mo/a cousin
principal preen·see·pal main
prisionero/a ⓜ/ⓕ pree·syo·ne·ro/a prisoner
privado/a ⓜ/ⓕ pree·va·do/a private
probar pro·bar try (attempt)
producir pro·doo·seer produce
productos ⓜ pl **congelados** pro·dook·tos kon·khe·la·dos frozen foods
profesor(a) pro·fe·sor/pro·fe·so·ra teacher • lecturer
profundo/a ⓜ/ⓕ pro·foon·do/a deep • profound
programa ⓜ pro·gra·ma programme
prolongación ⓕ pro·lon·ga·syon extension (visa)
promesa ⓕ pro·me·sa promise
prometida ⓕ pro·me·tee·da fiancee
prometido ⓜ pro·me·tee·do fiance

pronto pron·to soon
propietaria ⓕ pro·pye·ta·rya landlady
propietario ⓜ pro·pye·ta·ryo landlord
propina ⓕ pro·pee·na tip (gratuity)
proteger pro·te·kher protect
propuesta ⓕ pro·pwes·ta proposal
protegido/a ⓜ/ⓕ pro·te·khee·do/a protected
protesta ⓕ pro·tes·ta protest
protestar pro·tes·tar protest
provisiones ⓕ pl pro·vee·syo·nes provisions
proximo/a ⓜ/ⓕ prok·see·mo/a next
proyector ⓜ pro·yek·tor projector
prueba ⓕ prwe·ba test
— **del embarazo** del em·ba·ra·so pregnancy test kit
pruebas ⓕ pl **nucleares** prwe·bas noo·kle·a·res nuclear testing
pub ⓜ poob pub
pueblo ⓜ pwe·blo village
puente ⓜ pwen·te bridge
puerro ⓜ pwe·ro leek
puerta ⓕ pwer·ta door
puerto ⓜ pwer·to port • harbour
Puerto ⓜ **Rico** pwer·to ree·ko Puerto Rico
puesta ⓕ **del sol** pwes·ta del sol sunset
pulga ⓕ pool·ga flea
pulmones ⓜ pl pool·mo·nes lungs
puntero ⓜ **láser** poon·te·ro la·ser laser pointer
punto ⓜ poon·to point • dot • full stop
puro/a ⓜ/ⓕ poo·ro/a pure

Q

que ke what
quedar ke·dar stay (remain)
quedarse ke·dar·se stay (remain)
quejarse ke·khar·se complain
quemadura ⓕ ke·ma·doo·ra burn
— **de sol** de sol sunburn
quemar ke·mar burn
querer ke·rer love • want
queso ⓜ ke·so cheese
— **crema** kre·ma cream cheese

quien kyen *who*
quincena ① keen·*se*·na *fortnight*
quiosco ⓜ kee·*os*·ko *newsagency*
quiste ⓜ **ovárico** *kees*·te o·*va*·ree·ko *ovarian cyst*
quizás kee·*sas maybe*

R

rábano ⓜ *ra*·ba·no *radish*
— **picante** pee·*kan*·te *horseradish*
rabo ⓜ *ra*·bo *tail*
radiador ⓜ ra·dya·*dor radiator*
rana ① *ra*·na *frog*
rápido/a ⓜ/① *ra*·pee·do/a *fast*
raqueta ① ra·*ke*·ta *racquet*
raro/a ⓜ/① *ra*·ro/a *rare*
rata ① *ra*·ta *rat*
ratón ⓜ ra·*ton mouse*
ratonero ⓜ ra·to·*ne*·ro *buzzard*
razón ① ra·*son reason*
realista re·a·*lees*·ta *realistic*
recibir re·see·*beer receive*
recibo ⓜ re·*see*·bo *receipt*
reciclable re·see·*kla*·ble *recyclable*
reciclar re·see·*klar recycle*
recientemente re·syen·te·*men*·te
recently
recogida ① **de equipajes**
re·ko·*khee*·da de e·kee·*pa*·khes
baggage claim
recolección ① **de fruta** re·ko·lek·*syon*
de *froo*·ta *fruit picking*
recomendar re·ko·men·*dar recommend*
reconocer re·ko·no·*ser acknowledge* ·
recognise
recorrido ⓜ **guiado** re·ko·*ree*·do
gee·*a*·do *guided tour*
recto/a ⓜ/① *rek*·to/a *straight*
recuerdo ⓜ re·*kwer*·do *souvenir*
recuerdos ⓜ pl re·*kwer*·dos *memories*
red ① re *net*
redondo/a ⓜ/① re·*don*·do/a *round*
reembolso ⓜ re·em·*bol*·so *refund*
referencias ① pl re·fe·*ren*·syas
references (work)
refrigeradora ① re·free·khe·ra·*do*·ra
refrigerator

refugiado/a ⓜ/① re·foo·*khya*·do/a
refugee
regalo ⓜ re·*ga*·lo *gift*
— **de bodas** de bo·das *wedding
present*
régimen ⓜ *re*·khee·men *diet*
registrar re·khees·*trar check-in (hotel)*
reglas ① pl *re*·glas *rules*
reina ① *ray*·na *queen*
reírse re·*eer*·se *laugh*
relación ① re·la·*syon relationship*
relajarse re·la·*khar*·se *relax*
religión ① re·lee·*khyon religion*
religioso/a ⓜ/① re·lee·*khyo*·so/a
religious
reliquia ① re·*lee*·kya *relic*
reloj ⓜ re·*lokh clock*
— **de pulsera** de pool·*se*·ra *watch*
remo ⓜ *re*·mo *rowing*
remolacha ① re·mo·*la*·cha *beetroot*
remoto/a ⓜ/① re·mo·*to*/a *remote*
reparar re·pa·*rar repair*
repollo ⓜ re·*po*·lyo *cabbage*
reproductor ⓜ **de compacts portátil**
re·pro·dook·*tor* de kom·pakts
por·*ta*·teel *portable CD player*
reproductor ⓜ **de MP3**
re·pro·dook·*tor* de *e*·me pe tres
MP3 player
república ① re·*poo*·blee·ka *republic*
República ① **Dominicana**
re·*poo*·blee·ka do·mee·nee·*ka*·na
Dominican Republic
requesón ⓜ re·ke·*son cottage cheese*
reserva ① re·*ser*·va *reservation*
reservar re·ser·*var book (reserve)*
residencia ① **de estudiantes**
re·see·*den*·sya de es·too·*dyan*·tes
college
residuos ⓜ pl **tóxicos** re·*see*·dwos
tok·see·kos *toxic waste*
respirar res·pee·*rar breathe*
respuesta ① res·*pwes*·ta *answer*
restaurante ⓜ res·tow·*ran*·te
restaurant
revisar re·vee·*sar check*
revisor(a) ⓜ/① re·vee·*sor*/re·vee·*so*·ra
ticket collector

revista ① re·vees·ta *magazine*
rey ⓜ ray *king*
rezar re·sar *worship (pray)*
rico/a ⓜ/① ree·ko/a *rich*
riesgo ⓜ ryes·go *risk*
río ⓜ ree·o *river*
ritmo ⓜ reet·mo *rhythm*
robar ro·bar *rob*
roca ① ro·ka *rock (stone)*
rock ⓜ rok *rock (music)*
rodilla ① ro·dee·lya *knee*
rojo/a ⓜ/① ro·kho/a *red*
romántico/a ⓜ/① ro·man·tee·ko/a
  romantic
romper rom·per *break*
ron ⓜ ron *rum*
ropa ① ro·pa *clothing*
  — **de cama** de ka·ma *bedding*
  — **interior** een·te·ryor *underwear*
rosa ro·sa *pink*
roto/a ⓜ/① ro·to/a *broken*
rueda ① rwe·da *wheel*
rugby ⓜ roog·bee *rugby*
ruidoso/a ⓜ/① rwe·do·so/a *loud*
ruinas ① pl rwe·nas *ruins*
ruta ① roo·ta *route*

S

sábado ⓜ sa·ba·do *Sabbath*
sábana ① sa·ba·na *sheet (bed)*
saber sa·ber *know (how to)*
sabroso/a ⓜ/① sa·bro·so/a *tasty*
sacacorchos ⓜ sa·ka·kor·chos
  corkscrew
sacerdote ⓜ sa·ser·do·te *priest*
saco ⓜ sa·ko *coat*
  — **de dormir** de dor·meer *sleeping
  bag*
sal ① sal *salt*
sala ① sa·la *room*
  — **de espera** de es·pe·ra *waiting room*
  — **de tránsito** de tran·see·to *transit
  lounge*
salami ⓜ sa·la·mee *salami*
salario ⓜ sa·la·ryo *salary*
salchicha ① sal·chee·cha *sausage*

saldo ⓜ sal·do *balance (account)*
salida ① sa·lee·da *departure · exit*
salir sa·leer *go out (exit)*
salir con sa·leer kon *date (a person)*
salir de sa·leer de *depart*
salmón ⓜ sal·mon *salmon*
salón ⓜ **de belleza** sa·lon de be·lye·sa
  beauty salon
salsa ① sal·sa *sauce*
  — **de ají** de a·khee *chilli sauce*
  — **de soya** de so·ya *soy sauce*
  — **de tomate** de to·ma·te *tomato
  sauce · ketchup*
saltar sal·tar *jump*
salud ① sa·loo *health*
salvaeslips ⓜ pl sal·va·e·sleeps *panty
  liners*
sandalias ① pl san·da·lyas *sandals*
sandía ① san·dee·a *watermelon*
sandwich ⓜ san·weech *sandwich*
sangre ① san·gre *blood*
santo/a ⓜ/① san·to/a *saint*
sarampión ⓜ sa·ram·pyon *measles*
sartén ① sar·ten *frying pan*
sastre ⓜ sas·tre *tailor*
sauna ① sow·na *sauna*
secar se·kar *dry*
seco/a ⓜ/① se·ko/a *dry*
secretario/a ⓜ/① se·kre·ta·ryo/a
  secretary
seda ① se·da *silk*
seguir se·geer *follow*
segundo ⓜ se·goon·do *second (time)*
segundo/a ⓜ/① se·goon·do/a *second
  (place)*
seguro se·goo·ro *insurance*
seguro/a ⓜ/① se·goo·ro/a *safe*
sello ⓜ se·lyo *stamp*
semáforos ⓜ pl se·ma·fo·ros *traffic
  lights*
semana ① se·ma·na *week*
Semana ① **Santa** se·ma·na san·ta
  Holy Week
sembrar sem·brar *plant*
semidirecto/a se·mee·dee·rek·to/a
  non-direct
señal ① se·nyal *sign*
sencillo/a ⓜ/① sen·see·lyo/a *simple*
sendero ⓜ sen·de·ro *path*

senos ⓜ se·nos *breasts*

sensibilidad ⓕ sen·see·bee·lee·*da* *film speed • sensitivity*

sensual sen·*swal* *sensual*

sentarse sen·*tar*·se *sit*

sentimientos ⓜ pl sen·tee·*myen*·tos *feelings*

sentir sen·*teer* *feel*

separado/a ⓜ/ⓕ se·pa·*ra*·do/a *separate*

separar se·pa·*rar* *separate*

ser ser *be*

serie ⓕ se·rye *series*

serio/a ⓜ/ⓕ se·ryo/a *serious*

seropositivo/a ⓜ/ⓕ
se·ro·po·see·*tee*·vo/a *HIV positive*

serpiente ⓕ ser·*pyen*·te *snake*

servicio ⓜ ser·*vee*·syo *service • service charge*

— **militar** mee·lee·*tar* *military service*

— **telefónico automático** te·le·fo·nee·ko ow·to·*ma*·tee·ko *direct-dial*

servilleta ⓕ ser·vee·*lye*·ta *napkin*

sexismo ⓜ sek·*sees*·mo *sexism*

sexo ⓜ sek·so *sex*

— **seguro** se·*goo*·ro *safe sex*

sexy sek·see *sexy*

si see *if*

sí see *yes*

SIDA ⓜ see·da *AIDS*

sidra ⓕ see·dra *cider*

siempre syem·pre *always*

silla ⓕ see·lya *chair*

— **de ruedas** de rwe·das *wheelchair*

sillín ⓜ see·*lyeen* *saddle*

sillita ⓕ see·*lyee*·ta *child seat*

similar see·mee·*lar* *similar*

simpático/a ⓜ/ⓕ seem·*pa*·tee·ko/a *nice (person)*

sin seen *without*

— **plomo** plo·mo *unleaded*

— **techo** te·cho *homeless*

sinagoga ⓕ see·na·*go*·ga *synagogue*

Singapur seen·ga·*poor* *Singapore*

sintético/a ⓜ/ⓕ seen·*te*·tee·ko/a *synthetic*

SMS *e·se em·e e·se* *SMS*

sobre ⓜ so·bre *envelope*

sobre so·bre *about • over (above)*

sobredosis ⓕ so·bre·do·sees *overdose*

socialista ⓜ&ⓕ so·sya·*lees*·ta *socialist*

sol ⓜ sol *sun*

soldado ⓜ sol·*da*·do *soldier*

soleado/a so·le·*a*·do/a *sunny*

sólo so·lo *only*

solo/a ⓜ/ⓕ so·lo/a *alone*

soltero/a ⓜ/ⓕ sol·*te*·ro/a *single (unmarried)*

sombra ⓕ som·bra *shade • shadow*

sombrero ⓜ som·*bre*·ro *hat*

soñar so·*nyar* *dream*

sondeos ⓜ pl son·*de*·os *polls*

sonreír son·re·*eer* *smile*

sopa ⓕ so·pa *soup*

sordo/a ⓜ/ⓕ sor·do/a *deaf*

soroche ⓜ so·ro·che *altitude sickness*

sorpresa ⓕ sor·*pre*·sa *surprise*

su soo *his • her • their*

sostén ⓜ sos·*ten* *bra*

subir soo·*beer* *climb*

submarinismo ⓜ
soob·ma·ree·*nees*·mo *diving*

subsidio ⓜ **de desempleo** soob·*see*·dyo de des·em·*ple*·o *dole*

subteráneo ⓜ soob·te·ra·*ne*·o *metro • subway*

subtítulos ⓜ pl soob·*tee*·too·los *subtitles*

sucio/a ⓜ/ⓕ soo·syo/a *dirty*

Sudamérica ⓕ sood·a·*me*·ree·ka *South America*

sudamericano/a ⓜ/ⓕ
sood·a·me·ree·*ka*·no/a *South American*

sudar soo·*dar* *perspire*

suegra ⓕ swe·gra *mother-in-law*

suegro ⓜ swe·gro *father-in-law*

sueldo ⓜ swel·do *wage*

suelo ⓜ swe·lo *floor (ground)*

suerte ⓕ swer·te *luck*

suéter ⓜ swe·ter *jumper • sweater*

suficiente soo·fee·*syen*·te *enough*

supermercado ⓜ soo·per·mer·*ka*·do *supermarket*

superstición ① soo·per·stee·*syon* superstition

sur ⓜ soor south

surf ⓜ soorf surfing
— **sobre la nieve** so·bre la nye·ve snowboarding

T

tabaco ⓜ ta·*ba*·ko tobacco

tabla ① **de surf** *ta*·bla de soorf surfboard

tacaño/a ⓜ/① ta·*ka*·nyo/a stingy

tajo ⓜ *ta*·kho chopping board

talco ⓜ *tal*·ko baby powder

talla ① *ta*·lya size (clothes)

taller ⓜ ta·*lyer* garage (car repair) • workshop

tamaño ⓜ ta·*ma*·nyo size (general)

también tam·*byen* also

tampoco tam·po·ko neither

tampones ⓜ pl tam·*po*·nes tampons

tapón ⓜ ta·*pon* plug (bath)

tapones ⓜ pl **para los oídos** ta·*po*·nes *pa*·ra los o·*ee*·dos earplugs

taquilla ① ta·*kee*·lya ticket office (cinema, theatre)

tarde *tar*·de late

tarjeta ① tar·*khe*·ta card
— **de crédito** de kre·dee·to credit card
— **de embarque** de em·*bar*·ke boarding pass
— **de teléfono** de te·*le*·fo·no phone card
— **SIM** seem SIM card

tarta ① **nupcial** *tar*·ta noop·*syal* wedding cake

tasa ① **del aeropuerto** *ta*·sa del a·e·ro·*pwer*·to airport tax

taxi ⓜ *tak*·see taxi

taza ① *ta*·sa cup

té ⓜ te tea

teatro ⓜ te·*a*·tro theatre
— **de la ópera** de la o·pe·ra opera house

techo ⓜ *te*·cho roof

teclado ⓜ te·*kla*·do keyboard

tela ① *te*·la fabric

tele ① *te*·le TV

teleférico ⓜ te·le·*fe*·ree·ko cable car

teléfono ⓜ te·*le*·fo·no telephone
— **móbil** *mo*·bil mobile phone
— **celular** se·loo·*lar* cell phone
— **público** *poo*·blee·ko public telephone

telegrama ⓜ te·le·*gra*·ma telegram

telenovela ① te·le·no·*ve*·la soap opera

teleobjetivo ⓜ te·le·ob·khe·tee·vo telephoto lens

telesquí ⓜ te·le·*skee* ski lift

televisión ① te·le·vee·*syon* television

temperatura ① tem·pe·ra·*too*·ra temperature

templado/a ⓜ/① tem·*pla*·do/a warm

templo ⓜ *tem*·plo temple

temprano tem·*pra*·no early

tenedor ⓜ te·ne·*dor* fork

tener te·*ner* have
— **hambre** *am*·bre be hungry
— **prisa** *pree*·sa be in a hurry
— **resfriado** res·*frya*·do have a cold
— **sed** se be thirsty
— **sueño** *swe*·nyo be sleepy

tenis ⓜ *te*·nees tennis

tensión ① **premenstrual** ten·*syon* pre·mens·*trwal* premenstrual tension

tentempié ⓜ ten·tem·*pye* snack

tercio ⓜ *ter*·syo third

terible te·*ree*·ble terrible

terminar ter·mee·*nar* finish

ternera ① ter·*ne*·ra veal

terremoto ⓜ te·re·*mo*·to earthquake

testarudo/a ⓜ/① tes·ta·*roo*·do/a stubborn

tía ① *tee*·a aunt

tiempo ⓜ *tyem*·po time • weather

tienda ① *tyen*·da shop
— **de fotografía** de fo·to·gra·*fee*·a camera shop
— **de provisiones de cámping** de pro·vee·*syo*·nes de *kam*·peen camping store
— **de recuerdos** de re·*kwer*·dos souvenir shop
— **de ropa** de *ro*·pa clothing store
— **deportiva** de·por·*tee*·va sports store

Tierra ① *tye*·ra Earth

tierra ① *tye*·ra land

tijeras ① pl tee-*khe*-ras *scissors*
tímido/a ⑩/① tee-mee-do/a *shy*
tío ⑩ *tee*-o *uncle*
típico/a ⑩/① tee-pee-ko/a *typical*
tipo ⑩ *tee*-po *type*
— **de cambio** de *kam*-byo *exchange rate*
toalla ① to-*a*-lya *towel*
toallita ① to-a-*lyee*-ta *wash cloth • flannel*
tobillo ⑩ to-*bee*-lyo *ankle*
tocar to-*kar* touch • *play (an instrument)*
— **la guitarra** la gee-*ta*-ra *play the guitar*
tocino ⑩ to-*see*-no *bacon*
todavía (no) to-da-*vee*-a (no) *(not) yet*
todo *to*-do *everything*
todo/a ⑩/① to-do/a *all (singular)*
todos/as ⑩/① pl to-dos/as *all (plural)*
tofú ⑩ to-*foo tofu*
tomar to-*mar* take • *drink*
tomate to-*ma*-te *tomato*
tono ⑩ *to*-no *dial tone*
torcedura ① tor-se-*doo*-ra *sprain*
tormenta ① tor-*men*-ta *storm*
toro ⑩ *to*-ro *bull*
torre ① *to*-re *tower*
torta ① *tor*-ta *cake*
tos ① tos *cough*
tostada ① tos-*ta*-da *toast*
tostadora ① tos-ta-*do*-ra *toaster*
trabajar tra-ba-*khar work*
trabajo ⑩ tra-*ba*-kho *work (occupation)*
— **a tiempo parcial** a *tyem*-po par-*syal* part-time work
— **a tiempo completo** a *tyem*-po kom-*ple*-to *full-time work*
— **administrativo** ad-mee-nees-tra-*tee*-vo *paperwork*
— **de limpieza** de leem-*pye*-sa *cleaning*
— **eventual** e-ven-*twal casual work*
traducir tra-doo-*seer translate*
traer tra-*er bring*
traficante ⑩ **de drogas** tra-fee-*kan*-te de *dro*-gas *drug dealer*
tráfico ⑩ *tra*-fee-ko *traffic*
traje ⑩ *tra*-khe *suit*
— **de baño** de *ba*-nyo *swimsuit*

tramposo/a ⑩/① tram-*po*-so/a *cheat*
tranquilo/a ⑩/① tran-*kee*-lo/a *quiet*
tranvía ① tran-*vee*-a *tram*
tratar de ligar tra-*tar* de lee-*gar chat up*
tren ⑩ tren *train*
trepar tre-*par scale • climb*
tribunal ⑩ tree-boo-*nal court (legal)*
triste *trees*-te *sad*
tú too *you* sg inf
tumba ① *toom*-ba *grave • tomb*
tumbarse toom-*bar*-se *lie (not stand)*
turista ⑩&① too-*rees*-ta *tourist*

U

uniforme ⑩ oo-nee-*for*-me *uniform*
universidad ① oo-nee-ver-see-*da university*
universo ⑩ oo-nee-*ver*-so *universe*
urgente oor-*khen*-te *urgent*
Uruguay ⑩ oo-roo-*gway Uruguay*
usted oos-*te you* sg pol
ustedes oo-*ste*-des *you* pl pol&inf
útil *oo*-teel *useful*
uvas ① pl *oo*-vas *grapes*

V

vaca ① *va*-ka *cow*
vacaciones ① pl va-ka-*syo*-nes *holidays • vacation*
vacante va-*kan*-te *vacant*
vacío/a ⑩/① va-*see*-o/a *empty*
vacuna ① va-*koo*-na *vaccination*
vagina ① va-*khee*-na *vagina*
vagón ⑩ va-*gon train carriage*
— **restaurante** res-tow-*ran*-te *dining car*
validar va-lee-*dar validate*
valiente va-*lyen*-te *brave*
valioso/a ⑩/① va-*lyo*-so/a *valuable*
valle ⑩ *va*-lye *valley*
valor ⑩ va-*lor value*
varios/as ⑩/① pl *va*-ryos/as *several*
vaso ⑩ *va*-so *glass (drinking)*
vegetariano/a ⑩/① ve-khe-ta-*rya*-no/a *vegetarian*

vegetariano/a estricto/a ⓜ/ⓕ
ve·khe·ta·*rya*·no/a es·*treek*·to/a *vegan*
vela ⓕ *ve*·la *candle* • *sail*
velocidad ⓕ ve·lo·see·*da speed*
velocímetro ⓜ ve·lo·*see*·me·tro
speedometer
vena ⓕ *ve*·na *vein*
vendaje ⓜ ven·*da*·khe *bandage*
vender ven·*der sell*
venenoso/a ⓜ/ⓕ ve·ne·*no*·so/a
poisonous
Venezuela ⓕ ve·ne·*swe*·la *Venezuela*
venir ve·*neer come*
ventana ⓕ ven·*ta*·na *window*
ventilador ⓜ ven·tee·la·*dor fan
(machine)*
ver ver *see*
verano ⓜ ve·*ra*·no *summer*
verde *ver*·de *green*
verdulero/a ⓜ/ⓕ ver·doo·*le*·ro/a
greengrocer
verdura ⓕ pl ver·*doo*·ra *vegetable*
verja ⓕ *ver*·kha *gate*
vestíbulo ⓜ ves·*tee*·boo·lo *foyer*
vestido ⓜ ves·*tee*·do *dress*
vestuario ⓜ ves·*twa*·ryo *changing
room* • *wardrobe*
vez ⓕ ves *time (occasion)*
viajar vya·*khar travel*
viaje ⓜ *vya*·khe *trip*
vida ⓕ *vee*·da *life*
— **nocturna** nok·*toor*·na *night life*
video ⓜ *vee*·de·o *video*
vidrio ⓜ *vee*·dryo *glass (material)*
viejo/a ⓜ/ⓕ *vye*·kho/a *old*
viento ⓜ *vyen*·to *wind*
vinagre ⓜ vee·*na*·gre *vinegar*
viñedo ⓜ vee·*nye*·do *vineyard*
vino ⓜ *vee*·no *wine*
— **blanco** *blan*·ko *white wine*
— **espumoso** es·poo·*mo*·so
sparkling wine
— **tinto** *teen*·to *red wine*
violar vyo·*lar rape*

virus ⓜ *vee*·roos *virus*
visado ⓜ *vee*·sa·do *visa*
visitar vee·see·*tar visit*
vista ⓕ *vees*·ta *view*
vitaminas ⓕ pl vee·ta·*mee*·nas
vitamins
viuda ⓕ *vyoo*·da *widow*
viudo ⓜ *vyoo*·do *widower*
víveres ⓜ pl *vee*·ve·res *food supplies*
vivir vee·*veer live*
volado/a ⓜ/ⓕ vo·*la*·do/a *stoned
(drugged)*
volar vo·*lar fly*
voleibol ⓜ vo·*lay*·bol *volleyball*
volver vol·*ver return*
votar vo·*tar vote*
voz ⓕ vos *voice*
vuelo ⓜ *vwe*·lo *flight*
— **doméstico** do·*mes*·tee·ko
domestic flight

W

WAP ⓜ gwap *WAP*

Y

y ee *and*
ya ya *already*
yip ⓜ yeep *jeep*
yo yo *I*
yoga ⓜ *yo*·ga *yoga*
yogur ⓜ yo·*goor yogurt*

Z

zanahoria ⓕ sa·na·o·rya *carrot*
zapatería ⓕ sa·pa·te·*ree*·a *shoe shop*
zapatos ⓜ pl sa·*pa*·tos *shoes*
zodíaco ⓜ so·*dee*·a·ko *zodiac*
zoológico ⓜ so·o·*lo*·khee·ko *zoo*
zoom ⓜ soom *zoom lens*

don't just stand there, say something!

To see the full range of our language products, go to:
lonelyplanet.com

What kind of traveller are you?

A. You're eating chicken for dinner *again* because it's the only word you know.

B. When no one understands what you say, you step closer and shout louder.

C. When the barman doesn't understand your order, you point frantically at the beer.

D. You're surrounded by locals, swapping jokes, email addresses and experiences
– other travellers want to borrow your phrasebook or audio guide.

If you answered A, B, or C, you NEED Lonely Planet's language products ...

- **Lonely Planet Phrasebooks** – for every phrase you need in every language
you want
- **Lonely Planet Language & Culture** – get behind the scenes of English as it's
spoken around the world – learn and laugh
- **Lonely Planet Fast Talk & Fast Talk Audio** – essential phrases for short trips and
weekends away – read, listen and talk like a local
- **Lonely Planet Small Talk** – 10 essential languages for city breaks
- **Lonely Planet Real Talk** – downloadable language audio guides from
lonelyplanet.com to your MP3 player

... and this is why

- **Talk to everyone everywhere**
Over 120 languages, more than any other publisher
- **The right words at the right time**
Quick-reference colour sections, two-way dictionary, easy pronunciation,
every possible subject – and audio to support it

Lonely Planet Offices

Australia
90 Maribyrnong St, Footscray,
Victoria 3011
☎ 03 8379 8000
fax 03 8379 8111
✉ talk2us@lonelyplanet.com.au

USA
150 Linden St, Oakland,
CA 94607
☎ 510 250 6400
fax 510 893 8572
✉ info@lonelyplanet.com

UK
2nd floor, 186 City Rd
London EC1V 2NT
☎ 020 7106 2100
fax 020 7106 2101
✉ go@lonelyplanet.co.uk

lonelyplanet.com